Reporting in Counselling and Psychotherapy

Trainee therapists need to show practical competence through the production of client reports and case studies – an area that can be a source of anxiety to many students.

Reporting in Counselling and Psychotherapy is a unique, hands-on guide to this element of practical work. Using clinical examples to guide the reader, and a detailed analysis of case study and process report writing, it shows how to create clear, concise and properly presented reports.

This book is an invaluable tool, not only for those embarking on practical training in psychotherapy, counselling and psychology, but also for trainers in these areas and for clinicians writing clinical reports and case presentations.

Linda Papadopoulos is a reader in psychology and a chartered counselling and health psychologist working as a Programme Director for Counselling Psychology Courses at London Metropolitan University.

Malcolm C. Cross is a Chartered Counselling Psychologist and UKCP Registered Psychotherapist, and works as the Director of Counselling Psychology Programmes at City University, London.

Robert Bor is a Consultant Psychologist at the Royal Free Hospital, London. He is a Chartered Clinical, Counselling and Health Psychologist, as well as a UKCP Registered Family Therapist.

Reporting in Counselling and Psychotherapy

A trainee's guide to preparing case studies and reports

Linda Papadopoulos,
Malcolm C. Cross and
Robert Bor

Brunner-Routledge
Taylor & Francis Group

HOVE AND NEW YORK

First published 2003 by Brunner-Routledge
27 Church Road, Hove, East Sussex BN3 2FA

Simultaneously published in the USA and Canada
by Brunner-Routledge
29 West 35th Street, New York, NY 10001

Brunner-Routledge is an imprint of the Taylor & Francis Group

Typeset in Times by Mayhew Typesetting, Rhayader, Powys
Printed and bound in Great Britain by MPG Books Ltd, Bodmin,
Cornwall
Cover design by Lisa Dynan

British Library Cataloguing in Publication Data
A catalogue record for this book is available from the British Library

Library of Congress Cataloging-in-Publication Data

Papadopoulos, Linda.
  Reporting in counselling and psychotherapy : a trainee's guide to
preparing case studies and reports / Linda Papadopoulos, Malcom
Cross, and Robert Bor.
      p.   cm.
  ISBN 0-415-23194-9
1. Psychiatry—Authorship. 2. Psychiatry—Case studies. 3. Report
writing. 4. Neuropsychological report writing. 5. Psychiatric
records. I. Cross, Malcolm C., 1966– . II. Bor, Robert. III. Title.

RC455.2.M38 P374 2003
808'.066152—dc21   2002151450

ISBN 0-415-23194-9

Contents

List of illustrations

About the editors

Linda Papadopoulos is a reader in psychology and a chartered counselling and health psychologist working as a Programme Director for Counselling Psychology Courses at London Metropolitan University. She received her undergraduate degree in psychology from York University in Toronto, and went on to obtain an MSc in Health Psychology from Surrey University and a post-MSc Diploma in Counselling Psychology from City University where she completed her PhD. She has published extensively in the fields of medical and counselling psychology and her clinical interests include counselling people with body image disorders in medical settings.

Malcolm C. Cross. Although originally trained as a clinical psychologist in Australia, Malcolm is Chartered as a Counselling Psychologist and UKCP Registered Psychotherapist, working as the Director of Counselling Psychology Programmes at City University, London. He currently divides his time between his academic post, supervisory work and therapy provision in private practice and primary care. Intensely interested in personal construct psychology, Malcolm has published and presented numerous conference papers, relating this apporoach to the execution of research and work with a variety of client groups.

Professor Robert Bor is a Consultant Psychologist at the Royal Free Hospital, London. He is a Chartered Clinical, Counselling and Health Psychologist, as well as a UKCP Registered Family Therapist. He is a member of the Tavistock Society of Psychotherapists, Institute of Family Therapy, London, Association for Family Therapy, American Psychological Association as well as the American Association for Marital and Family Therapy. He is formerly a course director of counselling psychology courses at City University, London and London Metropolitan University and is extensively involved in counselling psychology training. He serves on the editorial board of several international journals and has published several books and numerous papers on his research and clinical interests. He is also a pilot, with an interest in aviation psychology, and is a Fellow of the Royal Aeronautical Society. Robert Bor is also a Churchill Fellow.

Note on confidentiality

Throughout this volume client names, and other significant identifying information, have been changed to protect the anonymity of the clients.

Chapter 1

Introduction

Although teaching methods in psychology and counselling may change and new theories emerge one thing that stays relatively constant is students' anxiety about the assessment of their practical and clinical work. In many ways, the training of therapists is a relatively new academic strain and as such there is a dearth of practical academic literature in field. In order to qualify as a registered or accredited therapist, trainees have to complete a certain number of practice hours with a range of client groups. Practical competence in these clinical placements is usually assessed through the production of client process reports and case studies. Unfortunately, relatively little guidance is given to trainees about what is expected of them when writing client reports, and this can be a further source of anxiety for students who are already feeling insecure about their emerging competencies.

We hope that this text will help to remedy these problems. We have set about providing a detailed analysis of case-study and process-report writing in the field of professional therapy training. This book is intended for all those currently in, or embarking upon, practical training in psychotherapy, counselling and psychology. It is also intended to serve as a guide for trainers in these areas and for clinicians who face the prospect of writing clinical reports or preparing case presentations.

In the following few chapters we examine both the practical aspects of developing a competent and integrated client report and the theoretical positions and structure required in order to help students express their ideas creatively and coherently. We begin in Chapter 1 by deconstructing the various parts of case studies and process reports and discussing in detail a range of topics such as selecting case material and structuring case studies. Chapters 2 to 18 are examples of real case studies and process reports written by trainees at different stages of their professional development. They reflect different levels of developing competence among trainee therapists and encompass a wide variety of theoretical models applied to work involving different presenting problems. Each colleague who contributed a chapter to the book was asked to describe their thoughts about revisiting their case material months, or in some cases years, later. These accounts are genuine and illuminating. These cases serve to ground the reports both in terms of psychological process and professional development. While reading these accounts it may be helpful for the reader to pay attention to the views expressed by the authors, their frank admission of insecurities and idiosyncrasies and, most of all, their ability to reflect upon their own process.

Each of the cases presented in the book begins with a brief editorial introduction. We describe why we chose each particular case, what we see as its merits and, in some cases, even its shortcomings. Our analysis in these sections is not intended to serve as a critical assessment of the reports but rather to highlight the most pertinent and salient aspects of client reports that trainers and clinicians look for.

In Chapter 19 we turn our attention to what NOT to do when writing a client report. This chapter aims to provide an informative account of where case material written up as coursework can go wrong. Our analysis here is not intended to be critical of trainees' efforts but rather to highlight how easy it is to 'miss the mark' when trying to put one's point across. In each case, practical suggestions and advice are given on how to rectify problem areas.

The final chapter is devoted to a summary of the work we have presented in the book. We discuss the main lessons that our students have taught us over the years and make our final recommendations on how to write a good case report.

We hope you get as much enjoyment and knowledge from reading this as we have had compiling it. Good luck with your own work in this area.

Case studies

The principle aim of a client case study is to allow the therapist to exhibit the link between practice and theory. It takes the form of a written summary of the principle aspects of the interaction between the counsellor and the client over a number of therapy sessions. A good case study will be represented by a careful and sensitive integration of clinical practice and theory rather than a simple verbatim description of therapy sessions. Therapists will write case studies at several points in their career and for different reasons. Some will do so for training purposes, others for clinical presentations and yet others as a means of justifying assessment or treatment. Trainees often need to create client case studies in order to demonstrate professional clinical competence whereas an experienced therapist may write a study for teaching or training purposes or for an academic text.

This section looks at:

- The details that need to be included in the case study.
- How to choose a case to present.

- How to structure and present a case study.
- How to prepare a case study.

One of the first and most important things to know about case studies is that they can vary from course to course and from practitioner to practitioner but there are common themes which link them. The aim of a case study is not to give a simple case history of the client but to give the reader a clear and concise account of the therapist's ability to select and apply theoretical concepts in practice. It will also serve as an account of the therapist's clinical skill and judgement.

The overall theme behind all case studies is the illustration of the integration of theory and clinical practice. This will require the therapist to illustrate how their choice of intervention was guided by a coherent theory of psychological change and explain the way in which that theory helped the therapist to understand the case. It is important that case studies show:

- A good understanding of the psychological principles of the chosen orientation.
- A level of synergy between this theoretical approach and the actual work with the client.

With respect to the preparation of a case study, it is crucial that the therapist has clearly defined criteria for the case study so that a specific purpose is outlined.

Theoretical position

It is important that the therapist has established a coherent theory, which can be clearly and concisely described to the reader. One of the main problems with writing case studies is that the therapist has a limited space within which to allow the reader to understand the case and the principles of the therapist's approach. As Bor and Watts (1999) point out, most case studies used in the training arena tend to be between 1,000 and 3,000 words, but students often have great difficulty in staying within these limits. In this respect, it is important to remember that the purpose of the case study is not to show everything that has happened in the therapy sessions but to provide a concise summary, with appropriate examples of therapeutic interaction, that illustrates the case that the therapist is making. A useful way of approaching the writing of a case study is to prepare a summary of the core theoretical principles of the approach used. This summary can be altered if the therapist moves to a more integrated approach as therapy proceeds. Bor and Watts (1999) point out that it is important that the therapist tries to avoid submitting case studies that are based on common-sense principles, which most therapists tend to share. These can take the form of 'listening to what client's say' or 'structuring the session to allow adequate time'. The example that follows gives an illustration of the theoretical summary that might be appropriate for a person-centered approach to a therapy session:

> Due to the work of Carl Rogers (1990), person-centered therapists believe that there are conditions that are not only necessary but sufficient to bring about therapeutic change. By sufficient, this approach means that the conditions will allow the client to self-actualise at the cost of other drives such as the drive to protect and defend their self-concept. The three qualities that Rogers emphasised were unconditional positive regard, empathy and genuineness on the part of the therapist. He noted that person-centered therapy was really a special type of interpersonal relationship between the client and the therapist and that it is this relationship that helps the client to move on. Although other traditions of therapy also emphasise the importance of these three tenets of person-centered therapy, they only see them as part of the establishment of a therapeutic environment in which to implement other treatments (such as cognitive behavioural therapy) rather than as sufficient for therapeutic change on their own.

This summary of the therapist's theoretical orientation should be clear, concise and cover the essential and basic tenets of the approach. It should also include full references.

Which case to illustrate

The most important decision facing any therapist creating a case study is that of which case study to select. Although it may appear to be mere common sense, it is important to establish the grounds on which certain cases may be suitable or unsuitable. First, it is important to know exactly to whom the case is being presented. In deciding which cases to present, therapists must look at cases which give a clear idea of which approach to therapy was being used and show that this particular approach was maintained throughout the course of the therapy. The choice of case should be amenable to the specific therapeutic approach used and should exhibit the core theoretical principle of this approach. The case that the therapist chooses to present in the study should highlight the use of some of the methods specific to the theoretical approach rather than only using approaches that are generic to multiple psychotherapies. It is always useful for the therapist to explain what led them to the use of the particular therapeutic tradition. When the therapist has decided on an approach to represent in the case study it is essential that the study is consistent with this therapeutic approach.

It is also important that the chosen case highlights the issues that the therapist wishes to illustrate in the case study. As such, a case that is particularly difficult may not be suitable for a case-study approach where the therapist's task is to highlight the use of case studies in a training context or where the therapist has limited text space. Under such circumstances, the case should be the right length so that there are sufficient sessions discussed to provide a detailed picture of the case without too much material being presented. It is important to be aware that it can be easy to overwhelm the reader with the details of the case, and a fine balance has to be reached where rich detail can be included but not to the detriment of the reader's comprehension of the case.

Finally, it is important to remember that seeking and using help from other practitioners is an essential part of safe and effective professional practice and any use of supervision should be appropriately documented within the case study. This can help to highlight the effectiveness of supervision in a case context.

Case studies should highlight learning on behalf of the therapist but within the specific paradigm used. The main utilisation of a case study will be to enable other professionals to monitor and comprehend the process within a given context.

The presentation of the case study

As with other pieces of structured writing, a case study should exhibit a discernable introduction, middle and end. This structure will allow the reader to get the most out of the given study. Bor and Watts (1999) suggest the following guidelines for headings and sections for trainee counselling psychologists and these suggestions provide a good general template:

1 Introduction and start of the therapy.
   - Introduction.
   - Summary of theoretical orientation.
   - The context of the work.
   - The referral.
   - Convening the first session.
   - The presenting problem.
   - Initial assessment and formulation of the problem.
   - Negotiating a contract and therapeutic aims.
   - Summary of biographical details of client and genogram.
2 The development of the therapy.
   - The pattern of therapy.
   - The therapeutic plan and main techniques used.
   - Key content issues.
   - The therapeutic process.

- Difficulties in the work.
- Making use of supervision.
- Changes in the formulation and the therapeutic plan.
- Changes in the therapeutic process over time.
3 The conclusion of the therapy.
- The therapeutic ending.
- Evaluation of the work.
- Arrangements for follow-up.
- Liaison with other professionals.
- What you learnt about psychotherapeutic practice and theory.
- Learning from the case about yourself as therapist.
4 References.

This guide is broad and may need to be amended in line with the therapist's theoretical approach. With respect to the actual practicalities of creating the case study, it is recommended that the therapist gathers the following as source data for the write-up:

- Copies of notes from sessions.
- Supervision notes.
- Client biographical data.
- Referral letters.
- Any subsequent reports on the client that the therapist may have compiled.
- Consent form from the client, giving permission for the trainee to use the work.

Genograms (family trees) can be extremely useful tools, both in the therapeutic context and during the preparation of a case study. They act as brief summaries of essential client data that can be presented in such a concise fashion that more space is made available to comment on other aspects of the case. Finally, when approaching the stage of writing the study, the therapist needs to focus on the following three points:

- Emphasise the way that the given evidence explains the work.
- Emphasise patterns and processes rather than just descriptive details.
- Mention key stages in the therapeutic process where various options were available to the therapist. Discuss why certain avenues of enquiry were followed at the expense of others.

Bor and Watts (1999) point out that the careful use of evidence will help the therapist avoid stereotyping and making unfounded claims and over-generalisations. An example might be, 'Like most children whose parents are going through a divorce, James felt that he was partly responsible'.

This would be inappropriate for two reasons. First, little meaning can be attached to such a generalisation without any supporting evidence and, second, there is no information suggesting that this is James' experience. As such, this aspect of James' feelings could be due to guesswork only on the part of the therapist.

One of the crucial, and easily overlooked, tenets of writing a case study concerns an emphasis on *why* the therapist worked as they did rather than merely reporting *what* they actually did. The therapist needs to document their reasons for taking certain paths of enquiry or interventions based on sound theoretical grounds. This point should be borne in mind at all stages of the case study.

Process reports

As a therapist, it is not only the words that are spoken in a session that hold import for the client. Of equal importance is the way in which those words are said, why those words were used, the issues that are not mentioned, the body language of the client and general non-verbal communication. These are all crucial determinants of any therapeutic session and form the process of the session, that is what actually happens in the therapy. A process report is a written meta-account of the communication and techniques that the therapist used in the therapeutic encounter. It portrays the methodology used by the therapist and highlights the therapist's post-hoc views about the influence that their behaviour had on their client and on the relationship. It is based on a recorded segment of therapy which is analysed retrospectively and the rationale behind the report is to enable the therapist to be reflective about their own work and to monitor their own ability to put theory into practice. The process report is not intended to be a perfect account of the 'ideal session' but a general training exercise to enhance the therapist's awareness of their ability to influence the therapeutic process. They tend to be in the region of 2,000 to 3,000 words in length, but can occasionally be longer.

With respect to this report, the therapeutic process is the crucial level of analysis and content is only included if it helps to illuminate the process taking place. Process reports differ from client case studies in that the focus of the client case study is content. As mentioned earlier, the case study focused on the relationship between the therapist's therapeutic work and their theoretical foundation. Bor and Watts (1999) conceptualise the difference by considering case studies as a macroscopic view of the therapeutic encounter while process reports represent a microscopic view. The process report requires constant appraisal and reappraisal of what is actually happening in the session. Each of the two approaches focuses on different, but complementary, aspects of the therapeutic analysis and together they give an illuminating view of the therapeutic encounter and the therapist.

Process reports are especially important in the training process where therapists can learn to become more reflexive and proactive with regard to their own therapeutic approach. Indeed, the ability to analyse and alter their own practice is fundamental to the approach of therapists as professionals. In order to achieve this, therapists must be aware of the processes that occur in the session with each and every technique and intervention used because these processes define the relationship between the therapist and the client. Only by using questions such as, 'Why did I say that?', 'What is happening here?' and 'What did I try to do there?' can the therapist grow as a professional and create a wealth of resources that can be used in future practice.

Recording

The first aspect to be noted about creating a process report is that taping is conditional on the client being comfortable with the recording process even though the transcript is crucial to producing the report. Some clients, such as those presenting with issues relating to sexual abuse, may be extremely apprehensive about discussing their histories with anyone let alone about having these taped. It is important that the therapist always remembers that the client's need comes first and if this involves a refusal to tape the therapeutic process then so be it. The client's consent must be gained before using a recording device and the therapist needs to introduce the idea of recording by emphasising the fact that it will help the therapist to obtain further insight into how the therapist and client can achieve their goals together. When introducing the idea, therapists must also discuss the absolute confidentiality (other than the therapist's supervisor) under which the transcript will be protected. The audio/video tape will give the therapist opportunities to refocus on nuances which may well have been missed, and re-examine aspects of the process that were difficult to absorb, during the session. These include issues of timing, clarifications of therapist and client interactions, non-verbal communications, tones of voice and intonation.

Which part do I use as the process?

When deciding this, the therapist must consider two issues in particular. First, the therapist will have to decide which session would be most appropriate to choose to highlight and, second, following on from this, the therapist must decide which segment from within this session would be the most appropriate to use.

Several considerations are appropriate at this stage. Familiarity will allow the therapist to focus on the process of the session, whereas choosing a session that is fairly unique will prompt a more content-focused appraisal.

In the first instance, choosing a session that is more representative of your work is likely to help you report the therapeutic process more easily. With respect to the chosen segment, any problems with choosing an appropriate session can be aided by asking if the segment contains the criteria that the therapist wishes to illustrate. This includes ensuring that there is clear theory involved in the segment and asking if the segment highlights the issue at hand. The therapist needs to find a segment where the theory behind the intervention is clearly recognisable; where the therapist can focus on what they were trying to achieve by a particular intervention and how they thought this particular intervention was useful.

The practicalities of the process report:

The following points address some crucial practical issues involved in transcribing the report:

- The process of transcription can be lengthy and a good guide is to assume that it could take around four minutes of written transcription for every minute of therapy.
- With respect to the detail of the transcription, Bor and Watts (1999) suggest that the therapist should not be overly concerned with the 'ums' and 'ahhs' of the tape, as these can often be markers of the emotional intensity of a therapy session.
- Be aware of hesitations, both yours and the client's.
- Be aware of non-verbal communication. That is, note eye contact, body language, movements and silences, as these often affect the decision-making process of the therapist. Also, note your own communications in response to these.
- It is essential to reread the transcription several times as new insights can occur on repeated study.
- Finally, no matter how tempted you may be, do not 'doctor' the transcription or leave sections out. It is important that the transcription is a verbatim documentation of the original tape.

It is helpful for the therapist to make notes as they reread the material. These notes will serve as very useful pointers when it comes to setting out the report.

With respect to documenting the details of the counselling session, there are specific interactions that the therapist should focus on. As well as the impact of therapeutic interventions, mentioned above, the therapist should be aware that their feelings are just as important as what was said and how this affected the client. A record of the therapist's feelings can help the reader to understand the way in which the session may have developed and why certain interventions were deemed appropriate.

Regarding events that may occur within the session it is important to highlight any dilemmas that occur. This could include the therapist noting points at which they, therapist and client, were unsure of how to proceed and why they felt that way. How did they cope with the dilemma and, in retrospect, how suitable was the therapist's reaction.

The structure of the process report

The following points can be useful when attempting to structure the introductory format of the report. Start with a client profile. This should be anonymous and provide an overall portrait of the client such that the reader has an understanding of the client's demographics (in prose style) as well as their personality and interpersonal behaviour style. Allow the reader to understand the way that the client was referred and the presenting problem. This should cover the issue(s) that brought the client into therapy but should be from the point of view of the client rather than the therapist. What does the client perceive as the issue? How does this trouble the client? Does this issue express itself physically as well as psychologically?

An initial assessment should propose an explanation for the presenting problem in a thorough but concise manner. This is the section where the therapist outlines his or her understanding of the issue at hand and so helps the reader to understand the development of the therapeutic process and the way in which the therapist chose to interact. It can be viewed as similar to the kind of information described in a case study. A therapeutic contract then needs to be created so that the client understands the approximate details of the therapy. Along with the preceding information, this helps the reader to formulate an idea of the type, length and aims of the therapy. This should then lead into the selected session. Should the segment chosen involve the middle of a session, or the middle of a group of sessions, a brief history of the sessions so far can be outlined. With respect to the main section of the report, speaker turns must be marked clearly and a double space between turns is an effective marker. The dialogue is commented on immediately after each segment of the session.

This main segment of the report contains several therapist interventions and not all of these interventions will be grounded in the congruent/consistent theoretical precept. Just like non-therapists, therapists may make responses due to boredom, instinct and frustration, among other reasons, and if this is the case then they should report it. It is normal and human for the therapist to be prone to the above reactions or even to simply lose their concentration. Should this happen, do not fail to mention it. It is more useful to the reader to give an account of *why* the therapist thinks this may have happened, than to gloss over it and hope that no-one notices.

An additional factor to remember when analysing the therapeutic segment is the influence of body language. This can take the form of eye contact, fidgeting or posture, and may convey an important insight to the therapist. For example, a depressed individual may avoid eye contact with the therapist. Therapists will be affected by body language and so the therapist should be aware of, and comment on, the way that they feel they reacted to a given body language. As well as noting body language, it is also important for the therapist to reflect on their own thoughts and feelings towards the client. These will affect the therapeutic relationship and it is important to note that the therapist's feelings towards the client may reflect other people's feelings toward the client and hence give valuable insight.

The pace of a session is a further consideration for the therapist. Novice therapists may feel under pressure to produce results with their clients and so move them through therapy at a greater speed than the client feels comfortable with. Any disparity in the pace of the therapy between therapist and client should be commented on. It may be that the therapist feels that the client is ready to move on to the next level but the client could feel otherwise. Reasons for this conflict in opinion are important and should be reflected upon in the report.

Finally, and as importantly as anything mentioned previously in this chapter, it is essential that the therapist's thoughts, feelings and evaluations are constantly noted in the report. Any evaluations made concerning the state of the client are of interest to the reader, as they will undoubtedly affect the therapist's intentions and interventions. The therapist's feelings toward the client and presenting problem will also impact upon the intervention chosen. It is often through the therapist's thoughts and feelings that the therapy is shaped and directed and a thorough reflection of this is essential if the author is to convey the experience of therapy in any real and immediate way.

Ethics

According to professional practice guidelines, it is a requirement when writing a client report that this is only done with the valid consent of the client, having taken all reasonable steps to ensure that the client has adequately understood the nature of the clinical report and its anticipated uses. There are certain guidelines that you should always try and follow so that your client has the capacity to provide informed consent without feeling compelled to agree as a consequence of their desire to please you as a therapist:

1   Explain to the client what a case study or process report is and what it will be used for. Make it clear to the client that they can see the report if they wish and that the final report will contain no name or identifying details.

2 Emphasise to them that, whether or not they agree to give consent, this will in no way affect the treatment they receive from you or your relationship with them.
3 In the situation where you are intending to do a case study or process report on a child or adult who is not in a position to give valid consent, you must establish who has legal authority to give consent and seek consent from that person.
4 Consent should always be given in writing; devise a consent form for this purpose.
5 Ideally, clients should be provided with a written account of what the client report is, who will have access to it, the purpose it is intended for and what will happen to it once it has served its purpose.
6 Clients should always be given sufficient opportunity to consider the implications of giving consent, prior to actually doing so.
7 Only make audio and/or video recordings of clients with their express agreement. Clients must be made aware of your intention to record sessions from the outset of therapy and also the conditions of subsequent access to any audio or video material recorded during sessions.
8 Make it clear to the client that at any time they can withdraw consent to being videoed or taped.
9 Take all reasonable steps to safeguard the security of all your client case studies and process reports. These should be at least as secure as clinical case records.
10 You must destroy '*not tape over*' all videotaped and audiotaped material once it has been used for the task that the client has given consent for.
11 In the event that you decide to use a case study or process report for another purpose (i.e. publication), then the client must be informed again and written consent given once again.

References

Bor, R. and Watts, M. (1999). *The Trainee Handbook: a guide for counselling and psychotherapy trainees*. London: Sage.

Chapter 2

A first session using the systemic approach

with a case study by Susie Robbins

PRELUDE

All trainees at some point agonise over having to choose an excerpt from a clinical session to present as a process report for evaluation. Most of us feel uncomfortable hearing ourselves on an audio recording or replaying a videotape of a session. We may have doubts as to whether our tutors will be sympathetic and persuaded to understand the process in the way we experienced it. The risk is that our fragile confidence will be knocked by the assessment of the report. It is entirely honest to recognise such feeling of doubt and anxiety and is the basis for preparing an honest and reflective account of your practice.

In the report Susie Robbins describes some of the feelings and dilemmas she experienced both in undertaking this piece of academic work and in her own assessment of what she believed she had done with the client. She conveys to the reader how time-consuming it can be to select a suitable piece of tape to present, revisiting her chosen excerpt many times and attending to different features and levels of interaction in the session. Of further value is the fact that Susie, having now completed her training to become a Chartered Counselling Psychologist, reflects back on a piece of work from the first year of her three-year training programme, offering the reader an exciting entrée into the therapist's reflections on her original assessments. The report is ultimately balanced in that it presents a carefully argued account of therapeutic process, and highlights both strengths and weaknesses alike. This is a core ingredient of reflective and mature practice.

A first counselling session presents unique challenges, and learning to apply a new therapeutic approach (in this case a systemic one) compounds these. In this case, Susie demonstrates a clear understanding of the core theoretical concepts and provides a list of appropriate references, describes a medical problem, states how this is related to the presenting psychological problem, and conveys a sense of curiosity and respect for the client through the use of questions.

Susie Robbins wrote this report at the end of a full-time MSc in Counselling Psychology. The comments were written at the beginning of the second year of a post-MSc practitioner diploma.

Preamble

This process report was written during my first year of training as a counselling psychologist. I hadn't found it easy to choose a tape for transcription, and had played several tapes over and over again while trying to make up my mind which one to use. In the end I chose this tape because while I felt the session had gone quite well, I also knew that I had found some aspects of the session difficult and believed that I could learn more from reflecting on the interactions that had concerned me.

In this session, I knew that I had developed an immediate rapport with the client and that I had asked some useful questions. However, I had also been nervous and concerned that I would somehow damage the client either by saying the wrong thing or by missing something important. My questioning was quite tentative and influenced by my own underlying fears and concerns. I missed some of the points that the client was making and, as a result, the opportunity to follow through on new lines of questioning presented by him.

This realisation not only gave me something to talk about in the process report, it gave me the opportunity to think about what kind of therapy I wanted to offer and how I could progress. After listening to the tape several times and writing the transcript, I was better able to understand not only what I had done well but also where and how I could improve. I learnt that I should take more care with my use of language and the way that I asked questions. More importantly, I learned that I needed to listen more attentively.

Looking back at the report now, I remember how painful it was to realise that I had made so many mistakes. I would have loved to produce a transcript that demonstrated complete competence as a therapist and showed that I had nothing to learn. However, I think that would have missed the point. There is always something to be learned from reflecting on our own practice. Although I have learnt better questioning techniques and have become better at judging when to listen and when to intervene, I know that I still make mistakes. I have simply had more practice now and have grown in confidence.

Overall, I am quite pleased with this piece of work. It is a useful reminder of my particular strengths and weaknesses and I think it highlights some of the difficulties faced by many trainees. For example, learning to ask open questions and to follow through appropriately. I also think it demonstrates the importance of empathic understanding and responsiveness. Clients need to feel understood and able to express their concerns if they are to benefit from therapy, and I believe that I achieved that with this client.

PROCESS REPORT

Introduction

This process report examines a transcript from a first counselling session that was conducted using a systemic approach. The report begins with an outline of the theoretical framework and a profile of the client. Following a lead in to the session, the report then examines the transcript in detail, analysing the thinking processes and interventions used in the session and assessing their validity and effectiveness. A summary of the work and an evaluation of the session is provided at the end.

Theoretical Framework

Systemic thinking in counselling psychology has its origins in cybernetics and began to develop in social work in the 1940s. During the 1950s, the work of Bateson, a philosopher and anthropologist, focused on the properties of systems and problems in communication. Later, Minuchin (1974) and his colleagues attempted to understand the structure and patterning of family interactions, while the work of the Milan school (Palazzoli et al. 1978) accentuated the collective construction of family beliefs and assumptions and introduced the idea of circularity (McLeod 1998). While these different strands of systemic theory employ different concepts with different areas of focus, they all share the common assumption that a family or group of people who are closely associated can be regarded as a self-regulating system. Human interaction and behaviour is viewed in the context of feedback loops that affect all levels of communication between all parts of the system (Hoffman 1981). Beliefs and behaviour are connected, so that change at either the level of belief or the level of behaviour can result in change at the other level. A major event affecting an individual in a system impacts on the relationship between all the other members of that system, with individual problems being highly influenced by family relationships and interactions (Bor et al. 1996). Behaviour is viewed in the context of all the other relationships in a particular setting (Altschuler 1997).

Systemic therapy aims to identify the meaning and function of a presenting problem within the context of the system and to provide a different perspective, opening up alternatives and possibilities. By supplying new information and connections between behaviours and beliefs, therapy may encourage clients to 'reframe' (Watzlawick et al. 1974) the problem and generate new patterns of behaviour. Circular interviewing is used to explore problems in terms of differences and to generate feedback to use as a basis for further questions.

Setting

A counselling service set within a GP unit that aims to provide support for patients registered at the surgery. Clients are usually referred by the GP's working at the surgery, but can also be referred by practice nurses or health visitors.

Profile of the Client

Referral

The client (Kevin) is a 47-year-old man who was referred by his general practitioner. He was concerned that Kevin had not yet come to terms with a diagnosis of polymyositis made six months previously. Kevin had also been diagnosed with systemic lupus erythematosus (lupus) five years previously and was becoming increasingly weak and unwell. The referral stated that Kevin had been prescribed a course of antidepressants by his general practitioner and had been taking these for two months. The referral also stated that Kevin was married with children. The ages of the children were not specified.

Polymyositis is an inflammatory disease affecting voluntary muscles, and causing weakened muscles and muscle pain. The condition is rarely fatal, but in severe cases patients may need a wheelchair. Systemic lupus erythematosus is an autoimmune disease having many manifestations, including skin rashes, kidney, heart and lung problems and anaemia (Shafer et al. 1979).

My aim for the first session was to learn more about Kevin's perception of his illness and the impact on his family. Information about the severity of his illness, his beliefs about the illness, his views regarding treatment, his concerns and his relationships with his family would help me to understand the problem and frame it within the systemic family environment.

Appearance and behaviour

Kevin arrived on his own and was dressed in black tracksuit bottoms, blue jumper and trainers. He walked steadily but rubbed his knees and ankles when he sat down and explained that his legs had been troubling him. The skin on his face and neck looked red and sore.

Contract and counselling plan

After introductions and clarification of my role within the counselling service, I explained to Kevin that we would make a decision at the end of the session about whether therapy should continue and negotiate a point at which therapy should end.

Lead in to the transcript

The transcript analysed lies some 30 minutes into Kevin's first counselling session. Initially Kevin had described the physical deterioration caused by his illness. Once very active, Kevin now found that increasing weakness and pain made every-day activities difficult and would soon force early retirement. Kevin had found these changes, coupled with wider family issues, very difficult to cope with. Kevin's initial rejection of the diagnosis of polymyositis had progressed to anger at the disease and its symptoms and then depression at his situation and the implications for the future. The prescription of an antidepressant had helped and enabled him to stabilise his relationship with his wife. Kevin now wanted help in coming to terms with the disease. Kevin had said that he had coped well with the problems caused by the lupus, and, as we move into the transcripted section, I was beginning to explore how the diagnosis of polymyositis had changed this ability to cope.

Analysis of transcript

COUNSELLOR 1: Um. Do you feel differently . . . how do you react differently now that you know that you've got the polymyositis as well and that that's causing you some problems, to when you reacted when you had lupus? 'Cos you've had that for a while now, you've had that for five years, haven't you?

Kevin had become increasingly disabled as a result of the lupus, and further disability from polymyositis was becoming apparent. I had established that Kevin was often unable to distinguish which illness caused which symptoms. I now wanted to explore how the diagnosis of polymyositis had changed his ability to cope with the disability. I hypothesised that while Kevin had apparently coped well prior to the diagnosis of polymyositis, the thought of further illness and disability was overwhelming him and affecting his understanding of how well he could cope in the future. However, I asked the question rather clumsily, following an open question with a closed question before giving Kevin a chance to think. Kevin looked confused and unsure of what I had asked.

CLIENT 1: Yeah.

In fact Kevin answered my second question and was clearly uncertain about the first question.

COUNSELLOR 2: Do you understand the question? I'm just wondering um, how . . . you, you've had some sort of symptoms of deterioration in, in your ability to to, um, to play football and to do other things . . .

CLIENT 2: Mm.

COUNSELLOR 3: And . . . presumably it's a little bit worse with the poly-myositis, but how has the diagnosis changed your feeling about your sort of deterioration?

Since Kevin had not understood what I was asking, I tried to clarify the question. I don't think I did a lot better here than I had the first time. I also feel that the word 'deterioration' was rather harsh, 'worsening symptoms' would have been a better phrase. I was searching for words in my head as I said them and struggling. A better way of wording this question would be, 'How do you feel the diagnosis of polymyositis has changed your ability to cope with the disability?'

CLIENT 3: (*Pause*) Well . . . really because it, it's going to get worse.

Kevin appeared to understand the question and answered it. He immediately referred to the future, revealing his belief that the polymyositis would add to his disability and his problems would increase. I had the sense that Kevin was feeling completely overwhelmed by his illness and unable to consider in detail how he might cope in the future.

COUNSELLOR 4: And you feel it's sort of an added . . .

I began to clarify my understanding of what Kevin had just said.

CLIENT 4: I mean it's, it's been getting worse over the two and a half years. I mean it's, um, you know I, I get problems with my knees now . . .

Kevin began to elaborate on what he had said.

COUNSELLOR 5: Mm.

(I remained silent but let Kevin know that I was listening.)

CLIENT 5: Um . . . but I mean it may not get worse . . .

Kevin appeared to be comparing past and present symptoms and thinking about the future progress of the illness.

COUNSELLOR 6: Mm.

(I continued to confirm to Kevin that I was listening.)

CLIENT 6: I mean that's one of the things about it. But, um, it it can stabilise but, I mean, it's going to get worse, probably. I mean, I expect it to get worse.

Kevin's answer was not very specific. He said that he expected things to get worse but he did not say in what ways or how that made him feel. I focused on the fact that Kevin was talking about the future and decided to explore what 'getting worse' meant to Kevin.

COUNSELLOR 7: What's your biggest fear, concern?

Kevin had indicated that he was concerned about the future, and about the extent to which the disability would progress. I wanted to understand his specific concerns so that I might then encourage him to consider how he might cope. Once future difficulties and concerns have been acknowledged, individuals can be helped to come to terms with these and prepare for the future (Altschuler 1997).

CLIENT 7: Well, that that you know, I was coping with the lupus but, you know, I suppose I had accepted it what it did to me and thought I could cope, but this I can't face.

Kevin continued to compare the impact of the polymyositis with the lupus, in line with the question asked at turn 1. He revealed that while he understood that the lupus was debilitating in itself, he did not view this as acutely threatening, whereas he felt that the polymyositis was a more significant threat.

COUNSELLOR 8: Mm.

(I let Kevin know I was still listening but tried not to interrupt his train of thought.)

CLIENT 8: But, my biggest concern really is with the, um, with the polymyositis I could be, end up in a wheelchair really.

Kevin clearly expressed the concern that he would become severely disabled, possibly needing a wheelchair as a result of the polymyositis

COUNSELLOR 9: Mm, and, and what about that is . . . is worrying you?

I was concerned that I was failing to get in touch with the emotional aspects of Kevin's illness and that while he was telling me he was worried, I did not have a sense of how this made him feel or how he felt his life was going to be affected. Kevin was frowning as he spoke and I suspected that he had not spoken to anyone before about his fears. I wondered if he had thought about the future in detail, or whether he had avoided this. I wondered if the image of the wheelchair was preventing him from considering how he might cope if his disability progressed to this extent. I suspected that Kevin was feeling a great sense of loss, both of his health and of his sense of identity. I asked him for more details about his concerns so that we could explore his emotions more fully.

CLIENT 9: (*Pause*) . . . Well, I, I suppose that I won't be able to do anything . . . you know, I'll basically be disabled . . . so I'm, I'll be, I'll be . . . I'll have to be helped every, every I mean, I won't be able to do anything . . .

COUNSELLOR 10: Mm.

CLIENT 10: . . . Everything, I'll have to be helped . . .

COUNSELLOR 11: Mm.

From turns 9–11, Kevin had paused several times and I sensed that he was struggling to find the words to express how he felt about the possibility of being in a wheelchair. I wanted to give him time to think and to consider what this might mean to him. I realised this was very difficult for Kevin and I tried to encourage him by nodding and verbally confirming that I was listening.

CLIENT 11: . . . And I think my, um, that would be very difficult for my wife as well. I mean, although, you know, she, she says, well as I say, she says not to worry about it but, um, I do worry about it.

Kevin clearly stated that that he was worried about the future impact of his disability and the effect this would have on his wife. He told me quite clearly that while his wife had told him not to worry he did worry, letting me know that this was a current concern that was affecting his ability to cope. He introduced the concerns he had for his wife and how she would cope. His sense of helplessness and loss of control was clear, a key concern being the idea of becoming dependent on others.

COUNSELLOR 12: So, are you worried about the impact of that, of actually being in a wheelchair on the family?

This question was intended to clarify what Kevin had just been telling me. However, it failed to pick up on his concerns for his wife. I feel I should have explored Kevin's fears for his wife at this point, and also how he felt each member of the family would cope in the future. Circular questioning could have explored the different reactions of family members, highlighting changing relationships in the family (Burnham 1986). The question was also a closed question and could have led to a simple, one-word answer.

CLIENT 12: Yeah, in more ways than one. I mean in the ways that I can't, that they'll have to do, they'll have to change their life around to to help me if that happens, but also I . . . I can't do the things I used to to help them. You know now, last week we had a problem with, um, the lawnmower and I used to go to the shed to get the tools and fix the mower and I tried to do it last weekend and I couldn't and the mower's still broken and I had to put it back together again. I just couldn't fix it so just simple things where, where . . .

COUNSELLOR 13: Mm.

CLIENT 13: . . . My wife can't do it, or the children . . .

COUNSELLOR 14: Mm.

CLIENT 14: So, um, its, um, you know, they'll be, they can't rely on me any more, they won't be able to rely on me any more for things they used to rely on me for.

Kevin explained the impact his illness was having on the family. He described how his role in the family was changing and would continue to change. He expressed his concern that the family would find this adjustment difficult and the sense of guilt resulting from the affect that that his illness was having on everyday life. He indicated that his role in the family before his illness was one of a protector and provider who could be relied upon to take care of things. The illness had challenged this important 'relational rule' (Altschuler 1997) and Kevin appeared to be feeling increasingly isolated and concerned about his future identity in the family.

COUNSELLOR 15: So, you're sort of generally worried about, um, the future and what it will hold?

I failed to pick up on the issue of changing relationships or Kevin's feelings of guilt and asked a general, closed question that could have led nowhere.

CLIENT 15: Mm. Yeah, I mean my children are going to move away. One has moved away already – she's married and moved away. Well, she's not far away but she's got a life of her own. And the 17-year-old's, I mean she'll move away as well, in time, and the 12-year-old he's not so, you know, it . . . the burden, it . . . I'm going to be a problem for my wife really.

Although I had asked a closed question, Kevin took it in the context of our discussion and expanded his previous answer. He referred to his awareness that the family would soon enter a new stage of the family life cycle, so that he and his wife would need to adjust to his illness in the context of the family managing without him. He continued to reveal his feelings of guilt, considering that he would be a 'burden' for his wife. He viewed the 'problem' as being how his wife was going to manage rather than his own difficulties.

COUNSELLOR 16: Mm. And how do you see her coping with with things if they do come to that stage?

I regretted saying 'Mm' as soon as I said it, feeling that I had somehow agreed with Kevin's statement that he was going to be a burden for his wife. An appropriate empathic response might have been to reflect on Kevin's feelings by saying, 'You feel as if you are going to be a burden for your wife'. This 'basic formula' (Egan 1998) may have helped to pinpoint Kevin's emotions and to reduce his anxiety. I could then have followed through with the question.

The hypothetical question that followed was designed to explore Kevin's views about how his wife would react if he became wheelchair bound. Kevin appeared to be consumed with guilt and worry that he had created problems for his family. I hypothesised that Kevin may be mistaken about his wife's capabilities but was unable to consider the possibility. In systemic theory, mind-reading questions such as this are often used to explore the extent to which family members are conscious of each other's thoughts and feeling, and thus the quality of communication in the family (Burnham 1986).

CLIENT 16: I don't know. I just think it's going to be a problem for her and, and I really don't want to be a problem for her. You know, I don't want to have to be looked after to that extent . . . I mean, I don't really want to have to be like that. If, if I end up like that I'd rather be dead really. I mean it's . . . it's bad enough now.

Kevin let me know the extent to which the thought of further disability, particularly a wheelchair, was affecting him, clearly stating that he would rather be dead than in a wheelchair. My immediate feeling was that I would need to clarify the extent to which this thought was playing on Kevin's mind and I decided to explore this further with him. However, for the moment, Kevin was continuing to talk.

COUNSELLOR 17: Mm.
CLIENT 17: Because I don't know, know when I'm at home, I mean at the weekend . . .
COUNSELLOR 18: Mm.
CLIENT 18: She goes out to work and, um, the kids aren't there and I . . . usually they're out and I'm on my own and it's um . . . you know, I just think about things and I, the more inactive you are the more time you have to think about things and . . . you know the television makes it worse because the television's on, and people go and people are playing football and I . . .
COUNSELLOR 19: Mm.
CLIENT 19: Used to play football and, you know, it just reminds me all the time, or I pick up a newspaper and it just reminds you all the time of what you can't do . . . and it just doesn't seem any life at all.

COUNSELLOR 20: Yeah.

Several questions came to mind as Kevin was talking from turns 16 to 19. He was clearly emotional and revealing the extent to which his illness was playing on his mind. However, Kevin was eager to talk at this point and I wanted to enable him to express his feelings.

CLIENT 20: But, you know, it, as my wife says, it might not happen, you know, some, um, in fact the chances are that it won't happen because only 15 per cent apparently end up in a wheelchair, you know, other people it stabilises but you don't where it'll stabilise, it could stabilise now and it'll just stay like I am or, but I could get worse and worse and it could stabilise, in a, you know, somewhere down the line.

Kevin revealed that he frequently thought about the future, especially when his family was out and he was on his own. A key concern was clearly the 'threat' of a wheelchair and he again mentioned his wife. This made me wonder whether the pattern of communication between Kevin and his wife was actually making him worry more. It appeared that, to some extent, his wife may be avoiding discussion about the future, so that Kevin was unable to consider ways in which the family might cope and to move on from his feelings of hopelessness.

COUNSELLOR 21: Mm. What does your . . . so your wife says it may never happen, but what does she say, do you, do you, what do you think she would say about, about the, about you being in a wheelchair? If you were?

I asked this hypothetical question to explore the extent to which Kevin was aware of his wife's thoughts and feelings, and therefore how much his illness had affected the communication between them.

CLIENT 21: Well, I think she'd think she'd be positive about it but . . . she's that sort of person but, um, but, you know, I don't really want her to have, have, to have her be positive about this, you know I mean?

Kevin let me know that he and his wife had not really talked about this aspect of his illness. He stated that he believed she would be positive, but hinted that he believed this would only be because she would have no choice, clearly exposing his feelings that he was imposing his illness on other people.

COUNSELLOR 22: Mm.

I was letting Kevin know that I was listening and understood what he was saying.

CLIENT 22: I think, I think she'd be, I think she'd say it was alright and I think in practice she'd, it would be alright, but I, I don't want her to have to to deal with that really, and I know she'd find it very stressful . . .

Kevin expressed the fact that he wanted to protect his wife and prevent her from having to cope with the consequences of his illness, continuing to reveal the extent to which his feelings and his ability to cope with his illness were linked to the impact on his family. While I was thinking about what Kevin was saying, I was also considering the statement Kevin had made at turn 16, that if things got too bad he would rather be dead.

COUNSELLOR 23: Mm.

I continued to indicate to Kevin that I was listening.

CLIENT 23: I mean, even if she says she would say, she wouldn't. I know she'd find it stressful because she worries a lot about things.

Kevin expressed his belief that his wife would find difficulty coping because she tended to worry about things. The implied assumption was that she would find it difficult because she had tended to worry about things in the past. I realised from the tone of Kevin's voice and the expression on his face, which was one of great sadness, that he was feeling very emotional. I was concerned that difficult questions would distress him further but I was also aware that I needed to clarify how low he was feeling, and the extent to which his concern for his wife and his worries about the future may cause him to consider whether life was worth living. I needed to find out whether Kevin had any suicidal intentions.

COUNSELLOR 24: And I, I'm sorry, I know I'm pushing you, and you say that you, you think your wife would find it stressful and you feel that, you know, it would be so awful that you'd rather be dead. Is that something you've thought about a lot, that, that, you know, perhaps it'll get to the stage that you'd rather be dead?

I had difficulty asking this question, and, in fact, didn't ask it very well. I started quite well by re-stating my understanding of what Kevin was telling me and then asking the question, but I used a closed question yet again and could have elicited a one-word answer.

CLIENT 24: Well, when I'm depressed, I mean, I've not been so depressed recently that, the, um, the antidepressants that they gave me help.
COUNSELLOR 25: Mm.
CLIENT 25: And I, I try to occupy my mind, I read a lot.
COUNSELLOR 26: Mm.
CLIENT 26: And, uh, what have you, um, I read a lot actually. I've read now but, um, yes but you you, yes, I mean it, it well, but yes I mean it, it's,

it's easier but I suppose to say I'd rather be dead but I don't, don't see the point of going on but even, you know, if it got like that but even the, that would, I couldn't say that to my wife she would just get . . .

COUNSELLOR 27: Mm, but . . .

CLIENT 27: Angry with me.

From turns 24 to 27, Kevin struggled to express his feelings and to some extent appeared to be unsure both about what to say and about how he felt about the future. His final comment was perhaps the most illuminating so far, revealing that he believed his wife would feel angry if she knew that he was feeling uncertain about the future.

COUNSELLOR 28: You wouldn't actually, would you, would you actually ever contemplate doing something about that, doing something to end it?

My concern about Kevin's previous statements was dominating my thoughts. At turn 27 I missed his comment about his wife becoming angry. I was not paying enough attention to what he was saying and 'jumped in' to confirm whether or not Kevin had considered, or thought he would consider, suicide. This point needed to be clarified, but my anxiety over this issue caused me to miss the point about Kevin's relationship with his wife.

CLIENT 28: No, I don't think so.

Kevin replied quickly and firmly, immediately allaying my fears. His non-verbal behaviour, shaking his head and looking surprised, also indicated that suicide was not something he had considered. However, I made a mental note of this piece of our conversation and decided to further check my understanding at a later time. I also discussed the conversation with my supervisor and recorded my observations and understanding in the client notes.

COUNSELLOR 29: No, good. It's not something . . .

CLIENT 29: No, I just, no. I just, no. You just feel that way sometimes.

Again, Kevin confirmed that he has not seriously considered ending his life, but referred to a state that 'you', i.e. 'people', experience on occasions.

COUNSELLOR 30: Yeah, it's just, yes and I, and I don't think that's unusual for people to feel that way when, when things are happening and, and it, it appears to be out of your control um . . . you know it's, it's very difficult and that's why it's, it's positive to come to here and talk about these things and sort of try and and look at them perhaps in a different way.

I tried to convey to Kevin that I understood and that he was not alone in feeling the way he did, thus normalising his situation to an extent. This can help to reduce feelings of isolation, exclusion and difference (Bor et al. 1998). I also wanted to acknowledge the positive step Kevin had taken in seeking help, and promote the idea that there may be a different way of looking at the family's difficulties.

According to Minuchin and Fishman (1981) any change in a family structure will inevitably cause a change in the family's world-view, and their own, narrowed perception of reality will cause them to believe that no other view is possible. By enabling Kevin to look at other possibilities and take a different view of his problem, the effect on his family could perhaps be minimised.

CLIENT 30: Mm.

As he answered, Kevin was looking thoughtful and appeared to be considering what I had said.

COUNSELLOR 31: How, how is it affecting the sort of family life. I know that it's, um, you say that you're not able to, to play sport and to do things as much yourself, what sort of impact is it having in general on the family?

Having established that Kevin was not feeling suicidal, I wanted to return to exploring Kevin's view of how the illness had affected the family. Earlier in the session, Kevin had explained that his initial reaction to his diagnosis had been to become frequently frustrated and angry, often storming out of the house. He had found it impossible to talk to other members of the family. His wife had become very distressed and his children had not known what to do and had avoided him. Kevin had said that these episodes had now subsided, but I wanted to discover how family life in general had been affected by the changes that they had been going through.

CLIENT 31: Well, to start with, as I said, it, it was really not very good because of my reaction to it.

COUNSELLOR 32: Mm.

I confirmed to Kevin that I was listening but waited for him to continue.

CLIENT 32: But funnily enough it sort of almost normal now, um, in fact in some ways it's brought me and the, the youngest child closer together 'cos I make a point now, when he's going to play football, or something.

Kevin let me know that the initial impact of his diagnosis and the sense of chaos and distress felt by the family at that time had given way to a more 'normal' pattern of family behaviour. He also commented on the positive effect of his changed relationship with his son. This indicated to me that Kevin was able to rationalise and would therefore potentially be amenable to looking at his problems in a different way, therefore opening up alternatives and possibilities (Burnham 1986).

COUNSELLOR 33: Mm.

CLIENT 33: Going along to watch him.

COUNSELLOR 34: Mm.

CLIENT 34: And if I go to the shops or something, if I go out, he'll come with me to make sure, you know, that I don't, that I don't fall over or what have you.

Kevin referred again to the changing relationships and roles in the family. He spoke more quickly and enthusiastically at this point and appeared to be touched by his son's attention and concern.

COUNSELLOR 35: Mm. Mm.

CLIENT 35: And so, funnily enough, it's brought us close together but, um, the 17-year-old is at college, so I don't see so much of her really. I mean, she's not, I suppose she kind of almost ignores, and that sounds negative to say she ignores it, and I don't mean it that way, but I suppose for her, you know, she's got other interests.

Kevin's narrative at this stage suggested that the family had to some extent 'settled down' to a kind of normality, and was already in the process of adjusting to his illness and increasing disability.

COUNSELLOR 36: Mm.

CLIENT 36: Um, so he's, he's, he helps when he can and for my wife, as I say, it's kind of almost at the moment it's almost normal because this doesn't . . . you, you, since I've taken the antidepressants I've not been so irritable some things, sometimes things will set me off, like if I, if I drop something or . . .

COUNSELLOR 37: Mm.

I confirmed to Kevin that I was listening but waited for him to continue.

CLIENT 37: If I can't do something I'll get a little angry but I tend not to be as depressed and, um, and it doesn't, the illness doesn't get, it gets worse slowly so, you know, it's almost it's almost at the moment, we're in a kind of a . . . it's fairly normal . . . it's almost a normal . . .

Kevin continued to express his belief that there was a sense of normality in the family. He indicated that he recognised the benefits of taking antidepressants and clearly stated that he was less depressed and irritable since taking them. He also demonstrated awareness of the most common 'triggers' to bouts of depression or frustration.

COUNSELLOR 38: Yeah, so, so actual sort of family life hasn't changed that much except that in actual fact there has been something positive because your relationship with your son has, has possibly got a bit closer.

I picked up on Kevin's observation at turn 35 about his relationship with his son. At the beginning of the session, Kevin had punctuated his son's concern and help as a sign of weakness and deterioration. At turn 35 he had begun to reframe and, therefore, re-punctuate this change in their relationship as a positive one. I wanted to reinforce this change in attitude and promote the view that his illness may facilitate some gains as well as losses, enabling Kevin to develop a feeling of hope for the future.

During the remainder of the session we continued to discuss Kevin's beliefs regarding his illness and the effects on the family.

Summary

Kevin's main concern was uncertainty about the future. In the short term his expected early retirement from work concerned him and he was worried about the 'space' created by not being at work. He was generally concerned about his changing role in the family, the associated change in relationships and his loss of identity. In the longer term, Kevin was concerned about increasing loss of independence and, particularly, the prospect of becoming confined to a wheelchair. He appeared to be more concerned about the impact on his family than about himself, and was particularly worried about how his wife would cope in this scenario.

I hypothesised that the diagnosis of polymyositis had thrown Kevin and his family into a state of turmoil and confusion. Kevin's initial reaction had been one of immobilisation, in which he denied his feelings of fear and confusion and refused to discuss the situation with his family. This upset Kevin's wife who wanted to discuss the situation and help Kevin. Kevin had quickly become angry and irritable, especially when signs of his increasing disability were apparent. The family had then settled into a state in which Kevin's illness was not discussed for fear of upsetting him. The resulting effect was that Kevin was becoming increasingly isolated and depressed and the family had no idea how to react. Although the family system had stabilised, this stability was dysfunctional. Kevin agreed with this summary, and his expectations regarding counselling were explored. When discussing the point at which counselling should end, Kevin decided that he would know he was feeling better if he could talk more readily to his wife and explore his concerns with her. An initial contract of six further sessions was then agreed upon.

I chose to use this session and transcript for the process report since it provided a good learning experience for me in the application of systemic counselling. It highlighted a number of issues regarding my own development as a counselling psychologist that I was able to address in future practice.

Overall, I felt I achieved my aims for the session. I gained a good understanding of Kevin's beliefs regarding his illness, his concerns for the future and the impact of the situation on the family. I was also able to note the physiological effects of his illness, the effect on his employment status, and the quality of social and professional support available to him. I developed a rapport with Kevin and thought that he felt both understood and able to express his concerns.

However, to an extent I feel that the session achieved its objectives primarily because Kevin wanted to talk about his problems, rather than because I was expert in asking appropriate questions and then in following through on the issues prompted by Kevin's responses. My tendency to ask closed questions restricted my exploration of his relationship with his family and could have affected my understanding of his problem. There were a number of points at which a more circular style of questioning should have been applied to explore the issues raised by Kevin in terms of how those issues were viewed by different members of the family. This could have extended to exploration of how Kevin thought his relationships with his family were likely to change as his illness progressed.

The session also demonstrated how the counsellor mentally focusing on one issue can impact the quality of the session and the information gained. At one point, I became so concerned with finding an opportunity of clarifying Kevin's feelings about suicide that I was not paying attention to the dialogue. As a result I failed to pick up on statements made by Kevin that would have enabled me follow through on comments he made and explore relationships in the family. I need to reflect on my ability to cope with such personal concerns while still 'paying attention'. I learnt a great deal about myself from this tape and was able to use the learning process to improve future sessions.

References

Altschuler, J. (1997). *Working with Chronic Illness*. Basingstoke: Macmillan.

Bor, R., Legg, C. and Scher, I. (1996). The systems paradigm. In R. Woolfe and W. Dryden (eds) *Handbook of Counselling Psychology*. London: Sage.

Bor, R., Miller, R., Latz, M. and Salt, H. (1998). *Counselling in Health Care Settings*. London: Cassell.

Burnham, J.B. (1986). *Family Therapy*. London: Tavistock.

Egan, G. (1998). *The Skilled Helper. A Problem-Management Approach to Helping*, 4th edn. Pacific Grove, CA: Brooks/Cole.

Hoffman, L. (1981). *Foundations of Family Therapy*. New York: Basic Books.

McLeod, J. (1998). *An Introduction to Counselling*, 2nd edn. Buckingham: Open University Press.
Minuchin, S. (1974). *Families and Family Therapy*. London: Tavistock.
Minuchin, S. and Fishman, H.C. (1981). *Family Therapy Techniques*. Cambridge, MA: Harvard University Press.
Palazzoli, M., Cecchin, G., Boscolo, L. and Prata, G. (1978). *Paradox and Counter Paradox*. New York: Aronson.
Shafer, K.N., Sawyer, J.R., McCluskey, A.M., Beck, E.L. and Phipps, W.J. (1979). *Medical Surgical Nursing*. St Louis: The C.V. Mosby Company.
Watzlawick, P., Weakland, J. and Fisch, R. (1974). *Change: Principles of Problem Formulation and Problem Resolution*. New York: Norton.

Chapter 3

CBT as applied to anxiety: a process report

with a case study by Lorraine Garden

PRELUDE

One of the most rewarding experiences for any trainee therapist is reaching a point where they are able to recognise their personal and professional progress. The journey for any therapist is paved with learning milestones and none is more significant than the acquisition of self-reflection and self-discovery that comes with one's development as a therapist. This case eloquently captures that journey for Lorraine Garden who discusses how upon revisiting the report she is reminded of the anxieties and insecurities of a new trainee but also that she recognises the reflectivity, which has contributed to her professional development so far.

This process report is very well written and Lorraine Garden makes clear links between the underlying theory that she uses and the practical methods she employs. Her work is frequently referenced, and her arguments are well substantiated by relevant theory or research within the field of cognitive behavioural therapy (CBT) and abnormal psychology. The other major feature of this process report is the professional maturity shown in her self evaluation and when evaluating the efficacy of the treatment.

This case captures the essence of what a process report should be. Lorraine not only reflects upon her work with her client but also upon the frustrations of choosing, transcribing and analysing a piece of work. Her account is honest and well contemplated and she invites the reader to learn about the process of therapy in the same way that she does, with an open mind and a clear agenda to gain the most out of the experience of writing the process report.

Lorraine Garden wrote this report at the beginning of a full-time MSc in Counselling Psychology. The comments were written at the beginning of the first year of a post-MSc Practitioner Diploma in Counselling Psychology.

Preamble

In deciding which client to write my process report on, I was guided by a combination of clinical, theoretical, personal and purely practical reasons. I found this case fascinating, as the client's presenting problem of panic attacks seemed to take on a whole new dimension in the light of other factors, gleaned from her history, concerning a personal trauma. This meant that we had a lot to cover in a short space of time. The process report seemed like a useful tool in helping to meet these treatment aims and could help to buy me more therapeutic time with the client. Having a recording of the sessions would enable me to attend to the other parts of the session that I may have missed, and explore the process for clues, fresh insights and modifications that I could then bring to future sessions to make them more efficient. On a personal level, as a relative newcomer to CBT, I was finding the art of applying theory, skills and techniques to practice, quite a challenge. Was I actually 'doing CBT' and how comfortable did I appear to be with the process of carrying it out? What impact was this having on my client? On a practical level, I chose this case as the client appeared to be both a suitable candidate for CBT and comfortable about being recorded.

Revisiting this report I am reminded of my anxieties concerning my inexperience, uncertainty and competence as a trainee therapist. Reading the report now, quite a healthy level of maturity comes through in my reflective comments and ability to evaluate my strengths and weaknesses critically. Despite feeling quite angst-ridden about exposing my credentials as a CBT practitioner (where I had come across as being quite dominant and bossy at times) I took care to think about these and how they impacted upon the client and to consider alternative ways of intervening. I think it was this that made me feel that I had produced some good work.

From drafting this report I learned so much! While, at the time, it can feel quite a laborious process, transcribing and analysing every utterance, sigh and silence, the end results are worth it. I gained some very different perspectives to the ones that I had come out of the session with, namely: (1) my presence and manner as a therapist and its impact upon the client; and (2) the client's experience of her difficulties and their impact upon me. I realised that listening to what your client is telling you is a much more active, and deeper, process than I had previously imagined. The way words were spoken, the tone, pace and rhythm, gave me a much deeper insight into the different levels of communication going on in any interaction. Although some, that are too fleeting to be able to attend to, may contain the most telling and therapeutically informative material. What I learned the most was how by being tuned into these levels of communication and actively noticing the clues in the process, we can learn how to interact with our clients in a way that is more congruent and clinically effective.

PROCESS REPORT

Introduction

In this process report Beck's (1976) cognitive-behavioural therapy model was used as a framework for intervention. Section 1 overviews the main principles and techniques. Section 2 outlines psychological assessment and is followed by a 10-minute transcription from the first session following assessment. In Section 3 commentary is included in the transcript and Section 4 summarises and evaluates the work covered in the session where an evaluation of the counsellor's role is given.

Section 1: theoretical framework

CBT is an integration of cognitive therapy (Beck 1970, 1976) and behaviour therapy (Bandura 1977) whereby the client is helped to recognise distorted patterns of thinking and dysfunctional behaviour. The basic premise is that dysfunction arises out of an individual's interpretation of events. Moreover, behavioural responses emerging from those interpretations are important factors in the maintenance of emotional problems.

Emotional disorders such as anxiety and depression are hypothesised to be maintained by distortions in thinking. This dysfunctional processing is manifested at a surface level as a stream of negative automatic thoughts. Distortions reflect the operation of underlying beliefs and assumptions stored in memory structures or schemata (Bartlett 1932). Once activated schemata can influence information processing, shape the interpretation of experience, and ultimately affect behaviour.

Counselling was conducted from a time-limited, solution focused approach to treatment. For effective treatment, 'collaborative empiricism' is relied upon where specific problems of priority are worked upon. Using Socratic dialogue, the therapist is able to explore the client's understanding of their experience and challenge their belief in dysfunctional assumptions and negative thoughts.

Anxiety

Preoccupation with the concept of danger and an associated underestimation of the ability to cope is what is viewed as the 'disorder' underlying anxiety vulnerability and anxiety maintenance (Beck et al. 1985). The locus of the disorder is not in the affective system but in the hypervigilent cognitive schemata relevant to danger that are continually presenting a view of reality as dangerous and the self as vulnerable (Beck et al. 1985). Such overestimates automatically and reflexively activate the anxiety programme (Beck 1976). Research suggests that two different types of anxiety can be usefully distinguished (Clark et al. 1988). In the first the predominant problem is recurrent panic attacks, which can occur unexpectedly and in almost any situation. The cognitive model of panic states that individuals experience panic attacks because they have a relatively enduring tendency to interpret a range of bodily sensations in a catastrophic fashion (Clark 1986). The catastrophic misinterpretation involves perceiving these sensations as indicative of an immediately impending physical or mental disaster, e.g. perceiving palpitations as evidence of a heart attack. A further increase in apprehension occurs, producing a further increase in bodily sensations and so on, in a vicious circle which culminates in a panic attack.

Section 2: psychological assessment

Referral

The client was referred by her GP to the Brief Therapy Team for help with panic attacks and anxiety management. The client requested counselling.

Medication

None prescribed.

Appearance and behaviour

Susan, a 29-year-old married mother of two children aged 4 and 2, was sitting in the waiting room in a hunched up and nervous way and appeared quite apprehensive. Throughout the session, however, she was able to relax and was easy to engage with.

Presenting problems

Susan explained how she had been experiencing mild panic attacks, over the past year. Susan's last attack happened 1 month ago, while driving with her children. Somatic sensations included breathlessness, heart palpitations, shaking and sweating. Unable to pull over, Susan found the experience extremely unnerving and has since avoided that particular route. Susan described the attack as happening 'out of the blue' and thought that she was having a heart attack.

In addition to panic attacks, Susan described how her daily functioning is affected by chronic bouts of worry and constant fears about dying. She revealed that she had found the premature birth of her (now 4-year-old) son and his subsequent hospitalisation traumatic and harrowing. Susan witnessed moments when her son stopped breathing, alarms went off, doctors and nurses rushed around the cot, and she was led away. Susan described difficulties in being able to recover from this event despite her son making a slow, but full, recovery. Susan described feelings of guilt and blame, explaining how she had become convinced that she had given him some life-threatening illness, and was responsible for his premature birth and near death.

Background and family history

Susan was brought up in a 'loving, close and happy Catholic family', though she described how her Nan, whom Susan had been afraid of, had occupied a very dominant role in the family. Susan described how she grew up appeasing those around her, feeling that she was to blame for things that were not her fault. The family's style of coping seemed to be characterised by catastrophisation of small issues into larger ones. Susan described being close to her mother, whom she also described as a worrier.

Life stressors

1996 Grandmother died; husband made redundant.
1997 Birth of son (with complications).
1998 House move – financial difficulties.
1999 Daughter born.

Cognitive behavioural profile

Cognitive factors

'Dysfunctional' thinking in her interpretation of non-threatening events and situations as threatening. This appeared to be characterised by an overestimation of the danger inherent in any situation. Cross-sectional analysis revealed how belief in negative thoughts and the possibility of their catastrophic consequences ('I am going to die') would serve to activate Susan's somatic anxiety programme (heart palpitations; dry mouth), which she would then appraise as further sources of threat ('Oh God, I'm having a panic attack') as in the vicious cycle of panic (Beck 1995).

Dysfunctional assumptions (Hawton et al. 1989)

Responsibility: 'If anything is wrong, it is my fault.'
Perfectionism: 'Everything has to be 100 per cent perfect, otherwise it will be all wrong.'
Competence: 'I'm not good enough; I'm a bad mum.'

Behavioural factors

Avoidance of situations such as the route to her mother's house. Susan demonstrated using distractive coping strategies, such as crossword puzzles, that had been successful until recently. However, with the increased severity of her attacks, these strategies were not enough. Safety behaviours included telephoning her husband, not being alone and seeking reassurance.

Emotional factors

Susan described feeling stupid and inadequate for not having got over what happened to her son, and for experiencing panic attacks at all. She described how it was difficult to express her true emotions with her husband and family. This may have implications for her ability to utilise support, as she has not told her husband, close friends or mother that she is preoccupied with death and constantly afraid.

Depression

Susan did not present with any real evidence of depression, though admitted to feeling low when worrying, and considering the prospect that her life may be blighted by panic attacks affecting her more and more.

Physical symptoms

Tiredness and feeling tense, plus somatic symptoms of panic as already described.

Case formulation

Susan appears to be suffering from a traumatic stress reaction to the complications experienced by her son shortly after his premature birth. While her symptoms do not fully satisfy the DSM-IV criteria for post-traumatic stress disorder (PTSD), no true avoidance and dissociation, this does not mean that her experience of the trauma is any less real. The continued belief in negative schemata surrounding this event ('it is my fault, I am to blame; I am a bad mother') may serve to contribute to, and maintain, Susan's vulnerability to experiencing the persistent anxiety and panic attacks. Having witnessed the near death of her son, Susan has developed the belief that any unexpected physical symptoms could lead to sudden death. Susan's preoccupation with death, evident in the scanning of events to find evidence of their potential danger, could in some way be an expression of her need to seek forgiveness or relief from her own sense of guilt about the event. This could be a kind of reassurance-seeking type of behaviour. While in reality Susan is a competent mother, she can never fully believe this, because of the underlying belief in her responsibility for her son's illness. This act of scanning is futile as it fails to satisfy her feelings of guilt, reinforces her negative self-beliefs, and may become a kind of vicious circle of self-punishment. 'What if?' ruminations appear to lead to catastrophic consequences, not only rekindling graphic memories of the horror of the event, but also triggering Susan's own anxiety and panic programme.

It is considered that Susan's beliefs about her involvement in the birth event may be linked to some core beliefs about her own sense of worth and adequacy.

Contributing factors to Susan's vigilance over danger and anxiety have been the death of her grandmother, the loss of her husband's job, the loss of their comfortable lifestyle and their home (to a more modest one) and with those the possible loss of her self confidence and control. Such losses can only have had a disempowering effect and served to undermine Susan's sense of security and stability, variables considered critical to the experience of the vulnerability felt in anxiety and panic disorders.

Contract and counselling plan

Contracting was influenced by the bounds of service. Following two assessments, eight weekly, hour-long sessions were agreed. Confidentiality was addressed in terms of self-harm, supervision, taping and written correspondence with the client's GP.

Goals of treatment

- Preventative and coping techniques via: psychoeducation; the vicious circle of panic; challenging-negative-thought exercises; rational self-talk exercises; distraction and relaxation techniques; desensitisation.
- It is hypothesised that in traumatic response reactions, memories are split off from consciousness and stored instead as sensory perceptions and obsessional ruminations (Siegel 1995). Continued experience of such intrusive and obsessive thoughts is considered critical to the continued experience of Susan's panic attacks. Therapy was directed at promoting emotional processing around this traumatic event via cognitive restructuring aimed at reducing the overestimation of responsibility and guilt, in order to integrate the trauma into Susan's life to enable Susan to accommodate the trauma in existing schemata in a meaningful and adaptive way.

Aims for session 1

- To motivate Susan's involvement in the collaborative process of CBT and to ensure that she fully grasps the conceptual links between thoughts, affects and behaviours.
- To work through NATs (Negative Automatic Thoughts) on affects and behaviour to be able to introduce the concept of countering them together with rationalisation as both a preventative and coping strategy.
- To summarise points of learning, gain feedback and set homework on challenging NATs exercises.

Lead-in to the session

The transcription is taken from the first session (following two assessment sessions) and begins where I am using the client's example of a recent panic attack, which was triggered by her re-evaluation of her role in looking after her friend's baby.

Section 3: transcript

THERAPIST 1: As you said before they're (NATs) negative and frightening and they kind of spin out with things a bit . . . so if we identify what they are, then we can get into the practice of actually knowing that you're aware that they're there . . .

Again I am trying to show more reasons why NATs are so important. However, I am aware throughout the whole session that I have been talking a lot and that Susan is the one listening and nodding. I feel aware that I have been dominating the session, and being very directive, yet at the same time I feel that it is vital that clients grasp the concept of the treatment and are motivated to collaborate. I wonder whether through Socratic questioning I should be helping the client to arrive at these conclusions herself without me actually being so didactic.

CLIENT 1: Right.

THERAPIST 2: Because you go through life and you're not going to be really naturally aware of the thought processes you're having, you have them but you're not going to sort of question them . . .

Again I am trying to prime Susan for what to expect and why it may feel unusual, first to identify your own thoughts and then second to challenge them. On reflection, I am aware that I am preparing and priming Susan for a lot of things. I wonder whether I am being too involved and wonder whether this is actually 'therapy'. However, on the other hand the literature on CBT suggests that a systematic structure and approach is essential. I rationalise this dilemma and make a decision to try to redress the balance by using more Socratic questioning.

CLIENT 2: No.

Susan shows me she follows.

THERAPIST 3: Now um, let's say OK, so can we go back to that situation.

I gain Susan's collaboration by asking her permission to go back to her most recent emotional experience to elicit her thoughts.

CLIENT 3: Yeah.

While I am aware of being so directive, her response informs me that she is receptive to the exercise and engaged.

THERAPIST 4: And see what, so what was kind of going through your mind? Was it the fact that he . . . there was a cot death, did you say, in the family?

I say this and wish immediately afterwards that I had not led Susan. I should have just asked her openly what was going through her mind? It may not have been the cot death, something else may have precipitated it.

CLIENT 4: Yeah . . . they . . . the . . . her mum won't have him until he's one because of the cot death and I was just like . . . and she's fallen pregnant again and he's only six months, and so she's not sleeping, so I was like, 'Oh, I'll have him' . . . and I . . . um, I can understand why his mum, her mum wouldn't have him, but that, that didn't worry me when I was saying, 'Oh, I'll have him'.

Here Susan demonstrates that her appraisal of any danger in possible situations has not escalated to a proportion whereby she will avoid situations in advance. This gives me some insight into the developmental stage of her anxiety/panic difficulties. This helps me to consider the course of treatment and will help me to select which interventions may be more useful than others. For example, had she got into a cycle of avoidance, then that may predict that she would find it harder to relinquish hold on any safety behaviours. This has implications for the setting of realistic goals and expectations.

THERAPIST 5: Mmm.

I show Susan that I'm listening and from the tone of my voice encourage her that it's safe to continue. From the quite positive tone of voice I am trying to reflect and bolster Susan's own self-admission that she does not worry all the time and that she is capable and competent. Also, I want to make her feel safe about disclosing these thoughts as she has demonstrated earlier that she does not share these fears with her partner for fear of sounding 'silly'. It is therefore important that Susan feels comfortable to disclose them now.

CLIENT 5: And then in bed I was, after I'd had him that I started to feel panicky . . . and thought God, what if something had happened, you know, and he's in my care . . .

Here Susan demonstrates catastrophic thinking associated with anxiety 'disorders'. The way Susan says the last few words reveals the possible amount of guilt Susan still feels for her own little boy's illness and hospitalisation around the time of his birth.

THERAPIST 6: Right so what if . . .

As I'm writing down what thoughts Susan tells me I echo them, in order to try and prompt her and elicit any catastrophic consequences of her thinking style.

CLIENT 6: Something had happened to him . . . (*Susan continues*)

THERAPIST 7: (*Writing down her thoughts*) OK. What would it mean if something, what was going on in your mind?

I use repetition deliberately to try to make this more real for Susan and then ask her directly what she was actually thinking in order to draw out her thoughts.

CLIENT 7: If I . . . maybe I'd done something . . . well, you know . . . if he had of died . . . well, you know, a cot death, would it be because I hadn't done something right?

This shows how Susan's thoughts may stem from some dysfunctional core beliefs about her abilities, and possibly involve self-blame.

THERAPIST 8: OK, and what other things were you thinking around that?

I ask Susan to go further with this, dropping my voice to reflect how serious this is and personal for her.

CLIENT 8: Just then that maybe I shouldn't have left him to cry so, 'cos he . . . he doesn't sleep very well, so but she . . . she said, you know, that don't just pick him up the first time, every time, leave him to cry for a bit and then so you do leave him to cry and, you know, if I . . . nothing happened to him so . . . (*Looks to me*)

Susan's thoughts seem to reflect a kind of hypervigilence and preoccupation with the concept of danger, common to anxiety symptoms. She reveals how she has rewound and played back the night before in real detail, and attended to the elements where danger could have presented itself. This in itself makes me question the degree to which she has experienced emotional trauma around her own son's hospital episode and

I hypothesise that selectively focusing on a non-dangerous event, and re-appraising her own behaviour in it, may be serving the function of punishing and blaming herself for what happened to her own son. Such cognitions may be critical factors in maintaining her anxiety and panic attacks.

THERAPIST 9: Sure.

I try to let Susan know that I am with her, and that it is safe to continue.

CLIENT 9: But if I had left him to cry then something had happened, then you think, 'Oh if only I hadn't left him to cry', but . . . saying it sounds really silly now, nothing happened so why should I have . . .

This reveals how Susan's thinking style is characteristically full of 'what ifs', serving the function of constantly attending to the possibilities of danger being present around her. She tails off.

THERAPIST 10: Thought about it?

Susan's facial movements and eyes look at me as though she needs some validation for what she is saying and I finish her sentence for her to show that I understand how she feels.

CLIENT 10: Yeah. (*Nodding*)

Susan says this resolutely and somewhat sadly, and from this I get a strong sense of her conflict and frustration; of being trapped in a perpetual state of self-examination and self-blame, which appears to be serving no functional purpose. This is an important discovery, as it suggests that this constant act of scanning (for possible events which can activate Susan's schemata of responsibility and blame) reflects the extent to which the trauma of her son's birth has not been sufficiently processed and integrated into memory, and is thus being relived and reactivated in different situations.

Section 4: summary

This session met the aims of socialising the client further to the CBT approach and to the influence of thoughts, affects and behaviours in anxiety and panic difficulties. This was achieved by reviewing the client's homework, which had helped to identify situational, affective and behavioural triggers for the client and the presence of any assistant negative thoughts. Working through the client's own examples of recent anxiety/panic attacks helped to make the client aware of an emerging pattern of her anxiety. Having helped the client to identify NATs, using the downward arrow, we elicited negative core beliefs of perfectionism, fear of losing control and feelings of inadequacy, failure and responsibility. From these beliefs it was possible to demonstrate their emotional impact in addition to their physical impact (physiological arousal). This enabled us to move on to the means of challenging negative thoughts and accessing alternative views. In keeping with the scientist–practitioner model, the material elicited enabled me to confirm my preliminary hypotheses and formulation of the client's problem, and to proceed with my chosen treatment plan, and to make modifications where necessary.

Evaluation of session and self-assessment of counsellor

On leaving this session I came away feeling that the session had gone well and that the client had benefited from the interventions used. This was evident from the client's feedback and ability to grasp concepts, to express her emotions and to identify thoughts and cognitions. In addition, the atmosphere of the session had seemed safe and, in terms of the therapeutic alliance, that the client was engaged in the process and motivated to use the techniques and ways of thinking suggested.

However, on reflection of my role within the session I feel quite divided. In the session I took quite a directive role. This is interesting because the client is quite softly spoken, though not timid. However, I feel that the reasons for taking such a directive stance are based on two main issues.

First, I felt compelled to socialise and educate Susan to the CBT models, in order for us to build the foundations of therapy. I have looked at the pattern of our interaction in these exchanges and noticed that I am often speaking more than the client is. The question arises here as to whether or not I should be telling the client such things, for example, the need to record several NATs, or whether I should be guiding the client towards making the discoveries herself. In the session I was aware of this discrepancy and tried to adjust the balance by using more Socratic questions. This automatically shifted the focus over to the client and helped to elicit underlying assumptions and beliefs (turns 23 to 29) and (turns 47 to 49). This session demonstrates some of the difficulties I was having in implementing CBT 'techniques' and how, at times, I was trying too hard to do the work for the client. Since then, I have learned to hold back and listen more, and to resist the temptation to jump in.

The second reason for my directive stance concerns the process between myself and Susan. I try to sound concrete and as grounded as possible as I am aware of her anxieties and of the possibility that she may panic within the session. This seems to appeal to the need to keep to a structured and safe CBT framework. However, having analysed the interaction, it would seem that at several stages I am over compensating and clinging too rigidly to this framework at the expense of the client's words. What does this say concerning my own anxieties about the prospect of the client panicking? At one point in the transcript, Susan show signs of anxiety and effectively diverts me away to avoid talking about the traumatic incident. Instead of sensitively and safely confronting this, I changed the subject in the hope that she would feel safer and calmer and distracted. This is counterproductive and may even collude with the client's own repertoire of avoidance. Having reflected on my role in this respect while on a conscious level I feel no anxiety about the prospect of the client panicking, the tape reveals that some anxiety on my part must have been present. How would I have reacted then if the client had panicked for real? As a means of addressing and anticipating this problem with future clients, I have resolved to use role-play to simulate a client panicking in a session, in order to confront any fears of my own and desensitise myself to this event, so that I may respond appropriately should it ever happen for real.

References

Bandura, A. (1977). Self-efficacy: toward a unifying theory of behavioral change. *Psychological Review*, 84, 191–215.

Bartlett, F.C. (1932). *Remembering*. Cambridge: Cambridge University Press.

Beck, A.T. (1970). Cognitive therapy: nature and relation to behavior therapy. *Behavior Therapy*, 1, 184–200.

Beck, A.T. (1976). *Cognitive Therapy and the Emotional Disorders*. New York: International Universities Press.

Beck, A.T., Emery, G. and Greenberg, R. (1985). *Anxiety Disorders and Phobias: A Cognitive Perspective*. New York: Basic Books.

Beck, J.S. (1995). *Cognitive Therapy: Basics and Beyond*. London: Guilford Press.

Clark, D.M. (1986). A cognitive approach to panic. *Behaviour Research and Therapy*, 24, 461–70.

Clark, D.M. (1988). A cognitive model of panic attacks. In S. Rachman and J.D. Master (eds). Hillsdale, NJ: Lawrence Erlbaum Inc, pp. 71–90.

Hawton, K., Salkovskis, P.M., Kirk, J. and Clark, D.M. (1989). *Cognitive Behaviour Therapy for Psychiatric Problems: a practical guide*. New York: Oxford University Press.

Siegel, D. (1995). Memory, trauma and psychotherapy: a cognitive science view. *Journal of Psychotherapy Practice and Research*, 4, 93–122.

Chapter 4

Achieving growth and change through the application of an integrative theoretical approach to address multiple client difficulties

with a case study by Nicola K. Gale

PRELUDE

We have chosen to include this study as it maintains a clear focus or theme in the context of a complex case, with multiple presenting issues and a therapeutic style that transcends more than one 'essentialist' approach. A particular strength of this case is that it does this in a considered and coherent fashion that reflects poise rather than panic in the selection of technique and the technical execution of the work. The author illustrates how it is possible to integrate directive, cognitive and behavioural (CBT) techniques into an exploratory approach grounded squarely in the therapeutic relationship. The author is confident and clearly conversant with the theoretical and empirical literature, she possesses the capacity to articulate a rationale for why she thinks and does what she does.

The client and the therapist in this case clearly share a spirit of joint enquiry that is so indicative of broadly constructivist approaches to developing understanding and facilitating change collaboratively. We are reminded that relational ways of working are critical where clients are ambivalent about, or unconvinced of, the possibility of change. In this case, behavioural interventions are interwoven into a therapeutic collaboration so that the power and impetus for change remains between the therapist and the client, rather than wholly within either party.

> *Nicola K. Gale wrote this case study during the early stages of her post-MSc in the Practice of Counselling Psychology; the final stage in the process of chartering at City University. Her reflective comments were written when she was invited to contribute to this text.*

Preamble

This case study describes a journey through multiple presenting difficulties towards growth and change. It is being presented to show how the course of that journey was charted by extending my usual ways of working, developing and applying an integrative approach to the therapy in order to address the complexity of the issues and take account of the client's preference regarding the type of counselling received. Achieving growth and change through the application of an integrative theoretical approach to address multiple presenting client difficulties.

How I came to choose this particular case

I remember that one of the most difficult parts of writing this case study was deciding which case to choose. Discussions in the course community at the time centred on factors to take into account, such as having a clear focus of interest for the reader, and how best to demonstrate our own practice at post-MSc level (this felt quite a challenge to me), and were helpful in arriving at a decision. In this case study, my aim was to show how I had needed to integrate quite extensive use of directive cognitive and behavioural (CBT) techniques into an overall more exploratory approach founded on the therapeutic relationship. This was in the context of complex client difficulties, that would benefit from the former, and a client preference for exploratory non-directive work.

How I think and feel retrospectively about what I have produced

Some three years on, I can see that writing this case pushed me to grow and consolidate the theoretical rationale behind my practice and was an example of an integrative way of working that I often find helpful to clients. It raises a number of themes that have since become more topical. The current requirements, especially in health settings, for evidence-based practice and the recent Department of Health guidance on treatment choice in psychological therapies support choosing interventions based on known effectiveness for the client's presenting difficulties. CBT is indicated for many. Because of the client's stated preference for an exploratory relationship-based therapy, this case also reflects some of the current debates about evidence-based efficacy versus client preference and about how both can be accommodated. It is also an example of the current debate among counselling psychologists concerning the use of diagnostic categories and the DSM-IV (APA 1994). I certainly found both of these helpful in this case for pointing to relevant interventions in the sessions, without detracting from the client's felt experience. While I recognise that they can both have limitations, I continue to use them to inform my practice where helpful.

What I learned from drafting and writing this report

In writing this report, as with other course work, I found that the main benefit was the need to reflect long and hard on a particular piece of work in order to do so, and to think carefully about and explicitly document integration of theory with practice. In terms of ongoing practice, it was an example for me of how important it is in client work continually to keep the hypotheses by which the work is proceeding under review, and to be prepared to revise and rethink, together with the client, when necessary. Because of this case study, I also reflected on the benefits of being able to interleave client-centred exploration of the client's particular situation, with information from a 'knowledge-based' perspective on some of what a person in this position might be going through. Often, though not always, this can be helpful to a client who then realises that they are not alone and that there is not only a natural course to a number of their difficulties but also that there are some well-founded ways of addressing some of them that can bring relief. This, in my view, does not replace individual exploration of the client's unique sense of being, though it can effectively supplement it.

CASE STUDY

Introduction

The setting for this case was a counselling service in the voluntary sector. The client had been referred directly to the individual counselling service, as described below. My usual theoretical approach to counselling practice is also relevant context for this case. A humanistic framework underpins my work, with person-centred theory at its core. I integrate this with a constructivist approach on how people see the world, and how their constructions affect the way they operate. I aim to develop a therapeutic relationship in which the client is an active and, as far as possible, equal participant. I also use techniques from the CBT traditions, working on how people's thinking styles can hold them back, and introducing behavioural experiments to generate options for seeing the world and to internalise change. This is in the sense that Winter (1992) refers to, citing the importance of 'an aggressive approach, emphasising active experimentation' (p. 323) in the personal construct psychology meaning of looking outwards and elaborating the client's perceptual field. What was different in this case was the salience of achieving change by integrating substantial CBT work.

The client and the referral process

The client was a 44-year-old woman living with a partner, whom she had met a year previously. I have called her Sally. She was in close contact with her family of origin (mother and two brothers). She had been married before, and divorced. She was currently doing some part-time typing work from home, having lost her job, and felt unable to get another post.

Sally had been referred by her general practitioner (GP). There was no further contact with the referrer or other professionals once the referral had been accepted, as it is the agency's policy not to do this unless there is a clear need. Sally was allocated to me for an initial assessment, and was told that this would be a mutual opportunity to assess her needs and see how they could be met by the counselling service.

Assessment and formulation

Sally appeared nervous in the assessment session, casting rapid glances in my direction from time to time, and fidgeting with her clothing. She talked a lot and very rapidly. In contrast, she came across as clear about what she wanted, in terms of the counsellor and appointment arrangements. I followed Culley (1991) in picking up on the importance of the observable aspects of Sally's presentation as well as what she said.

The same style of presentation continued in the counselling sessions, and was an important issue for the course of the therapy. Later in the therapy, communication became much more of a joint process. In the last few sessions, her presentation was much steadier and appeared more confident. Sally was very softly spoken in the sessions, smiling frequently and showing humour too.

In the initial assessment, Sally described how she wanted to get back to being more like her 'old' self. She explained that a series of events had left her feeling anxious, vulnerable and unable to cope with many aspects of day-to-day living. She recounted how she had been unable to stay in her job, as she no longer felt able to deal with angry and complaining customers. Two, in particular, had complained about Sally and she had been subject to an investigation, she felt unfairly, and was thereafter closely supervised. She had then decided to take up temporary work, and had increasing difficulties in several subsequent assignments, feeling that she could not relate to people, finding that she continually made mistakes, and eventually calling in sick so that she did not have to face going in. Using the telephone was a particular difficulty. She now disliked feeling dependent on her family. She also described how she felt that her marriage had been a mistake.

The problem was explored in the assessment appointment by creating an accepting environment empathically reflecting her own feelings in which Sally could tell her story. Kahn (1997) notes the importance of prizing the client in this way in the relationship, and I felt quite touched and trusted by her early openness. As a precursor to counselling work, I endeavoured to make the exploration a collaborative process, to establish a pattern of her leading her own process. A method endorsed by Culley (1991).

My initial view of the problem, largely from a person-centred framework, was that Sally needed to express her feelings about what had happened, and deal with the related elements of loss. It appeared that there was work to do on rebuilding her confidence and her self-esteem. I thought that within an accepting and empathic relationship, she would be able to work on this. I thought too that some specific behavioural interventions, such as relaxation and exposure techniques could help with the specific phobic responses and the level of anxiety, as would cognitive restructuring, but possibly only as an adjunct to the work.

I shared my initial ideas and provided Sally with an overview of these different ways of working, to give her an understanding of the options. She was not comfortable with a more active, directive approach, saying that it would not help her work on her feelings. Therefore, at the beginning of the counselling work, particularly given Sally's views on what she wanted from counselling, I approached our task together from a more person-centred perspective, focusing on building a therapeutic relationship. Clarkson (1990), on the basis of evaluating research in the field, suggests that the relationship, used intentionally, can be one of the most important factors in determining the success of therapy.

Kahn (1997) indicates that, working in a therapeutic relationship, diagnosis is not key, as moment-to-moment contact is being made with the client's needs. I felt Sally and I had good person-to-person contact and understanding. As the counselling progressed, however, I felt that a more specific diagnostic framework and a more detailed assessment would be helpful, as the complexity of the issues facing Sally emerged, and there seemed to be limited progress in the work. This was the start of what Clarkson (1996) refers to as a process of integrating, not a product of integration, driven by learning together with the client.

To make a more detailed assessment, I used the concept of behavioural interviewing (Kirk 1989). This was done over a number of sessions so that it was not incongruent with a relationship-oriented approach. In turn, we focused in detail on the issues Sally presented, especially on being unable to use the telephone or to work outside the home. I found it particularly relevant to look at the onset of Sally's difficulties, at what Kirk (1989) describes as the course of the problems (how they had developed since onset), and the cognitive, affective and physiological responses that were generating avoidance and maintaining the problem. A very full account emerged, as Sally appeared to feel increasingly more safe in the relationship and we developed trust.

There was a clear link between Sally's inability to work and the customer complaints against her. This appeared to have been a trauma for her, and she displayed some of the DSM-IV indications of post-traumatic stress disorder (PTSD): particularly intense psychological distress at cues and avoidance of stimuli and, arguably, there was some increased negative affect, but the activating event was not physically threatening, and she was not experiencing flashbacks (DSM-IV). PTSD did not seem to capture her experience.

Exploration also revealed a link from the telephone-work complaints to Sally's difficulty with using the telephone. Sally had become increasingly agitated about using the telephone, and had progressively become unable to carry out her role. The inability to use the telephone clearly arose from avoidance following the traumatic experience, but it also bore most of the characteristics of a specific phobia, as it was marked and persistent in relation to a clearly discernible object, caused anxiety perceived as excessive, was avoided or endured with dread, and interfered with normal functioning (DSM-IV). Anxiety was not invariable, however, and arguably could be better explained by the differential diagnosis of trauma onset. It seemed that, although neither diagnostic set of criteria was precisely met, therapy would benefit by being aware of both possibilities, and indeed Marks (1987) notes that PTSD can overlap with specific phobias that start after a trauma. Both involve specific fear cues, and both are mitigated by exposure. In the absence of other PTSD symptoms, therefore, it seemed reasonable not to seek further distinction.

Dysfunctional thinking became apparent, with Sally believing that whenever anything was going well for her there would be a disaster with which she would be unable to cope, for example Sunday family get-togethers were destined to be a disaster. Sally attributed any negative events to herself, for example the problem would be her cooking, not that her brother had just had an argument with his wife.

Making contact with other people was part of Sally's difficulty. She could go to classes at the gym as it was an organised activity, but was unable to make conversation. It seemed that there was an element of social phobia in this, i.e. anxiety invariably raised by social situations, which is seen as excessive, and is interfering with normal functioning (DSM-IV). The rapid but slight eye contact also seemed relevant here. Marks (1987) refers to the commonness of averted gaze in social phobia, and this was a noticeable issue for Sally. She said she felt unable to be herself with people. This lack of personal congruence (Rogers 1961) would, I thought, have important implications for how Sally might grow and become more congruent in therapy.

As a result of my attempts to piece the picture together in the more detailed assessment, I set out to incorporate cognitive and behavioural interventions in the work, given that they have been proven as interventions for some of the specific problem areas confronting Sally. Prochaska and Norcross (1994) imply that integrating these interventions in a person-centred relationship approach is likely to be compatible, since they view therapies as generally agreeing on the process of change and disagreeing on the content, and view combining awareness and action therapies as beneficial. Seeing a CBT approach as dealing with the 'how' of change, and the person-centred approach with the 'what', allows the person-centred theory to supply the theory of personality, and the origin and explanatory framework for the client's difficulties, and the CBT to provide some of the tools to bring change about. Horton (1996) sees this type of rationale as a beneficial move towards top-down deductive rather than case-driven inductive integration. Mahrer (1989) sees it similarly. This fits for me philosophically, yet I was motivated in this instance by the inductive requirement to help Sally in the therapeutic relationship in the most effective way.

The counselling sessions

In the early sessions Sally talked about not feeling confident, and moreover expressed negative associations around confidence in that confident people would also not be likeable people. For her, a person was either 'confident' or, in personal construct terms, its bipolar opposite – 'reliant' (Fransella and Dalton 1990).

From the seventh session onwards, Sally started to make some small gains. The first was being able to tell one of her friends about why she had left her old job, without feeling that this would cause her friend to look down on her. From that point on, in most sessions, there was incremental change, generally involving good handling of specific situations, which would have been very anxiety provoking at the start of therapy.

As these gains started to become more stable and success more predictable, the content of the sessions turned to what became the two core symbols of Sally's difficulty, namely using the telephone, and the thought of getting a full-time job again. The clear association of the two areas had become apparent during deeper exploration of the past work difficulties. Steady progress was made regarding the telephone and, as her approach changed, Sally experienced considerable release over both issues with the pace of change escalating. It was rewarding to observe Sally's delight in the wake of her considerable gains.

The remaining stage of the therapy was taken up with Sally planning for the future, gaining independence both in what she was doing (for example planning a surprise fiftieth birthday celebration for her partner, involving the telephone to an extent she could not previously have managed), and in her attitude to her relationships and approach generally. The counselling focus shifted from problems to opportunities for growth.

The process within the sessions was co-operative and collaborative, where we explored Sally's situation, her behaviour, and her thoughts and feelings. I saw this as establishing the working alliance or I/You relationship (Clarkson 1995), which comprising the person-centred core conditions (Rogers 1961), would be the foundation for the therapy. The sessions began with a lot of listening, letting Sally talk, and letting her know that I understood. Sally tended to start by talking about a particular event in the week that had concerned her in some way. Initially, the work remained at this somewhat superficial level of providing release and containment for the week's anxieties. As Sally's confidence in the relationship progressed, from discussing a current event, we would extend the exploration into her more core issues, more actively addressing how she might see the situation differently, and moderate how she was reacting to it.

Part of the overall process of the work was Sally becoming her own counsellor, generalising to other issues outside what she was doing in the sessions. Kelly (1965) said, 'the task of psychotherapy is to get the human process going again so that life may go on and on from where psychotherapy left off' (p. 223), continuing that the relationship and techniques that will achieve this are as varied as human relating. During the last sessions (the therapy lasted about six months in all), we reviewed and appreciated the work together, as a joint venture. Lindsay and Powell (1994) note the importance of transferring management progressively to the client.

In terms of psychological interventions, the foundation for the work was building the therapeutic relationship. As indicated earlier, I had expected that the person-centred core conditions for therapeutic change, empathy, congruence and unconditional positive regard, taken together with psychological contact, a client in a state of incongruence and communication of the conditions of empathy and respect (Rogers 1957), would be central to facilitating change. Although continued experience of the therapeutic relationship over time might well have produced psychological movement, after the more detailed assessment I suggested refining the approach to use more active interventions. We had developed an openness between us in which Sally would say directly what was and was not helpful to her, and given her own wish to move forward more quickly and with more focus, we agreed to make changes.

I first suggested to Sally that she do a self-characterisation sketch for homework, recommended by Kelly (1955) to get an overview of how a client sees themself. Sally appeared well motivated to do this, and talked about how much she had enjoyed writing at college. On review the following week, however, she reported being unable to do the task. She said that she could write about her interests, but not about her inner world. While, in one sense, this well summarised where she saw herself in psychological terms, it gave no more insight into any specific areas for further exploration.

From there, I adopted a strategy of using the specific events of Sally's week as a basis from which to work on aspects of her thinking style. Sally tended to attribute negative happenings to herself rather than to the situation, and I encouraged reality testing of many of these situations, including reversing the perspectives so that she was encouraged to express the situation from the other party's viewpoint. We discussed the thinking distortions that she was making in the terms used by Powell (1992), which are easy to understand and explain, and also, therefore, to work with. These included especially all-or-nothing thinking, catastrophising, having a negative focus, and jumping to conclusions in order to make negative interpretations without adequate evidence. There was, despite the challenging nature of this work, a lightness in how we went about it within the relationship, which supported the endeavour.

It was also important in deciding which areas to work on, to determine together if they were areas in which Sally wanted to make changes, or whether the expressed desire to change was the result of internalised conditions of worth, for example her going back to full-time work. This process has been described by Corey (1996) in person-centred terms as getting behind the facade of socialisation created by internalising external conditions of worth, to greater independence and integration using a personal frame of reference.

Role-play was another aspect of our work together. Corey (1996) indicated how helpful this could be for promoting active engagement from the client. Although Sally was initially nervous, the trust we had built up allowed her to relax in the work and be more open to the benefits. We worked through strategies for dealing with some of the core difficult areas, for example what she might say when asked in conversation why she had left her previous job. This role-play also contained an element of systematic desensitisation, as rehearsal and being able to deal effectively with the situation reduced anxiety. She also found it helpful to discuss the practical options open to her, for example reducing anxiety by doing less to prepare for family gatherings. This part of the work was quite practical and Sally saw immediate benefit from it, and so in turn I believe it strengthened our relationship for the harder work. Part of the aim was mastery in the here and now, noted by Palmer and Szymanska (1996) as an important goal of cognitive therapy.

Behavioural exposure was used for the specific telephone phobic response. We used the principles of fantasy exposure (Marks 1987), by talking through in detail during the session situations using the telephone. Sally would then try out the exposure tasks for homework. I encouraged Sally to develop a hierarchy based on the scale of her fears, in terms of when she answered the telephone and what she used it for. Another area where I adopted the principles of exposure was in relation to her avoidance of the topic of work in day-to-day interaction, encouraging her, for example, to talk with friends about their work. In achieving small successes, Sally's fear was reduced, as incompatible success information was being incorporated within the phobic fear schema (Brewin 1988). The reality testing eventually extinguished the phobia (Rosenhan and Seligman 1995).

In relation to the trauma Sally experienced at work, again both cognitive and behavioural strategies were used. Scott and Stradling (1992) note that desensitisation works when the avoidant behaviour is based on threat, and the exposure work in relation to the telephone was therefore part of this.

Cognitive restructuring was also adopted, talking through the complaints in great detail and reframing what Sally's part was in the events (Scott 1997). As noted by Rose (1996), such an event needs to be integrated cognitively, and restructuring appeared to achieve this. It helped Sally to do this to combine it with an empathic response to her feelings, resulting in the events becoming less salient.

Reinforcement of the gains Sally was making was helpful, as recommended by Lindsay and Powell (1994). I encouraged her to spend time talking about them, internalising them in doing so, and attributing them to her own agency. Quite often this was done with humour, as Sally had a tendency to laugh when she realised she was dismissing her achievements again. At the same time she recognised that the underlying change in perspective was an important, and increasingly self-directed part of this work. Brewin (1988) indicates that the therapist addressing this tendency is in fact an important part of the cognitive therapy, and linked to challenging dysfunctional thinking patterns.

At the end of therapy, Sally attempted the self-characterisation again, and it seemed to me it might be a marker of the work coming to a close. She wrote two short pages celebrating her achievements. This for me seemed to symbolise how Sally had freed herself from anxieties in the counselling process, and was ready for, and optimistic about, the future. It provided a focus for us to appreciate the work we had done together, and draw the therapeutic relationship to a close.

Reflections on the case and learning

My use of supervision in this case was helpful considering how best to pace the counselling, uncoupling psychologically the work outcome from the ending of counselling. I used supervision to talk through Sally's 'all or nothing' thinking style, and how that might be addressed. Towards the conclusion of the work, supervision was very beneficial in discussing the kind of ending that would be appropriate in view of the major place of the relationship in the work, and the pros and cons of offering a follow up appointment. I might have benefited, however, from having worked with my supervisor more specifically on more of the complexities of this case in relation to use of the diagnostic framework and interventions. Lindsay and Powell (1994) comment that some problems are complex, and that, reasonably, 'a large battery of treatments may be applied . . . in shotgun fashion, to make sure that all possible difficulties are tackled' (p. 36). In terms of the generic tasks of supervision put forward by Carroll (1996), the focus was on process and relationship rather than management.

That the therapeutic approach adopted was effective was assessed from Sally's reports of how she was handling day-to-day situations with very little difficulty, and feeling much more positive about herself. Sally had become more congruent, feeling much more herself with other people. Specifically, she had also moved away from distorted patterns of thinking, and had overcome avoidant behaviours.

In terms of my learning, this case showed me that I can effectively vary my style as a therapist and that the more extensive use of directive techniques as employed in this case does not need to be in conflict with an empowering and exploratory therapeutic relationship. A number of theoretical papers make sense of this, such as Horton (1996) who looks at a much broader model of counselling, comprising relationship, content and planning, across the various stages of therapy. In broadening my approach (in apparent contradiction, but making sense given the need to approach a personal integrative framework with more forethought than using an established model), I also found myself needing to be much more explicit about the techniques that I was using and how they were compatible with an integrative framework that was coherent overall. This was of benefit in developing a sufficiently flexible and extensive integrative framework to address the needs of a particular client with a diverse range of presenting issues, where the work demanded a wider repertoire. In relation to psychological counselling, I became much more at ease with diagnosis in the terms of DSM-IV. Greater precision of diagnosis had seemed important in order to match Sally's multiple presenting needs with an appropriate cognitive or behavioural intervention.

The successful application of specific interventions was achieved in the context of a therapeutic relationship. I felt that I was providing steadiness and support for Sally and also, because of the trust we built up, I was able to challenge her and help her move forward. It is clear to me both from the style of counselling she asked for overtly, and how the sessions proceeded, that Sally was unlikely to have made the progress that she did from a wholly technique-based approach that did not put considerable emphasis on the relationship itself. Equally, integrating quite extensive cognitive and behavioural work added considerable impetus to her process of change and growth.

References

APA (1994). *Diagnostic and Statistical Manual of Mental Disorders*, 4th edn. Washington, DC: American Psychiatric Association.

Brewin, C.R. (1988). *Cognitive Foundations of Clinical Psychology*. Hove: Lawrence Erlbaum Associates.

Carroll, M. (1996). *Counselling Supervision. Theory, Skills and Practice*. London: Cassell.

Clarkson, P. (1990). A multiplicity of psychotherapeutic relationships. *British Journal of Psychotherapy*, 7(2), 148–163.

Clarkson, P. (1995). *The Therapeutic Relationship in Psychoanalysis, Counselling Psychology and Psychotherapy*. London: Whurr.

Clarkson, P. (1996). The eclectic and integrative paradigm: between the Scylla of confluence and the Charybdis of confusion. In R. Woolfe and W. Dryden (eds). *Handbook of Counselling Psychology*. London: Sage.

Corey, G. (1996). *Theory and Practice of Counseling and Psychotherapy*, 5th edn. Pacific Grove, CA: Brooks/Cole.

Culley, S. (1991). *Integrative Counselling Skills in Action*. London: Sage.

Fransella, F. and Dalton, P. (1990). *Personal Construct Counselling in Action*. London: Sage.

Horton, I. (1996). Towards the construction of a model of counselling: some issues. In R. Bayne, I. Horton and J. Bimrose (eds). *New Directions in Counselling*. London: Routledge.

Kahn, M. (1997). *Between Therapist and Client. The New Relationship*, revised edition. New York: W.H. Freeman.

Kelly, G.A. (1955). *The Psychology of Personal Constructs*, vols 1 and 2. New York: W.W. Norton.

Kelly, G.A. (1965). The psychotherapeutic relationship. In B.A. Maher (ed.). *Clinical Psychology and Personality. The Selected Papers of George Kelly*. New York: Robert E. Krieger.

Kirk, J. (1989). Cognitive-behavioural assessment. In K. Hawton, P.M. Salkovskis, J. Kirk and D.M. Clark. *Cognitive Behaviour Therapy for Psychiatric Problems. A Practical Guide*. Oxford: Oxford University Press.

Lindsay, S.J.E. (1994). Fears and anxiety: treatment. In S.J.E. Lindsay and G.E. Powell (eds.). *The Handbook of Clinical Adult Psychology*, 2nd edn. London: Routledge.

Lindsay, S.J.E. and Powell, G.E. (1994). (eds). *The Handbook of Clinical Adult Psychology*, 2nd edn. London: Routledge.

Mahrer, A.R. (1989). *The Integration of Psychotherapies. A Guide for Practicing Therapists*. New York: Human Sciences Press.

Marks, I.M. (1987). *Fears, Phobias, and Rituals. Panic, Anxiety, and their Disorders*. New York: Oxford University Press.

Palmer, S. and Szymanska, K. (1996). Cognitive therapy and counselling. In S. Palmer, S. Dainow and P. Milner (eds). *Counselling. The BAC Counselling Reader*. London: Sage.

Powell, T. (1992). *The Mental Health Handbook*. Bicester: Winslow Press.

Prochaska, J.O. and Norcross, J.C. (1994). *Systems of Psychotherapy. A Transtheoretical Analysis*. Pacific Grove, CA: Brooks/Cole.

Rogers, C.R. (1957). The necessary and sufficient conditions of therapeutic personality change. *Journal of Consulting Psychology*, 21(2), 95–103.

Rogers, C.R. (1961). *On Becoming a Person. A Therapist's View of Psychotherapy*. London: Constable.

Rose, S. (1996). Counselling following trauma. In S. Palmer, S. Dainow and P. Milner (eds). *Counselling. The BAC Counselling Reader*. London: Sage.

Rosenhan, D.L. and Seligman, E.P. (1995). *Abnormal Psychology*. New York: W.W. Norton.

Scott, M.J. (1997). Post-traumatic stress disorder: a cognitive-contextual approach. *Counselling Psychology Quarterly*, 10(2), 125–137.

Scott, M.J. and Stradling, S.G. (1992). *Counselling for Post-Traumatic Stress Disorder*. London: Sage.

Winter, D.A. (1992). *Personal Construct Psychology in Clinical Practice. Theory, Research and Applications*. London: Routledge.

Chapter 5

Locating the locus of evaluation: the subtle processes of person-centred counselling

with a case study by Alex Hudson-Craufurd

PRELUDE

We are pleased to be able to present Alex Hudson-Craufurd's work within this volume. The process report illustrates how so much material can be generated within just a few minutes of a counselling session. Alex shows great sensitivity and insight into his own practice as he reflects on his work with his client James. It is clear from reading this process report how these exercises in structured reflection provide enormous opportunity for professional growth and development. The process report as an assessment tool is often criticised on the basis that because the report is written retrospectively the therapist has the opportunity to develop a rationale and hence justify their practice, thus suggesting that the commentary provided may have little similarity to the observations and experiences of the therapist and the client at the time of the recording of the session. Such arguments seem to miss the point of this learning exercise and would be more relevant if the aim of the report was to evaluate competency or 'good enough' practice. Rather the aim of a process report is to develop the trainee and assess characteristics of therapy that are much more subtle and dynamic.

This report in particular touches on the importance of the shift from an external to an internal locus of evaluation for the client (Mearns 1994). It is very interesting to note that there may be evidence of a parallel process in operation here, partially due to the nature of the task, that of critical reflection and the necessity to persuade assessors that you know what you are talking about, and partly because of the personhood of Alex, our therapist here. In particular we are struck with the tension that Alex experiences in accepting his practice as skilful and competent and criticising it minutely. Although he acknowledges that the critical function of person-centred counselling is to facilitate the client's process, rather than become overly focused on the detail of the content, his appraisal of his own practice has a tight focus, with significant attention to detail, being on the whole pretty unforgiving. What we hope Alex and others will learn from reading this report is that great therapists always have something to learn from reflecting on their practice and that should the day arrive when we believe that we have achieved perfection in our practice, we should perhaps consider taking on the role of client for a stretch.

> *Alex Hudson-Craufurd wrote this process report in the first year of his training as a counselling psychologist at City University, London. His reflective comments were added for the purpose of this publication just after his work was assessed and returned to him.*

Preamble

Why I chose this particular case

I had decided to start recording Jamie's sessions because I had a hunch that although he did spend a lot of time telling me the factual details of what had happened to him, there were subtle processes at work in our sessions which the detail of a process report could help elucidate. It could aid my empathic understanding, and thus, as well as my own learning, there might be real benefits to him from such a piece of work. I chose this particular passage because it illustrates the variety of his processes and also shows him reflecting on them.

What I think and feel retrospectively about what I produced

I do not regard this as a definitive account, or explanation, of what went on during those ten minutes. Rather, I see it as an attempt to pin down the ebb and flow of the interaction between myself, the client and the theoretical knowledge that informs my work. It opens up possibilities rather than being an account of how I fall short of any notion of the 'perfect counsellor'. These possibilities both excite me and make me anxious.

Having completed the task I was shocked by the amount of material that emanated from it. What struck me was how directly I stumbled across the key theoretical issues of person-centred counselling, and how much there was to discuss about them. I was also taken aback by how much could be implied by a casual aside, or even a sigh or pause. That is not to say that a sensitive counsellor would not notice these small signs; however it would certainly be more difficult to relate them to theory without the attention to detail involved in a process report.

On the other hand, when I read the transcript, or even listen to the tape, it does not seem to capture how hard it is to work in a truly person-centred way. To give my mental and emotional space to another person for an hour can be extremely tiring, and when someone is incongruent or anxious this seems to affect me as I reflect in my body and mind what is happening in theirs. With Jamie I had to work hard to keep my concentration on what he was putting across (interestingly he remarks in the transcript, turns 42 to 45, how difficult it was for him to keep his focus on his own needs).

What I learned from completing this and other client studies and process reports

I have learned about the person-centred model and also about myself as a counsellor. Especially, I have learned how the 'locus of evaluation' of a client (which of course is not something fixed) can inform, I think, any model of counselling. From all my pieces of work I have gained more insight into how being the person I am affects the work I do. For instance, I think I tend to contain rather than facilitate emotional expression. Thus, I am more aware in general how, as the person-centred tradition considers (Mearns 1994), our limitations as counsellors are our limitations as human beings. I have also gained a great insight into how to put over what I have learned.

PROCESS REPORT

The excerpt in summary

This excerpt shows Jamie reflecting on the past, the challenges of the present, and how he has responded to them, especially on his own. I have chosen this excerpt because Jamie's process varies as we talk about different subjects, therefore presenting different challenges to me. He also reflects on his own process of change in a way that illustrates many issues dealt with in person-centred theory. My expressed empathy facilitates this process and promotes his internal locus of evaluation.

The client and his background

Jamie is a man in his late fifties who has lived most of his life in a small town working as a self-employed builder. He was married and raised three sons there, but his drinking had become increasingly heavy and his wife of thirty-five years had requested a separation. He had started a relationship with a much younger woman and moved to London with her, but she had also asked him to leave after two years. Then he had moved to a large city in Scotland where one of his sons and his wife now lived. He had resided in a hostel for four months but recently moved to an unfurnished flat on his own. He had been trying to give up alcohol since being in the hostel, with periods of abstinence and periods of drinking 10–20 units of alcohol per day. He was also attending Alcoholics Anonymous meetings and the specialist alcohol service of a psychiatric hospital.

The context of the referral

He had referred himself to our service as part of his effort to remain abstinent. We are a specialist alcohol counselling service, for anyone concerned about their own or another's drinking. Counsellors use a mixture of the person-centred approach with other specific cognitive-behavioural approaches for substance misuse such as motivational interviewing (Miller and Rollnick 1991). I have fortnightly individual supervision. My supervisor is trained in person-centred counselling and supervision and has many years' experience counselling and supervising in an alcohol-counselling agency. She has also published research about working in a person-centred way with women who have an alcohol problem (Lillie 2002).

The person-centred approach

The person-centred approach to counselling and psychotherapy sees the relationship between the counsellor and client as the both the context and the source of therapeutic change. The relationship strengthens and nourishes the client's self-actualising tendency and his/her use of an internalised locus of evaluation (Mearns and Thorne 1987).

The person-centred counsellor aims to create a relationship based on Rogers' six conditions (Rogers 1990), which he considered both necessary and sufficient to create positive change in the client.

1   Psychological contact between client and counsellor.
2   The client is in a state of incongruence (being vulnerable or anxious).
3   The counsellor is congruent or integrated in the relationship.
4   The counsellor experiences unconditional positive regard towards the client.
5   The counsellor experiences an empathic understanding of the client's frame of reference.
6   The client perceives the last two conditions in the counsellor.

The goals of therapy and person-centred formulation

Jamie wanted help to remain abstinent and cope with setting up home on his own. For many years he had been in employment, with a partner, and had lived in comfortable home environments. Now he found himself in a strange city in a barely furnished flat living on benefits.

In person-centred terms he was certainly in a state of incongruence. He demonstrated some of the anxiety and vulnerability typical of someone who was beginning to deal with an alcohol problem. However, he needed to learn how to make his own way in the world.

I did not, in general, find it difficult to regard him positively. Jamie was polite and reliable. He had plenty on his mind and shared it freely.

My rationale for adopting a person-centred approach was that he needed to develop a sense of self-worth that was less dependent on other people's opinions. He often talked about how he had been used to doing things for other people, and how this was the source of much of his identity and self-worth. In person-centred terms his self-worth seemed conditional on external loci of evaluation. By engaging in person-centred counselling, his ability to use his internal locus of evaluation should be strengthened. He was receiving help focused on his alcohol from other agencies, so I thought it appropriate to offer something more open. Anyway, person-centred counselling is proposed by some as a useful general approach for people with alcohol problems (Bryant-Jefferies 2001, Lillie 2002). My supervisor agreed that this was appropriate.

The one possible difficulty might have been that I did sometimes find it difficult to feel in contact with Jamie. He would describe things in great factual detail, and often I felt only intermittently in contact with him.

I offered person-centred counselling to Jamie and he was happy with this. We agreed ten sessions and reviewed it, agreeing another ten as Jamie thought it had been helpful.

The lead-in to this excerpt

This session is number twelve. At this session Jamie had been abstinent for six weeks. He has been talking about how his wife had become angry with him for not supervising their son as she thought he should (the son has some kind of mental or physical problem and she gives him some support with this. She had gone away for a few days and Jamie had taken over this role while she was absent). She had refused to speak to Jamie. He said his mind had drifted back to the past and he had nearly bought some alcohol but stopped himself. Then he talked about how his wife had told him he was an alcoholic, while his ex-partner never mentioned that she was concerned about his drinking.

Transcription of the excerpt

JAMIE 1: Whereas, em, (*sigh*), the partnership I was in, she was, em, (*big sigh*) I mean at least, em, when my marriage was, I mean it was talked about, but I reckon it was talked about in the wrong way, whereas in the partnership, em, it wasn't really discussed, I think, em, you know, looking back there was a couple of references made . . .

ALEX 1: Yeah.

I am listening to him, and regard him positively although I must admit to a little bit of discomfort at him talking about how his partner and wife did not address his heavy drinking (Jamie 1). I cannot help thinking that he is not taking responsibility for his own drinking. In the person-centred model it is important to understand what it is like for the client rather than stand back and make a judgement, so I tried to stick with his concerns and let this pass myself. He is looking back and thinking that the external loci of evaluation (his wife and ex-partner) had failed him. However, if I were to make a judgement about those thoughts I would be continuing this process by becoming yet another external locus of evaluation for him to consider. Rather, by my allowing him to reflect on his experience, he can strengthen his ability to rely on his own point of view. Perhaps he will also learn that it might be more useful to develop his own judgement and resources (in person-centred terms his self-actualising tendency) than rely on the judgement of others. In addition, I am no more there to judge his ex-partner's behaviour than his; in person-centred work it is my job to be 'beside' the client not 'on the side of' the client (Mearns 1994).

JAMIE 2: I think one was that I shouldn't drink spirits, em.

ALEX 2: Right.

JAMIE 3: But then she would go out and buy, you know, a few cans of beer to take home, or when we went shopping or . . .

ALEX 3: Yeah.

JAMIE 4: So there was never real, any concern shown about the, er, the amount I was drinking, and I think my problem was, the, er, was the alcohol that I did take into the house. It was then that I, er, I didn't seem to be able to control the amount and looking back, em, when I was still married and staying at home, em, the amount of alcohol I used to consume . . .

ALEX 4: Uh huh.

JAMIE 5: . . . and it always seemed to be at night-time, you know I didn't really drink much during the day, it wasn't till the latter part in London that I started to drink in the morning . . .

ALEX 5: Mmm.

Both in this exchange (Jamie 1 to Alex 5) and previously, Jamie had been talking about his recently-ended relationship. My responses were to demonstrate that I was listening. However, as he talked about the past he looked down and to my right with hardly any eye contact and I felt that he was not really in much contact with me. As Tudor (2000) observes, the first of Rogers' (1990) necessary and sufficient conditions, psychological contact is present in degrees. As is evidenced from his sighing, he seemed to be quite tense as he spoke. I also felt tense, with a compulsion to fidget. It is likely that this was due to his presentation as I did not feel

*particularly tense before the session, and there had been a similar pattern
in my previous session with Jamie. My supervisor suggested that it would
have been appropriate to have shared this feeling of distance and tension
with Jamie as a congruent reaction. Mearns and Thorne (1987) suggest
that feelings in response to the client that are relevant and persistent or
striking should be shared. As I have described, this was a persistent
feeling, and it was certainly relevant; lack of contact or communication
was a major difficulty for Jamie, and it seemed to be reflected in our
relationship at this time, as well as in the content of what he was saying.*

*An alternative would have been simply to reflect to him what I had
noticed about his behaviour: 'you're sighing when you say that', 'you're
looking at the floor'. This would be like Prouty's (1976) 'contact reflections', which he uses to establish contact with clients who have communication difficulties.*

JAMIE 6: . . . and on my way to work I would go and get a couple of cans of
beer, em, during working hours I would have access to some tins of
beer, at lunchtime I would go and have a pint up at the pub, (*intake of
breath*) and on the way home, er, at night I would go and, em, buy a
few cans to take home with me.

ALEX 6: And, I mean, you were saying this was when you were working as a
handyman . . .

*My response here (Alex 6) was simply to demonstrate my empathic
understanding. It also demonstrates to him that what he said about this
before was important enough for me to remember.*

JAMIE 7: Yeah.

ALEX 7: . . . When you were, you were saying you thought you were, em,
doing too much really, or you, there was always something you could
be doing, but there . . .

*My reply here (Alex 7) is quite vague and tentative. This illustrates
something about my personal style that can be both useful and unhelpful.
As Mearns and Thorne (1987) point out, a tentative style has the
advantage that it allows the client to correct me and thus keep to his
frame of reference. On the other hand too much vagueness can be confusing and long-winded and thus impede communication. In this case it did
seem to register with Jamie. However, as psychological contact was not
as good as it could have been, I think that it would have been wiser to be
clearer in my communication.*

JAMIE 8: Well that's it, em.

ALEX 8: . . . But you were having a lot of demands placed on you because
you could do most things.

In the same vein, I feed back (Alex 8) to Jamie something that he had told me in a previous session, about the situation he was in. It was my view that he was not just someone who had an alcohol problem, whereas perhaps he was thinking about himself at that time just as a drinker. My unconditional positive regard for him is important here. It is not about approving of all his behaviour, or even liking him as I might like a friend (Mearns 1994), but accepting him as basically a good person, and seeing that he has strengths as well as failings.

JAMIE 9: Well, I had all of that plus I had, em, er, divorce going on and, er, I had a couple of court cases, em, which I had to contend with, and, em, there was just lots of things, at the time . . .

ALEX 9: Yeah.

JAMIE 10: . . . Which I feel were really just too much for me to cope with, em, in fact I'm quite surprised that, er, I coped even to the extent that I have, em, being here in Glasgow, em, considering the, er, a lot of the circumstances, em, I've had to go through, which, you know, I'm not used to, em.

After my comment (Alex 8), Jamie starts to talk about the difficulties he faced (Jamie 9 to 10). The fact that he was drinking more is thus balanced against the fact that his situation was difficult for him. At this point, his more positive tone was reflected in his body language as well, as he began to have some eye contact with me. Also of note is that Jamie emphasised the 'I feel' in this statement (Jamie 10), emphasising that this is his point of view. In person-centred terms he is using his internal locus of evaluation (Mearns and Thorne 1987). By feeding back to him what he has previously said, and helping him to consider a fuller picture I hope that his confidence in using this locus has been strengthened.

ALEX 10: You mean being in the hostel and then having to get . . .

JAMIE 11: Being in the hostel, em, being moved into a flat with no furnishings, em . . .

ALEX 11: Mmm.

JAMIE 12: Em, just, er, the fact of having no money, em, there's lots of things that, er . . .

ALEX 12: You couldn't buy the things for the flat that you needed . . .

JAMIE 13: That's right.

ALEX 13: Without scrimping and saving . . .

JAMIE 14: Yeah.

ALEX 14: And going round asking people for this and that.

I am again feeding back (Alex 10 to 14) to Jamie what he has mentioned in previous sessions, demonstrating an understanding of his efforts to overcome a difficult situation. Another possible response would have been to reflect back his 'surprise' at being better than he thought at coping. His surprise suggests that he has discovered that his self-concept was not accurate, and he underestimated his coping skills. Had I fed this back to him it could have raised his awareness that he might in general be more capable than he thinks.

JAMIE 15: Mmm. (*intake of breath*) But other than that as I said, em, I've made the most of things, em, I have been, maybe, I don't know, I've been fortunate, more fortunate than some people. I have been helped out with, er, various, em, charitable organisations, and, em, er (*sigh*), I mean I do have a financial settlement to come because I sold my, my share of my house to my eldest son and, em, I'm still waiting on a settlement . . .

ALEX 15: Oh, right.

Jamie switches from talking about his difficulties to talking about how in some ways he considers himself lucky (Jamie 15). Again this is a more positive way of looking at his recent experiences, although one that focuses on factors external to him. Another thing of note is that Jamie adds 'as I said', referring back to his previous comment about how he has coped well in the circumstances. He picks up the thread of what he was saying, and it is perhaps a reflection of the fact that I said more than was necessary (three comments, all of which amounted to much the same thing.). He seems to want to get back to the fact that he has coped, rather than look at precisely what he has coped with. In this case, he is the one trying to reflect on his own process, despite my distractions!

JAMIE 16: . . . Which when I get I will use to pay off my credit cards, em . . .

ALEX 16: Right.

JAMIE 17: But, as I say, that seems to be taking forever and a day, em, it's not happening overnight.

ALEX 17: Yeah.

JAMIE 18: So, I mean I still have to cope with, with that, in fact I've actually got, em . . .

ALEX 18: What, having the debt?

JAMIE 19: Old debts and things to try and cope with each month.

ALEX 19: I mean, so, you were saying you thought in some ways, saying you were thinking, you know, perhaps you'd coped rather well, considering all the things that had been going on for you recently.

I made this remark (Alex 19) to feed back to him again his view of himself as able to cope in difficult circumstances, when he talks about the challenge he has with his debts.

JAMIE 20: Well, I think I have, I mean I'm not saying I have but, em, I feel as though I've coped reasonably well . . .

His response (Jamie 20) tentatively contrasts his own point of view, from an internal locus of evaluation, with some external or objective reference point. I think this demonstrates a rather limited confidence in his own point of view. The person-centred model sees such lack of confidence as due to introjected conditions of worth (Bozarth 1998). Certainly Jamie has experienced that the love of his wife and partner were conditional on him being able to restrict his drinking. However, he may also have lost confidence in his own viewpoint because he has had to admit that he has had an alcohol problem for a long time, despite the fact that he did not at the time see himself in this way. The person-centred model would reply that during this period of heavy drinking his self-concept (as someone without an alcohol problem) was losing touch with his 'organismic self' (his essential resources as a human being) (Thorne 1990). In other words, he was unable to recognise the problems arising from his drinking because to admit a problem would mean that he would violate his condition of worth (if I have an alcohol problem I must be a bad person). I am not sure about this way of looking at it but I can certainly agree that Jamie needs to strengthen his ability to use an internal locus of evaluation.

ALEX 20: Mmm.

JAMIE 21: . . . Under the circumstances.

ALEX 21: Well, you said, you said that you've been getting on with doing the things for the house, haven't you?

Again I remind him (Alex 21) of an example of this (Jamie 20), but this time more concisely.

JAMIE 22: Yeah, em, er. Considering my eyesight's still not one hundred per cent, em, I mean, I've decorated my . . .

This leads on to a list of the things he has accomplished despite challenges (Jamie 22 to 32).

ALEX 22: Mmm.

JAMIE 23: . . . Painted my bathroom. (*clears throat*) I've still got the woodwork to do, to finish it but, er . . .

ALEX 23: Yeah.

JAMIE 24: . . . I've fitted, er, a shower in it now, I've tiled the walls . . .

ALEX 24: Oh, right.

JAMIE 25: . . . Part of the wall and, er, where the shower is, I've fitted a shower, em, which I had actually used this morning, em. I've still got things, I've still got, like a shower curtain . . .

ALEX 25: Mmm.

JAMIE 26: . . . To get and a shower rail, em. At the moment I'm using as a shower rail, I'm using a roller pole, which would be used normally . . .

ALEX 26: Oh, what one of those extendable ones for painting the ceiling?

I say this (Alex 26) in quite an animated fashion as I really did think it quite an ingenious idea. I could easily have been more congruent and said something like, 'that's ingenious'.

I am not sure why I did not, but perhaps I feared distracting him from his internal locus of evaluation. Mearns (1994) writes that the person-centred counsellor should exercise extreme care when dealing with someone with a distinctly externalised locus of evaluation. As I have remarked above, this seems to be an issue for Jamie. However, on reflection it would not seem to have been harmful to be more congruent. Had I been so, it would have been more like an 'idiosyncratic empathy reaction' (Bozarth 1984).

JAMIE 27: Yeah.

ALEX 27: Oh, I know what you mean, yeah.

JAMIE 28: And, er, for the curtain I had a piece of polythene that come off something and I used it as a shower curtain . . .

ALEX 28: Yeah.

JAMIE 29: . . . Till such time as I can afford, em.

ALEX 29: Yeah.

JAMIE 30: I had been getting a piece of lino, er, for, from a charity shop, so I cut it up and used it in my bathroom so, the bathroom itself looks . . .

ALEX 30: Right.

JAMIE 31: . . . Quite reasonable now, you know it's, em, it's more inviting to go in than the, er, the drab, dark-blue colour that it was, em.

ALEX 31: The walls were all like that, were they?

JAMIE 32: The walls were all dark blue and, em . . .

ALEX 32: So, it's got a fresh coat of paint and everything now . . .

JAMIE 33: Yeah.

ALEX 33: And it's got new tiles . . .

JAMIE 34: Yeah.

ALEX 34: And a new shower unit, yeah.

JAMIE 35: Uh-huh.

ALEX 35: And 'cos you said last week, you were saying you were starting to, you know, look forward a bit more, and sort of, not too far forward, but . . .

In our previous session I had reflected this comment back to him and there was a change similar to the one in this session (around Jamie 10), but more dramatic, going from looking at the floor and talking about the past to looking at me and talking about the present and future. I reminded him (Alex 35) of this remark as he was talking about the decoration that he had done, which seemed to involve looking to the future.

JAMIE 36: No.

ALEX 36: . . . Em, you know, to get to do with the things you needed to do.

JAMIE 37: I think it's just, er, getting the motivation, em, 'cos I find that, er, I will go and do a bit, then I seem to lose it, run out of steam . . .

ALEX 37: Yeah.

JAMIE 38: Or motivation and I sort of stop and then I'll perhaps go and watch a bit of TV or whatever and listen to some music, then a little while later it will come back into my head that I was working on something and . . .

ALEX 38: Yeah.

JAMIE 39: I'll go back and do a little bit, em.

My remark about looking to the future (Alex 35) does spark something off in him and he talks about how he is taking positive steps to improve his life, although it is a difficult process.

ALEX 39: Yeah.

JAMIE 40: I say I find it very hard to do things because I've never been used to doing things for my . . . just for myself, em . . .

Interestingly, Jamie talks (Jamie 40) about how important it is for him to have someone else to do things for – this seems to confirm the need to strengthen his internal locus of evaluation.

ALEX 40: Well, that's right, you've said that before you know, it's nice to, to do, you know, even . . .

JAMIE 41: To do . . .

ALEX 41: . . . Working as a decorator, you, you, you'd do it not just for the money but for the appreciation.

I think my reply here (Alex 40 to 41) is overlong. I could have let him finish my sentence. I was determined to get what I wanted to say across, forgetting that the key thing is to stimulate his process of reflection.

JAMIE 42: Yeah, em, and I still find that, em, and I think that's where my concentration is, er, lacking . . .

ALEX 42: Yeah.

JAMIE 43: Is that, that I'm doing it for myself and not, that I'm not doing it for a wife or a partner or . . .

ALEX 43: Mmm.

JAMIE 44: . . . Someone I'm gonna get paid from, or . . .

ALEX 44: Yeah, yeah.

JAMIE 45: I just find it quite difficult still to, er, do things for myself.

Jamie confirms (Jamie 42 to 45) that the potential approval of others helps him concentrate, but the satisfaction of doing something does not; his concentration is conditional on a positive evaluation from an external locus.

ALEX 45: And you've just gotta do it and say I need to get it done for myself.

JAMIE 46: Well, that's it. I, I mean, I do try and as best as possible drive myself on . . .

ALEX 46: Mmm.

JAMIE 47: When I say drive myself, I mean I'm not working at it constantly, I'll do a bit of filling, I'll do a bit of painting, and I can leave it as quick as I started it, em. I haven't got the, em. You can have all the drive but if you don't have the motivation, em, I think both of them have got to go hand in hand. I think you've got to have both motivation and drive, em.

ALEX 47: But you, and you've got the motivation in small amounts but it tends to . . .

JAMIE 48: In small amounts . . .

ALEX 48: But it tends to come . . .

JAMIE 49: But I think if you don't get the two working hand in hand, em . . .

ALEX 49: Mmm.

JAMIE 50: You eventually gets done, it does eventually get done, em, it just takes an awful lot longer than what it should do.

Written down, this exchange (Jamie 47 to 50, Alex 47 to 49), seems quite incoherent but we understood each other. It is a difficult process for him to do things with no external locus of evaluation, but he keeps going. This is reflected in our work together as well. It is not a smooth process but it is one we are both committed to.

Evaluating the excerpt

Although I consider that the excerpt demonstrates good practice on my part, it also points to ways to which I could improve it.

First, it might have been helpful to use a congruent reaction to bring into the open how he distanced himself from me while talking about his past relationships. This would give him the opportunity to express his feelings about them if he chose to do so. He might not even be aware that he does this. This would also have given me the opportunity to demonstrate my unconditional positive regard, by showing that I was willing to remain in contact with him and be with him no matter what he talked about. As I did not do this, he may have got the impression that my regard was conditional on all his past actions being 'good'.

One lesson that I have been learning, and have continued to learn through this piece of work is that I am good at helping clients contain and channel the emotional content of their experience. The other side of this coin is that I am much less good at helping clients get in touch with this type of content. I can see in this excerpt that I am less likely to reflect client's feelings back to them, or feed them my own feelings in the form of a congruent response. It does not seem that I am insensitive to such content; rather that I tend to see it as potentially dangerous and overwhelming. I can see how my important relationships seem to reflect this, and it is good material for my personal therapy as well as my reflective practice.

This excerpt also reminds me that I could work on making my responses more clear and concise. I do have a tendency sometimes to overqualify what I am saying or labour the point. This is, I think, not particularly obvious here but I am conscious of the tendency. The point is that in person-centred counselling the key object is to facilitate the client's process rather than detailing my responses exactly. However, the main learning point for me is that in a person-centred framework the extent to which a person's locus of evaluation is internalised or externalised is of crucial importance to the way one works (Mearns 1994). By examining the process of this excerpt I have been able to appreciate the subtlety of the clues by which a client may express this.

I have continued to work with Jamie. He remarked later on how he had started to think much more about what he should be doing (thus he has developed his use of an internal locus of evaluation.) He also said that he has found life to be much easier since he started to be more open and honest, rather than worrying about what others might think. He was pleased that this process report was to be published, and that his experiences might benefit others in difficult circumstances.

References

Bozarth, J. (1998). *Person-centred Therapy: A Revolutionary Paradigm*. Ross-on-Wye: PCCS Books.

Bozarth, J. (1984). Beyond reflection: emergent modes of empathy. In R.F. Levant and J.M. Shlien (eds). *Client-centered Therapy and the Person-centered Approach*. New York: Praeger. Cited in Mearns and Thorne (1987).

Bryant-Jefferies, R. (2001). *Counselling the Person Beyond the Alcohol Problem*. London: Jessica Kingsley.

Lillie, N. (2002). Women, alcohol, self-concept, and self-esteem: a qualitative study of the experience of person-centred counselling. *Counselling and Psychotherapy Research*, 2(2): 99–107.

Mearns, D. (1994). *Developing Person-centred Counselling*. London: Sage.

Mearns, D. and Thorne, B. (1987). *Person-centred Counselling in Action*. London: Sage.

Miller, W.R. and Rollnick, S. (eds) (1991). *Motivational Interviewing: Preparing People to Change Addictive Behaviour*. New York: Guilford.

Prouty, G.F. (1976). Pre-therapy, a method of treating pre-expressive psychotic and retarded patients. *Psychotherapy: Theory, Research, and Practice*, 13(3): 290–295. Cited in Mearns (1994).

Rogers, C.R. (1990). The necessary and sufficient conditions of therapeutic personality change. In H. Kirschenbaum and V.L. Henderson (eds). *The Carl Rogers Reader*. London: Constable.

Thorne, B. (1990). Person-centred therapy. In W. Dryden (ed.). *Individual Therapy: A Handbook*. Milton Keynes: Open University Press.

Tudor, K. (2000). The case of the lost conditions. *Counselling*, February, 33–37.

Chapter 6

The use of CBT with complex client issues: accessing schemas

with a case study by Alice Sherman

PRELUDE

The context setting in which we practice as therapists directly determines how we work and, therefore, indirectly affects what we produce for assessment when writing up a case study or process report. In this study, Alice Sherman describes a case in which she offered a course of brief cognitive behaviour therapy to a client who expressed his anger both verbally and non-verbally.

Supervision played a crucial role in her therapy, which, in turn, improved her confidence as a therapist. Not only is this case study clearly written, it also offers the reader a useful template showing how to organise material and what it is appropriate to include under the different subheadings. The assessment section provides information on the referral, the client's background history, and the therapist's assessment of the presenting problem, including an anger rating scale, in which clinical material is depicted in this helpful figurative format. The 'voice' of the scientist-practitioner is in evidence throughout this case study, as impressions and ideas are checked against the available evidence and facts. This leads to an interesting and well-structured account of therapy, frequently illustrated by the inclusion of the client's actual utterances and her descriptions of his behaviour. The evaluation section invited the therapist to reflect on what she achieved with the client and her impressions of the process.

The case study that follows is, in every respect, a model one and the tutor is left in no doubt that the trainee has a firm grasp of the application of CBT and a high level of critical awareness.

> *Alice Sherman wrote this case study at the end of the second year of a part-time MSc in Counselling Psychology. The comments were written at the beginning of the first year of a post-MSc practitioner diploma.*

Preamble

Rationale

I have chosen to present this particular case study for a variety of reasons. First, the nature of my client's problem was particularly unusual, and this resulted in a complex and challenging case for me. My client experienced acute anger outbursts twice a day, which culminated in physical lashing out of his arms and legs and associated arm and chest pains, which he felt unable to control and which affected his quality of life. Second, a significantly successful outcome resulted from working within a brief cognitive behavioural therapy (CBT) framework, thus proving that five sessions can be effective even when a client presents with acute and complex complaints. The case study focuses upon how cognitive-behavioural techniques have helped alleviate such acute symptoms in a relatively short amount of time. Issues explored include my client's feedback about which therapeutic interventions were of most benefit in alleviating his anger, as well as my own postulations based upon CBT theory.

What I have learnt from this case study

Retrospectively, this case study has been a useful tool in improving my own future clinical practice in terms of working with similar complex cases within a time-limited framework. It has also demonstrated how client feedback can be a valuable and, indeed, essential tool in therapy. In writing this case study, I have taken the opportunity to examine my own specific practitioner skills, which helped to effect therapeutic change in my client in greater depth, than I would otherwise have done through supervision alone. As a result, my confidence as a trainee practitioner has increased and this has altered my work with other clients as a result of the knowledge gained through the issues explored within this case study.

The therapeutic framework

A CBT framework was employed for two main reasons. First, my client had found CBT useful in the past in tackling panic attacks, demonstrated a good understanding of the underlying principles, and felt both keen and confident in continuing to work within such a framework. Second, I hypothesised that CBT would be a useful approach based upon my previous work with clients who have presented with comparably complex problems such as anxiety and panic attacks, where there were also strong cognitive, emotional, physiological and behavioural components.

CBT assumes that one's thoughts are related to one's emotions, physiological state and behaviours (Pearsons 1989). This model proposes that one's core beliefs about oneself and one's environment are critically important in producing and maintaining one's behaviours, emotions, physiological responses and overt thought patterns. Therapy aims to intervene at each of these identified levels in order to promote corresponding change. This is undertaken by the use of exercises of a purely cognitive or behavioural nature as well as cognitive-behavioural exercises. Success is measured by behavioural, cognitive, physiological and emotional change in terms of symptom reduction. In this case therapy aimed to reduce the frequency and severity of the anger episodes experienced by my client.

CASE STUDY

Part 1: initial assessment

Referral details

'Dave' was referred by his GP to an in-house counselling psychology service, which offers brief therapy in an NHS Primary Care setting. The referral letter stated that Dave was a 42-year-old man suffering from stress, anxiety, irritability and associated chest pains with no medical cause. The client himself had requested counselling rather than the prescription of any psychotropic medication by his GP.

Therapist's initial impressions

On initial presentation Dave seated himself in a rather closed body position, with his arms and legs crossed and maintained minimal eye contact. I perceived engagement with Dave as difficult at first due to his body language and short, closed utterances. However, during the course of our first meeting, the conversation flowed increasingly freely, although he maintained a closed body posture. Focusing on the process of therapy, I changed my style of questioning to a more information-gathering style, which helped Dave talk more openly and expressively.

Client background information

Social history

Dave was a 42-year-old unemployed man living with his disabled wife and her teenage son from a previous marriage. Dave had been made redundant from working on the railways seven years ago; a job he had been doing for ten years. Since then Dave had been unemployed and explained that he had found it difficult to find long-term work on account of his age and limited skills. Dave regularly used to drink heavily during and after work and smoked twenty cigarettes a day, but he gave both these habits up approximately a year ago. He admitted that drinking helped him deal with stress and that he had felt generally more stressed and angry since abstaining. On the advice of his GP Dave had recently taken up a healthy-eating diet, given up smoking and had begun attending a gym three times a week in order to reduce his body weight and lower his blood pressure. Approximately a year ago, by attending CBT counselling, Dave successfully overcame panic attacks associated with travelling on buses.

Client's view of problem

Dave told me that his life had become intolerable over the last year due to 'anger attacks', which occurred at least twice a day. These attacks would typically come on extremely quickly (within a matter of seconds), without him being aware of any specific triggers. He described feeling 'out of control' at these times, quickly feeling extremely angry and concurrently experiencing arm and chest pains, headaches and the need to lash out with his arms and legs. These attacks were unpredictable, happening 'at any time', for instance when he was out alone walking the dog. He expressed concern that these attacks were damaging to his physical health regarding his heart and blood pressure, and stated that he wished to learn anger management techniques through coming for counselling.

Therapist's assessment of problem

In this first session, I explored with Dave how his anger affected him on cognitive, behavioural, physiological and emotional levels in order to make an assessment of his presenting complaint and to allow Dave to recognise how his anger manifested itself at various levels. I asked Dave to recall the temporal nature of his anger episodes, utilising an 'anger ruler' (Gottlieb 1999) to rate the changing severity of his anger over time, and to link each rating to its corresponding expression of anger. Dave was asked to describe his emotion at the different ratings of his anger (Figure 1).

Precipitating factors

Dave reported that an attack could happen 'at any time', although he did identify two specific triggers. These were: (1) having an argument with his partner; and (2) periods when he had 'time and space to think', such as walking the dog. This information led me to form an hypothesis that Dave's problems may have had a cognitive and emotional underpinning, which could be explored and dealt with within the context of therapy. I hypothesised that Dave was experiencing the effects of anger emotionally,

Passage of time	Anger ruler rating	Emotion experienced	Behaviour expressed	Physiological condition
	1	'Irritable'	Scratching his head	
	2			
	3			
	4			Sweating
	5	'Angry'	Clenched hands	
	6			Restricted breathing
	7			
	8			Headaches
	9		Thrashing of arms and legs	Arm pains
	10	'Explode!'		Chest pains

Figure 1   Anger ruler. In hindsight, this exercise formed the cornerstone of our therapy sessions as it introduced my client to the core CBT concepts of how one's problems can be understood in terms of symptom manifestation and course. This enabled both me and my client to tackle his problem from different angles using CBT interventions, according to each of the CBT 'levels' (i.e. emotional, behavioural, physiological and cognitive). Retrospectively, this exercise altered my client's perception that his attacks were unpredictable and happened 'all at once'. Rather, possible 'triggers' had been identified and a temporal pattern to the attacks emerged.

physically and physiologically and that in order for his anger to dissipate he might need to explore what specifically was making him angry.

Modulating variables

Dave reported never being angry on Thursdays, which was the day he collected his Social Security pay cheque, bought a gift for his wife and visited the gym, where work-outs and relaxation classes helped him to feel calm. At this stage, this information indicated to me a possible link between Dave's mood and the onset of his anger attacks.

Dave explained that he sometimes 'snapped out' of an episode when his wife shouted at him to calm down, and that this brought him 'back to reality'. Additionally, walking out of the room rather than arguing could de-escalate the situation. However, he was aware that 'bottling up' his emotions could be harmful too. The way in which Dave was expressing and dealing with his emotions was currently experienced as unsatisfactory. This information gave me some preliminary ideas regarding possible therapeutic interventions, such as improving communication patterns with his wife rather than 'bottling up' his emotions. It also highlighted possible exercises that might be useful to Dave, such as relaxation training to alter his emotional state.

Cognitive patterns

At this early stage, a cognitive assessment was felt to be essential in terms of understanding his anger. Typically, the thoughts preceding and maintaining an anger episode centred around his feeling frustrated with himself at being unemployed. For instance, 'I've missed out on lots of opportunities to get a good job'/'I'm never going to get a good job at my age'.

Behavioural interventions

Progressive muscular relaxation and breathing exercises were carried out in this first session in order to reinforce a sense of physiological control, in the face of his 'feeling out of control' with regard to his anger attacks. I recommended that he practice the breathing exercises during an anger attack, noting that such exercises were also useful at instilling a sense of wellbeing at his gym classes.

Educational interventions

At our first session, I found it necessary to put Dave's mind at rest concerning the effect his anger had upon his physical health. Dave expressed concern that his anger outbursts were detrimental to his cardiac function and blood pressure. I reassured him that although his heart rate increased at these times, his cardiac function and blood pressure were well controlled by his healthy diet and cessation of smoking and drinking. I also made it clear to him that his arm and chest pains were clearly brought on by these anger episodes, rather than any cardiac pathology, which had been excluded as a possible cause of discomfort by his GP. I explained that most headaches occur as a result of muscle tension and we explored his 'anger ruler' information which supported the link between his affect and physical symptoms.

Therapeutic formulation and plan

My hypothesis at the initial assessment stage was that Dave was suffering from frequent episodes of anger outbursts, which seemed to be a somewhat dysfunctional expression of frustration with himself at being unemployed and under-achieving in his life. The anger episodes seemed to follow a distinct temporal pattern (see Figure 1) yet the underlying cognitions maintaining these outbursts were unclear at this early stage, with initial assessment information pointing at both internal and external factors triggering the attacks. At this stage, my therapeutic plan was to explore, in further sessions, the specific triggers to attacks, and the underlying cognitions and core beliefs responsible for maintaining Dave's anger. Additionally, CBT interventions would be taught to allow Dave to break his habitual outbursts. Homework tasks would focus on behavioural, cognitive and cognitive-behavioural interventions, which are outlined below in Part 2.

HOMEWORK

1   To keep a 'thought diary' to document his cognitions preceding an anger episode in order to gain a more detailed cognitive assessment. (See Figure 2, Appendix A.)
2   To practise progressive muscular relaxation and breathing exercises.

Therapy contract

Issues of confidentiality had been explained during this session, including the requirement and role of therapist supervision and audio recording of sessions, to which Dave gave signed consent. Due to the complex nature of his problem and its severity, Dave and I agreed to meet for the full six sessions allowed within the counselling service setting. Each session lasted 50 minutes and the sessions were held on a weekly basis so that progress could be monitored regularly.

Part 2: development of therapy

Therapeutic interventions utilised

- Progressive muscular relaxation and breathing exercises (physiological).
- Distraction and visualisation techniques (cognitive).
- Monitoring stages of anger attacks and triggering events (behavioural).
- Dysfunctional thought recording and practising rational alternative thinking (cognitive-behavioural).
- Information provision regarding psychosomatic chest and arm pains and education regarding blood-pressure control (educational).

Key content issues for Sessions 2 to 5

Session 2

Dave began the session by expressing pleasure at having developed an increased awareness regarding his anger attacks at each temporal phase. However, he reported finding it difficult to do the breathing exercises during anger episodes as 'it all happens too fast'. He had filled out a diary sheet (Figure 2, Appendix A), which affirmed our conclusions regarding triggering situations, expression of anger and mediating factors, but did not provide any additional cognitive information. The second session therefore focused on eliciting more detailed information about the cognitive aspects of his anger attacks.

It transpired that internal cognitive triggers to his attacks concerned his anger and frustration towards himself with respect to losing his job, and his putting this down to his abuse of alcohol while working on the railways. In this respect he felt responsible for his current financial status, having spent too much time and money on alcohol when he could have focused on improving his career prospects. Drinking in the pub had allowed him to 'run away' from his problems and stress at home. He stated that alcohol had helped him cope with stress, and having given it up for health reasons he now found anger was expressed in his outbursts.

Having asked Dave how things might be different should his anger problem be resolved in the future, he replied that communication between him and his wife would be improved. This signified to me that communication was currently problematic and that this issue was related to his anger problem and would need to be explored in the current session. On further questioning it transpired that his wife had numerous stressors in her own life and arguments ensued easily for this reason. She suffered from chronic arthritis, which was painful and debilitating, and was unhappy with the lack of help she got from her son at home. Additionally, she was studying for an A-level.

In order to improve Dave's communication with his wife we focused on exploring typical arguments that they had. Dave came to realise that these tended to start when she was feeling ill or unhappy with her son. He told me that in a typical argument his common response would be to shout and feel anger and resentment towards her. On exploration of the possible underlying reasons prompting her 'argumentative' manner, he reported that his reaction might be too harsh and that he could be a little more 'considerate' in future, to see if this improved communication and de-escalated arguments. Another pattern Dave recognised was that he often 'switched off' and did not listen to his partner when she was angry with him. We looked at alternatives, such as listening to what his wife was complaining about and acknowledging her frustrations. At this stage, I hypothesised that 'switching off' in arguments was similar to his avoidance or blotting out of his difficult emotions through abusing alcohol. Instead, therefore, therapy could aim to introduce alternatives to avoidance, such as talking to his wife in a more constructive manner.

HOMEWORK

1   To practise alternative and more rational thinking when in an argument scenario, rather than 'switching off' or shouting at his wife.
2   To fill out a 'challenging dysfunctional thoughts' sheet (see Figure 3, Appendix B).
3   To continue practising relaxation and breathing exercises.

Session 3

Dave did not bring his dysfunctional thought record with him, and gave the reason that this was because he felt his anger was more under control at this stage and that he had not experienced many anger attacks over the past week. He also explained that communication with his wife had improved over the last week and that he had coped much better with arguments. He reasoned that this was because he was more aware of his dysfunctional communication patterns and realised that 'these bad habits can be broken'. Similarly, he told me that the frequency of anger attacks had decreased due to his increasing awareness of each phase of his anger. For instance, noting that he was scratching his head would now be an indication of an impending attack and he would be able to intervene at this point to stop an attack from progressing by utilising distraction techniques (such as breathing exercises) or practising alternative thinking styles.

Compared to the previous week, Dave seemed to have made a great deal more progress in terms of amelioration of his anger attacks and improving communication with his wife. At this stage, I felt that Dave might be becoming more aware of the nature of his anger and his potential for changing the dysfunctional habits underlying and maintaining his attacks. He was able to identify certain temporal behavioural and physiological triggers which signalled to him that an attack was pending, and had been able to put into practice some CBT techniques aimed at breaking the patterns of an attack and thus stopping it from progressing further. In hindsight, this session proved to be a most valuable one in terms of my client's increasing awareness of effecting change and regaining some control over his anger.

In this session, Dave reported his main complaint as being that his anger attacks were more prevalent when he had 'space and time to think'. We explored the typical thoughts that he had at these times, which clearly focused on personal underachievement. Examples were:

- 'My drinking habit ruined my career.'
- 'I have not achieved my full potential.'
- 'If I do get a job, it will have no prospects.'

It had struck me, in contrast to my client's feelings of underachievement, how much he had actually *achieved* in his life with regard to giving up smoking and drinking (having told me earlier, 'I never thought I would be able to give up the booze'), starting an exercise regime, embarking upon a healthy-eating diet and overcoming panic attacks. In discussing these achievements in this session, Dave realised that he had not given himself enough credit for these and that a useful intervention would be to get into the habit of acknowledging these achievements rather than continually focusing on his downfalls.

We listed Dave's five 'Golden Achievements':

1   Giving up drinking.
2   Giving up smoking.
3   Overcoming his panic attacks.
4   Starting a healthy-eating diet.
5   Going to the gym.

I asked Dave to write these on a small card, which he could keep on his person outside the counselling sessions. I then asked Dave to experiment with reading this card at times when he felt angry, so that he could challenge his dysfunctional self-concept of being an underachiever.

At the end of our session Dave stated, 'I've talked about everything I wanted to', and we therefore agreed to terminate therapy after our next session. This signalled to me that my client was pleased with the progress that he had made thus far and that he felt it unnecessary to continue with therapy for the entire six sessions.

HOMEWORK

1   To experiment with reading his 'five Golden Achievements' card at appropriate times.
2   To experiment with visualising an image of himself in the future, having succeeded in combating his anger attacks, when thinking about his past achievements.
3   To visualise a large 'STOP!' sign in his mind when aware of an early phase of an anger attack, in order to intervene at this phase and halt a full anger attack.

Session 4

Dave began the session by telling me that his anger episodes were dissipating more rapidly, especially when at home, where he was able to deal with things 'more rationally', explaining that he was looking at things from 'different angles' and was able to de-escalate potential arguments and anger attacks. He also mentioned that his wife had been helping him recognise his different anger phases, by pointing out his physiological and behavioural expressions of anger if he had not recognised them himself.

Dave explained that episodes were, however, still occurring, when he had space and time to himself. He told me he felt too embarrassed to carry his achievement card with him and had taken to writing the five points out on his hand in biro ink as an alternative! Within this session I felt that Dave's anger relating to his wife and home life was much improved. However, his self-perception at times when he was out alone still triggered attacks, although these were more controlled now by means of the cognitive-behavioural intervention of reminding himself of his past achievements.

Regarding his arm and chest pains, Dave told me that he now realised that these were related to anger rather than having any cardiovascular origin. In recognition of this, I stressed the importance of practising progressive muscular relaxation on a daily basis, to improve control over his physiology and state of mind.

Dave told me that he tended to forget to use the visualisation techniques during an attack. These were practised during the session and I advised him to use them as a direct response to recognition of an impending anger episode before reassessing his thought patterns, by coming up with more rational alternatives or reassessing his underachievements in light of his 'golden achievements'.

In light of these continuing issues, we agreed to have an extra session the next week, as a review, rather than terminating therapy at this stage.

HOMEWORK

1   To practise progressive muscular relaxation on a daily basis.
2   To use visualisation techniques to intervene at an early attack phase and to practise rational thinking.
3   To practise replacing thoughts of underachievement with his five 'golden achievements' before and during an attack.

Session 5 – termination

Dave reported having had no incidents of anger attacks at all over the past week and, at this stage, put this down to being able to recognise the early stages of an attack and intervene using various techniques to stop it progressing. He reported feeling more able to deal with stress and argumentative scenarios with his wife by looking for alternative, more rational, thoughts and not bottling up his emotions, as he had done previous to therapy.

Dave showed me his palm on which he had drawn an angry face in black and red biro ink! He explained that this helped stop attacks from progressing, more so than thinking about his achievements, in that when he looked at the picture he would tell himself that it represented his 'angry self', which he no longer wanted to be! Dave also mentioned that his arm and chest pains no longer occurred.

He felt confident that he would be able to cope in the future and felt prepared for this session to be his final one. I was happy to discharge Dave back to the care of his GP after this fifth session.

Part 3: discussion and evaluation

Therapeutic process and changes over time

Over the five weeks of therapy Dave demonstrated a great deal of progress with a reduction in the frequency and severity of anger attacks, fulfilling the main aims set at the outset of therapy. The utilisation of a CBT framework allowed a full appreciation of how Dave's anger attacks manifested themselves cognitively, behaviourally, physiologically and emotionally. This initial awareness proved to be a crucial factor in Dave's increasing understanding of his anger attacks, enabling him to decrease their severity, by intervening at early phases, and eventually to stop them all together. The variety of CBT techniques reinforced a sense of control which Dave felt he had lost during his attacks. Muscular relaxation and breathing exercises reinforced physiological control, while monitoring, visualisation techniques and altering dysfunctional thinking styles during arguments with his wife were most useful in breaking the behavioural and psychological components of his attacks.

Having hypothesised external and internal triggers to Dave's anger, we were collaboratively able to distinguish two different techniques to help reduce his anger. In terms of external triggers, such as arguing with his wife, Dave's cognitive reassessment of the situation through rational thinking helped dissipate the situation. However, in terms of the internal triggers to attacks, such as when he walked the dog, my hypotheses led me to encourage Dave to focus on his successes rather than failures. That is, to try and challenge his core belief system, which was dysfunctional with respect to triggering anger attacks.

However, in contrast to this, Dave reported that it was more useful to draw a picture of his 'angry self' on his hand in order to break his habit of outbursts during the early phases. In this respect, his core beliefs were acknowledged and challenged during our sessions, but failed to be of much use in the practicalities of dissipating his anger outbursts. Our sessions allowed for collaborative and experimental therapeutic work within a CBT framework. My client felt comfortable with altering and adapting various techniques that I had offered within our sessions, which reflected our good therapeutic working alliance and his enthusiasm for effecting change. He demonstrated a sound understanding of CBT and was able to be therapeutically creative within this paradigm.

In summary, therapy had been successful through the reinforcement of the control my client had in stopping his anger attacks, increasing his awareness of how the attacks manifested themselves in a recognisable temporal pattern, and through the use of cognitive-behavioural interventions at early phases, which were of most use at stopping attacks from progressing further.

Difficulties encountered

At our first session I perceived Dave's body language, style of talking and minimal eye contact to be indicative of defensiveness and, therefore, engagement in therapy to be quite difficult. By changing my style of asking questions and conducting the session Dave began to talk more freely. Through my mimicking, to some extent, of my client's conversational style, I was able to overcome this initial difficulty and I felt that Dave talked more freely and engaged better over the progression of sessions. To some extent, our therapeutic alliance rested upon my client's trust in me and the fostering of a collaborative and understanding mutual relationship.

After our first session I felt quite overwhelmed at the presentation of such acute 'symptoms' of Dave's problem! My confidence grew, however, over the next few sessions as Dave reported progress from interventions carried out in our sessions and during the interim periods. I found that the feedback provided by my client at each session helped the process of therapy so that I was able to work with Dave successfully.

In hindsight, I would have liked to have spent more time with Dave challenging his negative core belief system and schemata regarding his personal underachievements, as these seemed to be major internal cognitive triggers to his anger attacks. However, due to the brief therapy restrictions of the setting in which I worked this may not have been possible.

In future work with clients I feel that it would be useful to explain more fully the underlying reasons for each CBT intervention that I present to them. In this way homework tasks would be more fully understood and brought along to the sessions, as well as my clients gaining a better appreciation of the therapeutic interventions undertaken.

Evaluation of my work

In summary, this case study has demonstrated to me the usefulness of using CBT techniques with anger management issues, supporting the work of Gottlieb (1999), within a brief therapy framework. Through working with Dave I have realised the importance of listening and acting upon client feedback, and of altering my 'style' of therapy to suit each individual client, when difficulties are perceived. It has proved to me that although I might feel overwhelmed by acute and complex problems presented by a client at the outset of therapy, through a collaborative process based upon a good therapeutic alliance I am able to be therapeutically creative and experimental. This in effect has increased my confidence as a trainee practitioner.

References

Gottlieb, M.M. (1999). *The Angry Self: a Comprehensive Approach to Anger Management*. Arizona: Zeig, Tucker.

Pearsons, J.B. (1989). *Cognitive Therapy in Practice: a Case Formulation Approach*. New York: Norton.

Appendix A

Date	Situation	Angry thoughts and rating of anger	Physical effects	Calming down
Saturday	Shopping, laundry	Just general anger. Rating 30%	Headache, chest pains	Got the job done and relaxed
Sunday	Arguing with wife	Quite a lot of anger (60%) but kept buttoned up	Chest and some arm pains	Went into other room
Wednesday	Walking the dog	Mind wandered and got angry quickly (20%)	Not many	Went by itself

Figure 2   Thought diary (Session 2).

Appendix B

Date	Emotion	Situation	Automatic thoughts	Rational thoughts	Outcome
	What do you feel?	What was happening?	What exactly are your thoughts?	What are more realistic thoughts?	Rerate belief in automatic thought (0–100%)
	How bad is it? (0–100%)		How far do you believe them? (0–100%)	How far do you believe them? (0–100%)	Rerate emotion (0–100%)

Figure 3   Challenging dysfunctional thoughts sheet.

Chapter 7

Walking back to happiness: a couple's incongruent perception of chronic illness

with a case study by Russell Hurn

PRELUDE

The art of describing a particular case, of giving the reader insights into the workings of the therapeutic relationship and the development of understanding, lies in the therapist's ability to comment on how process informs and directs the contextual issues emerging from therapy. Russell Hurn's account of his work in this process report captures the subtleties of process that are so often ignored in client studies. He elaborates on the importance of the working alliance between therapist and patient and how this trusting bond serves as the foundation for the therapeutic progress that the patient makes. Russell also makes a point of describing his feelings when reviewing taped material, a daunting task for any trainee or indeed qualified therapist! His insights regarding his interventions are well thought out and constructively critical. He makes reference to the fact that, through listening to his interaction with his client, he is able to go beyond the mere content of the sessions and gain a wider perspective on his interactions with the client. In a way, this allows him to supervise his own work retrospectively; to gain insight through repositioning himself outside the ongoing dynamics of the relationship. This exercise not only informs his work with this particular client but also prepares him for future clinical/therapeutic encounters.

Finally, and very importantly, Russell refers to the realisation that hypothesising within the therapeutic context is an ongoing, collaborative, dynamic process between therapist and client, and that sometimes progress is not defined by the clear achievement of goals but rather by the ability to construct and reconstruct shared meanings of the client's reality, in a safe, nurturing environment.

> *Russell Hurn wrote this process report at the beginning of the first year of a part-time MSc in Counselling Psychology. The comments were written at the beginning of the first year of the post-MSc practitioner diploma.*

Preamble

Choosing the case

My choice to report the following intervention was based on a number of factors; the openness of the client, her partner's willingness to participate, the working alliance which I felt was very quickly established and, on a practical level, the quality of the recording. This case was my first real foray into the systemic paradigm, and, as such, has had a great impact on my professional development. It proved to be a steep, but interesting, learning curve. Luckily for me, it encapsulated many of the fundamental principles of the family therapy approach which I could relate easily to previous research. In a sense, I felt that this case truly enabled me to appreciate some of the issues of systems theory; specifically circularity, hypothesising and neutrality.

Retrospective appraisal of the report

During the documented session I found it difficult to remain neutral, but my awareness of the potential danger enabled me to continue, if not completely neutral, at least suitably enough to facilitate a working relationship. I also experienced what I thought was a struggle for power between the two opposing beliefs that the couple held. In a sense, I was used as a power broker bringing attention to how the power of these beliefs was at work in the system (Keeney 1979). At times my questioning was disjointed and unimaginative. This may be a result of this being my first systemic session. Initially, I felt that I was not at ease with the techniques of questioning and tended to rely more on direct approaches, rather more than may have been desirable.

I found this process report stimulating at all levels, from the therapy session itself to the deep reflection involved in this process report. I became immersed in the details of the conversation and the non-verbal behaviour. So much so that in my original draft I ended up transcribing and analysing far more than the required ten minutes. Naturally, I received an editorial rap across the knuckles concerning the importance of being concise in one's writing! This report made me aware of my limitations within the systemic framework, but it also uncovered the potential of this method of intervention when used properly.

The learning experience

This process report taught me the importance of reviewing taped material, which enabled me to go beyond the content. Having no immediate demand to communicate with my clients, I could more easily attend to the conversation and read between the lines to identify the inferences made through the communication. In this example, the tape recorder proved to be my reflecting team offering a different hypothesis for exploration, speeding up the therapeutic intervention and leading to an effective end. I accept that there are always alternative ways of understanding the content and process of the communication that has taken place (Pearce 1993), but my interpretations of the events in the session are based on my unique experience and the opportunity to relive the session by listening to the recorded material without having to be part of it. By doing this I could, in a sense, get inside the clients' system and look out from their point of view.

This case represents a number of important issues for therapeutic practice:

- The importance of recording and then reviewing sessions.
- The active role the therapist adopts in a familial system.
- The need to remain neutral while in the system.
- The power of individual beliefs on the working and communication within a family system.
- The incongruence of chronic illness perception between individuals.
- The dynamic nature of hypothesising.
- The effectiveness of brief intervention.

PROCESS REPORT

Introduction

This report addresses the concerns of a female patient who presented with anger and depressed feelings towards her life situation and her husband, following his brain haemorrhage. In the transcribed text and summary material I will discuss the issues of retirement and chronic illness within a systemic perspective following a session with the patient and her husband.

Theoretical Concept

The emphasis of the systemic approach is on the whole family as a medium of change (Burnham 1998), and an idea that communication and control within a system depends on the feedback it receives. Any tendency to move away from the equilibrium that the family has created is corrected through negative feedback to produce homeostasis. Families are described as healthy if they can respond in a flexible way to changing circumstances, altering their rules to fit the new situation. The individual is, therefore, understood in terms of their context. There is no underlying theory of personality or motivation (Bor, Legg and Scher 1997), the counsellor is thus not so concerned with why people act in a certain way but how they act and what reaction that causes. The family are described as partners in a dance. Their relationships are punctuated by beliefs and behaviours, and problems may occur at developmental stages of the individual or family life-cycle. Minuchin (1974) argues that lack of resolution skills disable the system, which usually gravitates to one of two tendencies: stability or change. Problems are viewed as parts of repetitive sequences which 'maintain and are maintained by the problem' (Burnham 1998, p. 7). Psychological symptoms are thus the system's attempt at solving the problems within the group or family.

Assessment from this theoretical perspective becomes part of the process and involves the therapist as an additional element to the system in which they are intervening. The counsellor, therefore, adopts a position of looking outwards at the world from within the system. Hypotheses are generated from the obtained information and these are starting points for lines of questioning to validate the original formulation (see Selvini Palazzoli et al. 1980), they also ensure the activity of the therapist to track the relationship patterns (Selvini Palazzoli et al. 1980). Information is always news of difference, there is not a search for truths but a continuous exploration of relationships, therefore no one person is viewed as the cause of a problem but rather as a characteristic of the relationship. To facilitate this the therapist remains in a neutral position with a continual state of curiosity which leads to different views and subsequently more curiosity (Cecchin 1987). The assumption is that change within the relationship is generated by disturbing the current system to bring forth a new stability. Burnham and Harris (1988) suggest solutions to family change are viewed as latent within the system and can be realised by introducing clarity to confusion and confusion to rigidity. The major function of the therapist is to look for the communicative function of symptoms (Keeney 1979), i.e. what is the meaning of the problem as seen from each individual's place within the system? They must then introduce new connections and information between behaviours and beliefs to stimulate the system to adopt a different dance.

Assessment

Mary is a 62-year-old, retired, white female who acts as a carer for her 65-year-old husband Rob, who suffered a brain haemorrhage 18 months ago. She appeared smart and well presented, lucid and alert. Mary has been married before and suffered physical and mental abuse during that 25-year relationship. She had also received some counselling prior to our meeting, following her mother's death six months before.

Presenting problem

She presented with a high level of frustration and anger at her life situation, feeling that it was progressively worsening and that she was being 'used and put upon'.

Problem formulation

Mary had high expectations for her time in retirement and had made many plans, all of which have been cancelled. She is experiencing uncertainty about her future and role as carer/wife following three major life events; her retirement, her mother's death and her husband's chronic illness.

Contract and therapy plan

I made an open-ended contract, which was to be based on a session that her husband attended. This was to ascertain whether a systemic approach would be more helpful than personal therapy, based on the significance of her relationship within the presenting problem.

Referral and setting

Mary was referred by a national charity, which offers support and rehabilitation programmes for brain-injured patients and their carers. The assessment and subsequent sessions were held at the charity's offices.

Aims of session

The aim of this featured session was to observe the relationship between Mary and her husband and to see her problem, of anger and frustration, in context. Mary had been keen at the assessment to attribute the cause of her consternation to Rob and his inactivity, I wanted, therefore, to ascertain for myself the possible extent of this incapacity and to formulate a treatment plan based either on systemic or a more personalised form of therapy, i.e. cognitive behavioural.

Lead into transcript

I had arranged the room so that there were two chairs fairly close to each other and another at an angle. When the clients came in I asked them to take a seat. Mary chose one of the two placed together and directed Rob into a spare seat in the corner by the door (I thought the only thing missing seemed to be a dunces hat). Within this set up I was placed between them. Mary began by expressing how much sleep she had managed to get by going away for a couple of weeks since the assessment, she attributed this to not being disturbed by Rob every night. He described her as being more relaxed since this holiday and said that their relationship was easier. They had, in his words, 'not been jibing' at each other so much. Mary confirmed this and noted Rob's difference for a few days after she came back, but stated that this more thoughtful attitude had stopped quickly as he readopted the daily routine. This involved him staying in bed most of the morning and spending the rest of the day sitting watching television, an action Rob himself described as boring. It was obvious from the first few minutes that they were very different in temperament. Mary is very energetic and on the go most of the day while Rob is very calm and relaxed, polite and friendly but somewhat lethargic. Mary is a keen walker and tries to get Rob out and about, apparently without much success. While on a separate holiday Rob had managed to go for a number of walks, the reason he gave was that he forced himself to go because he was on his own. It is following this confession that we begin the transcript.

Transcript

COUNSELLOR: Mary why do you think that Rob found those walks around (*holiday destination*) pleasurable and the ones (*near home*) not?

This use of circular questioning was an attempt at trying to get her to understand Rob's position and also to give him an insight into what Mary thinks and feels (see Selvini Palazzoli et al. 1980). This was also designed to give me some information on the state of the relationship and the possible opposing views each may hold.

MARY: I can't understand it. I don't know, I just don't know . . . unless it was just because he was away from me.

The first part of this response was expressed with some distress, a plea for help to me and to her husband to help sort out the mess she feels she is in. The second part is a move for some sympathy, a plea for some reassurance from her husband that the relationship is important to him.

COUNSELLOR: Rob, what do you think?

I was about to put the opposing question to Rob to make him think about Mary's thoughts when he doesn't go for a walk with her but this question was quickly interrupted by Rob who took his own initiative to answer his wife's plea.

ROB: No (*then unintelligible mumble*) . . . It was just that I was on my own and, uhh, there was nothing else to do kind of thing.

The mumble after he denied not wanting to be with Mary may reflect a difficulty he has in discussing matters of emotion. The following statement is an attempt to justify his behaviour and to nullify the importance of the topic.

MARY 1: (*interrupting*) Yes, but . . .

Here Mary is acknowledging that he wants to be with her in the relationship but is still searching for an answer that, in her mind, can justify his actions.

ROB 1: I forced myself to do it.

Rob is indicating his own autonomy here and indicating that he has some degree of motivation.

COUNSELLOR 1: So, if you were on your own you forced yourself?

I felt it necessary to clarify the point here. To reflect back to Rob what he had said and reaffirm his ability to be motivated at times.

ROB 2: Yeah.

The point is accepted and reinforced.

COUNSELLOR 2: So what stops you when you're with Mary?

This is the direct form of the circular question that I had put to Mary earlier. I felt this was needed after establishing the existence of motivating forces.

ROB 3: Well, nothing really. But it, uhh, we do occasionally do go out.

He is confused here. He has failed to find the answer that is congruent with his general behaviour, and therefore tries to change the direction of the conversation with a comment that puts a more positive connotation onto his behaviour. He finishes with a look towards Mary for support. There seems to be a blockage here for Rob and unwillingness or inability to accept that a problem exists.

MARY 2: Now don't, don't include me in this because I could [steady?] I could scream at what you are saying.

These last few words are more forceful and there is a degree of anger in her voice. This is obviously a situation she has experienced before and I got the feeling she was determined to punctuate the point for my benefit. She is possibly highlighting the anger of her problem as expressed at the assessment. This anger could be the symptom of an attempt at correcting the system (Burnham 1998).

ROB 4: Occasionally we go out.

This is repeated over the last few words Mary says and is an attempt to hold his ground, resisting any possible justification for a confrontation.

COUNSELLOR 3: (*pause*) She says she's going to scream at what you're saying.

I felt intervention was needed because the conversation seemed to be heading into a one-way street and would probably have taken its natural course towards exasperation for one of them. This question is reflective and looking for feelings behind the suggestion of a scream. Mary's previous words had contained a hint of laughter this was in response to the smile that had spread across Rob's face, possibly indicating his familiarity with her tone of voice.

ROB 5: (*laughs*) Yes, she would.

Rob's feelings are expressed in his laughter, to him the actions are predictable and he knows that Mary will become upset, but he is not prepared to say, or do, anything to prevent this. A more appropriate question from me may have been sequential, to explore his usual actions in such a context. This may have helped to expose a pattern of behaviour that we could have addressed in therapy.

COUNSELLOR 4: (*pause*) So, let's imagine a typical afternoon, maybe it's a day like today and, uhmm, Mary wants to go for a walk. You said that you're . . .

I was attempting to readdress not identifying the pattern of behaviour and so attempted to reset the scene and follow a usual situation through its natural progression.

ROB 5: (*interrupting*) We go round to Ash Hampton village that's about all, isn't it.

Rob is avoiding the possibility of any questions here by interrupting and trying to play down the importance of the investigation. The intonation also suggests that although he is bored at home with nothing to do, going out is also boring and not important.

MARY 3: He would go if it was an errand.

Mary tries to punctuate Rob's comments by indicating possible motivation for his behaviour. She seems to be suggesting his behaviour is either purely selfish or influenced by necessity, rather than a desire for a pleasurable relationship with her.

ROB 6: Yeah.

Rob admits this and apparently sees no problem with it.

MARY 4: He wouldn't go just for a walk.

This is another attempt at saying that 'he wouldn't just want to be sharing time with me'. It was directed at me and I began to feel that Mary was trying to recruit me to her side of the dispute and I was aware that I must try and remain neutral but curious (Cecchin 1987).

ROB 7: We've got the sto . . . You know Ash Hampton village at all?

This was Rob's attempt to connect with me. He directly uses the subject of his local village, not only as a way of changing the immediacy of the conversation, which he may have begun to find uncomfortable, but also trying to engage me in a separate conversation. I am aware that they are both now actively trying to recruit me to their side of the dispute, an indication that I am becoming part of the system.

COUNSELLOR 5: Yeah.

I let this side of the conversation continue for two reasons. First, I felt that I had, if anything, been harder on Rob than on Mary up to this stage and wanted to give him room to breathe, and second, I felt that he may provide some more relevant information if allowed to progress at his more relaxed pace.

ROB 8: We, I go up there.

This comment fell a little short of my expectations and seemed to take him back into a circular argument with Mary again. The change of pronoun indicates an individual at work, someone who has a motivation for his actions.

MARY 5: If we were going up to shop, yes, he would come with me.

With this comment Mary manages to agree with what Rob has said but seems to be setting something else up.

ROB 9: Yeah.

This is a quick agreement, he seems pleased with what Mary has just said.

MARY 5: But if just to go for a walk round he wouldn't want to.

This seems to reinforce her own comments from before, relating to his selfish motivation for going out.

ROB 10: Mmm.

An agreement, but unwillingness to expand further.

COUNSELLOR 6: So what, what do you think is the difference for Rob between an errand and . . . pleasure?

This is another attempt to get beyond the behaviour in order to identify beliefs and feelings through circular questioning.

MARY 5: I don't know . . . I just don't know how he ticks over no longer.

This is quite important as Mary's depressed mood and comments suggest that there is a general lack of communication between the two of them. This may relate to the physical effects of the brain haemorrhage on Rob's personality and subsequent social behaviour. Mary's depression and annoyance may also have a communicative function which Rob is not understanding (Keeney 1979).

COUNSELLOR 7: We, we said that, Mary said that she she felt like screaming. Why do you think Mary maybe gets uptight when you don't want to do these things?

I perhaps should have continued with Mary and used mind-reading type questions to foster a mental link in order to fill the void she was experiencing, instead I made an attempt to get back to the emotional content through circular questioning. I was hoping to make Rob think about the reaction his behaviour was causing rather than just remaining habitualised to the consequences.

ROB 11: I haven't a clue . . . really . . . no.

This response mirrors that of Mary. Neither of them seems to be able to relate to the thoughts and wishes of the other at this time, there is a communication breakdown.

COUNSELLOR 8: You can just imagine, it could be anything we could . . . just raid our imaginations for ideas.

This is an attempt to stay with this line of questioning. I felt sure that if they just took the time to consider the possibilities of the other in the relationship then they may be able to relate it to their own behaviour. At this point I am working with a hypothesis that they both have different wishes and aspirations for the future which are coming between them (Selvini Palazzoli et al. 1980).

ROB 12: Mmm.

Rob has not really grasped what I want of him and is considering what I have just said.

COUNSELLOR 9: I mean some might be right, some might be wrong, just see if you could name anything.

This was a plea to Rob to stop and think and not just pass this comment off and ignore the situation as he seems prone to do.

ROB 13: Well, we enjoy each other's . . .

Here Rob avoids the question as such, but this avoidance does suggest that they do enjoy being together. This is the first time I have received this type of information.

MARY 6: (*interrupting*) Why do you think, NO! Why do you think I get frustrated when you won't go to (*place name*) you won't go down to (place name) with me, you won't go out unless it's an errand to suit yourself.

Mary really wants this question answered. Possibly she feels that she has failed to get me on her side and thus has to pursue this information herself. This is good because it shows that I was to some degree remaining neutral and it also facilitated direct communication between them.

ROB 14: Well, we get on all right together apart from that.

This is a somewhat mumbled response, a possible resistance to sharing any emotions through direct confrontation.

MARY 7: That's not the point (*hits the table to punctuate the next two words*) Why. Do you think I get . . . (*stops abruptly*)

Mary really wants an answer that lies beyond Rob's usual dismissive comments. The banging on the table indicates the amount of emotion she is experiencing. This is a physical side of her wishing to scream. She is hitting out with words to get a satisfactory reply. There may be links here to Mary's previous marriage, which ended after she was physically abused, she was used to some outburst of emotion but here feels she is getting nothing and doesn't know how to react. The abrupt end shows a reluctance to verbalise the strong emotion she is feeling.

ROB 15: I don't know. I couldn't tell you.

Again a dismissal.

(*six-second pause*)

I let this silence continue. I could see that Rob was thinking and I wanted to use non-verbal communication to let him know that I was with him while he pondered on the exchange that had occurred. Mary had given me the impression that powerful emotions were at work and that she needed some reassurance from Rob. She was fighting for answers but only within emotional limits. Rob, on the other hand, was actively avoiding emotional content while appearing weary and almost distant. It was almost as though they were both afraid of their feelings.

ROB 16: Well, you think I ought to go out.

The wait paid off, as Rob identified a possible feeling of concern that Mary may be experiencing.

MARY 8: Well, of course you're quite capable. You can walk about . . . you don't realise how lucky you are that you can walk about, I mean you see Mark, Paul, George in wheelchairs at the day centre but even that doesn't click with you that you're fortunate.

Mary doesn't respond with concern but is more intent on clarifying her position by providing some information as to her behaviour and his lack of insight.

ROB 17: I know I'm fortunate, fortunate to be here, but uhmm . . . it's just that, it's one of those things isn't it, I mean, if you don't want to do a thing you don't do it. That's it. That's the way I look at it.

There was more expression in his voice at the beginning of this statement. He has obviously thought about his situation since the brain trauma and reflected on it. This means something to him but he ends with a plea that seems to say, I am ill and my life is precarious so I should make the most of it. At this point my hypothesis began to change (Selvini Palazzoli et al. 1980). They still seemed to be coming from opposite directions but may actually have a common goal rather than a separate one, as I had previously thought.

Summary

The conversation continued and I discovered how the couple's retirement had impacted on their relationship. Rob had been very active when he first retired up until his brain haemorrhage. Mary had been impressed with his level of fitness and had been looking forward to an active retirement with her husband. Rob had, however, been instructed by doctors to take life easy since his condition began and had taken these words as gospel.

We discussed any worries that Rob might have for the future. I also asked them to imagine that they could time travel and, if so, what advice they would give themselves in the past. Mary's advice was to live for the day and experience your dreams when you can. When linked with the material listed above, this information enabled me, on reflection, to hypothesise that she had become disillusioned and was experiencing some feelings of loss. Family relationships tend to become disturbed when significant life stages are reached, e.g. death or retirement. They are times to reshuffle the deck the family uses to play with and to re-evaluate the game (Burnham and Harris 1988). Relationships that once were close can become more distant.

Retirement is a release from previous commitments and a time when fantasies and plans for the future come into play. The initial activity of Rob on his retirement and the plans Mary had for an active and pleasurable time had been destroyed by the haemorrhage. Consequently they were both facing a retirement of uncertainty, quite the opposite to their initial plans. Rolland (1994) argues that the need to compromise plans due to the chronic illness heightens feelings of being robbed.

Mary and Rob's problem had a direct reference to my own life and the retirement plans that my uncle and aunt had made. These had been smashed when she died of cancer just as they started to enjoy their new life. This personal experience of loss associated with retirement may have fuelled my eagerness to help Mary and Rob. It may also have facilitated my reframing of the situation in that, although they had opposing starting points regarding health beliefs, they actually had the common goal of sharing a long and happy retirement together. To achieve this Rob believes that he must remain inactive and follow his doctor's advice rigidly, taking it easy. For him this is a step down from a lifestyle that was already more relaxed than Mary's. For her to 'take it easy' meant to go for long walks and embrace the benefits of fresh air and light exercise, this level of activity, she believed, would serve to lengthen Rob's lifespan and help to generate a better retirement for them both. As a result Mary and Rob had a belief system skew (Rolland 1994) regarding the way to live following a brain haemorrhage.

At work in this system were issues of age, ability and gender roles. For Mary, three significant events had affected her plans for the future:

- Her retirement had opened up possibilities for more pleasurable activities.
- The death of her mother had highlighted her own vulnerable age.
- Her husband's haemorrhage had seemed to steal from her the one person that would be with her in the years to come.

To her, Rob's inactivity was a waste of the opportunities that life presented to them. She failed to see that his actions may have been a separate attempt to prolong and enhance the time that they had left together.

At the subsequent session, I reframed the situation (Watzlawick, Weakland and Fisch 1974) so that they could gain insights into each other's thoughts and beliefs. This enabled them to place a positive connotation on their actions while highlighting their similar desires from opposing viewpoints. They agreed with my ideas, confirming my hypothesis, and stated that the tasks for sharing time that I had suggested in the first session had helped and that they were enjoying each other's company. These tasks had included Rob setting his alarm and getting up to share breakfast with Mary five days a week, on the same days she was not allowed to shout at him or complain until after lunch.

In this follow up, they seemed very much a couple. They sat closer together and there was no confrontation. They talked of a trip they had planned together and the times they had shared since our last meeting. They made me feel relaxed in their company, something I had been unable to feel at the initial session. This more congenial atmosphere prompted me to suggest that the couple take a therapeutic breathing space to allow their system time to settle down, as suggested by Selvini Palazzoli (1980). They seemed very agreeable to this, so I took a leap of faith and suggested that we should only meet again if they experienced a relapse. This was based on the family initiative after enlightening the couple to their interactions (Weber, McKeever and McDaniel 1985) and the assumption that the intervention, even though brief at three sessions, could be beneficial because the couple had made the mutual decision to stay and work together (Benjamin 1987). Families facing chronic illness have difficulty in imagining the future because of the potential for loss and the deterioration of the flexibility that may have existed in the system (Penn 1985). My intervention was to make them aware that they didn't need to change the structure of their relationship because they both wanted the same thing. I felt that to extend the therapy any more at this time would have been more detrimental than otherwise. Levey (1994) suggested that more is not necessarily better, a small step can make a big difference. In this case, I like to think that that is just what happened.

References

Benjamin, A. (1987). *The Helping Interview*. Boston: Houghton Mifflin.

Bor, R., Legg, C. and Scher, I. (1997). The systems paradigm. In R. Woolfe and W. Dryden (eds) *Handbook of Counselling Psychology*. London: Sage.

Burnham, J.B. (1998). *Family Therapy*. London: Routledge.

Burnham, J. and Harris, Q. (1988). Systemic family therapy: the Milan approach. In E. Street and W. Dryden (eds) *Family Therapy in Britain*. London: Sage.

Cecchin, G. (1987). Hypothesising, circularity, and neutrality revisited: an invitation to curiosity. *Family Process*, 26(4), 405–413.

Keeney, B.P. (1979) Ecosystemic epistemology: an alternative paradigm for diagnosis. *Family Process*, 18(2), 117–129.

Levey, K. (1994). Single session solutions. In M.F. Hoyt (ed.) *Constructive Therapies*. London: Guilford Press.

Minuchin, S. (1974). *Families and Family Therapy*. London: Tavistock Publications.

Pearce, W.B. (1993). *Interpersonal Communication: Making Social Worlds*. London: Harper Collins.

Penn, P. (1985). Feed forward: future questions, future maps. *Family Process*, 24(3), 299–310.

Rolland, J.S. (1994). *Families, Illness and Disability: An Integrative Treatment*. New York: Basic Books.

Selvini Palazzoli, M. (1980). Why a long interval between sessions? In M. Andolfo and I.I. Zwerling (eds) *Dimensions of Family Therapy*. New York: Guilford Press, pp. 161–169.

Selvini Palazzoli, M., Boscolo, L., Cecchin, G. and Prata, G. (1980). Hypothesising, circularity and neutrality: three guidelines for the conductor of the session. *Family Process*, 19(1), 3–12.

Watzlawick, P., Weakland, J. and Fisch, R. (1974). *Change: Principles of Problem Formation and Problem Resolution*. London: W.W. Norton.

Weber, T., McKeever, J.E. and McDaniel, S.H. (1985). A beginner's guide to the problem-orientated first family interview. *Family Process*, 24, 357–364.

Chapter 8

Treating the family: a process report on systemic therapy

with a case study by Rebecca Goldmeier

PRELUDE

Even though there are other case studies and process reports in this book which describe a similar theoretical approach, no two therapies, therapists or case studies are alike. Among many other factors, the art and science of therapy requires a unique blending of the rapport and relationship between therapist and client, therapist competence and confidence, client motivation, theoretical knowledge and experience. Rebecca Goldmeier was challenged to put new theoretical ideas taught on her course into practice. Through detailed reflection, as required in a process report, she reminds us how time-consuming this process is for trainees. She points out, however, how helpful it was to organise her ideas under different subheadings and to use suspension sessions both in developing an understanding of process and in writing-up the case. The excerpt she chose to present in her first year of study is, unusually, not from a first session. This is to her credit, as it is sometimes less of a challenge to present material from a first session. In this case, Rebecca first gives some background information to help the reader understand where she had got to in the therapy. Notice that *each* transaction between therapist and client is followed by her process comments. She also mentions how difficult it can be to work systematically with an individual when one is understandably curious about relationships and patterns of communication outside of the session. However, Rebecca does not lose sight of the fact that it is the material that is transacted within the session that constitutes therapeutic process.

> *Rebecca Goldmeier wrote this process report in the middle of a full-time MSc in Counselling Psychology. The comments were written during the beginning of the first year of the post-MSc practitioner diploma.*

Preamble

Why choose this case?

This process report was written towards the end of my MSc at which time I had completed the module in systemic therapy. This case was the first time that I had attempted to practise my newly acquired skills in systemic counselling. Although the outcome of counselling with this client was positive, I found the experience a challenging one, constantly applying new learning from lectures into practice. I therefore thought that using this case for my process report would allow me an opportunity to think about the process issues when working within a systemic framework and would enable me to observe some of my systemic interventions more closely.

Furthermore, I enjoyed working with this client. I felt that we had a strong therapeutic relationship and I looked forward to our sessions. I thought that it would be interesting to analyse this relationship more closely and to try and determine the factors that contributed to this alliance.

How do I feel about what I have produced?

Retrospectively, I feel fairly content with the report, especially since it was my first process report using a systemic orientation. I can see the time and effort that I must have put into writing it and I wonder how I found the time, considering the pressures of the MSc!

In particular, I notice the structure of the report and my use of headings. I think they are a useful way of guiding my writing and I would certainly make use of this structure again in the future.

I am aware of how many more counselling skills I have developed since the work with this client took place, both in my ability to utilise systemic questioning within sessions and to incorporate systemic thinking and ideas in my analytical comments.

What have I learned from drafting and writing this process report?

I think one of the key areas of learning from the writing of this process report was the use of supervision in drafting and writing the report. Supervision is a forum in which I am able to think about process issues and I always find it useful to note down what has been discussed with my supervisor. Rereading my analysis of the transcript I was reminded of how much my notes helped me in writing this report. They served as a foundation for further thinking on the case and made the task of writing the report less time-consuming.

I am increasingly aware of the helpfulness of taping sessions for my own personal development as a counselling psychologist. It provides me with a chance to review my skills critically and to look at alternative interventions that may have been more useful. As a trainee, it is sometimes difficult during a session to think about what intervention I am going to make and for what purpose. The writing of the process report helps to link my practice to theory and to ensure that I am not making interventions with no theoretical basis. I found that following the writing of the process report I began to become more aware of my practice and the need to try and follow up on areas of my work that I identified as needing some improvement. Thus, the report indicated areas where I might undertake some further reading and further practice.

The following process report begins with an account of the systemic approach, which has been used as the theoretical framework for the work with this client. The report is based upon the third session of a five-session contract and details the initial assessment and formulation of the client. It provides a detailed analysis of a ten-minute transcript from the session. The report concludes with an evaluation of the session and some personal reflections of a counselling psychologist in training.

PROCESS REPORT

Section 1

Theoretical orientation: systemic therapy

Since the 1950s, 'systemic' therapy has become somewhat of an umbrella term due to the expansion and development of new models and influences from other groups. Fundamentally, all models share core principles, however their explanations may vary. This section focuses on the theoretical concepts, which unite all models.

The development of systemic therapy demonstrated a paradigm shift, a break away from concerns with individual patterns. It radicalised the way clinicians worked as they began to focus their attention entirely on the 'family'. Goldenberg and Goldenberg (2000) suggest that systemic therapy has become more than simply another treatment method. It now represents a whole new way of conceptualising human problems, understanding behaviour, the development of symptoms and their resolution.

The 'system' refers to any group of elements in interaction with one another over time. Jones (1993) proposes that the system should not be seen as a closed unit but one that is in continuous interaction with others. The system, therefore, is arguably defined by the observer and in therapy this definition will relate to the implications of the boundaries set by the family and the therapist. She suggests that the open system has three main characteristics: wholeness, feedback and equifinality. *Wholeness* is dependent on the system being more than the sum of its parts and thus on the interrelation and interdependence of the behaviours of all the family members. *Feedback* assumes that the system will respond to input from all its members or from the environment. *Equifinality* is where the organisation or process part of the system has a prime function irrespective of different initial positions.

Selvini Palazzoli et al. (1980) conceptualised the family as a self-regulating system, which controls itself according to the rules formed over a period of time through a process of trial and error. Through the family's communication patterns and interaction the system rules are maintained.

Goldenberg and Goldenberg (2000) propose that the symptoms experienced by the individual who is initially considered 'dysfunctional' are not accidental but are skilfully fabricated to achieve particular systemic purposes. Therefore, central to systemic therapy is the notion that no behaviour is considered negative and no individual is blamed for his or her symptomatic behaviour. The goal of systemic therapy is to try and change family rules in order to change behaviour (Cecchin 1987).

Goldenberg and Goldenberg (2000) suggest that Milan theorists developed the concepts of three 'landmark intervention strategies', namely, hypothesising, circularity and neutrality. Cecchin (1987) depicts how all three principles are recursively linked, such that neutrality provides the context for constructing multiple hypotheses, which construct a context of neutrality. Without understanding the importance of successfully using all three tools, one will be unable to see the systemic rules, which maintain the symptomatic behaviours of the system.

Systemic therapy tends to be seen by many clinicians as an inappropriate approach to use when working therapeutically with individuals. Jenkins and Asen (1992), and Bott (1994) strongly advocate that a useful systemic framework can be maintained if the therapist aims to keep the therapy system 'open' for relevant others to join at any time. Concerns of the systemic therapist are, therefore, still concerned with the patterns of relationships in human systems and understanding problems in context.

Therefore, sessions were conducted as if other members of Avril's system were present, continually considering others' views about Avril's dilemmas as well as connecting the symptomatic behaviour.

Section 2

Client profile

The client presented in this process report is a 53-year-old lady presenting with symptoms of depression and anxiety. These symptoms are long-standing and have been exacerbated over the past twelve months.

Referral

When attempting to understand Avril's difficulties, it is vital from a systemic perspective to begin to understand the system that Avril belongs to, and the context in which her problems may have been discussed initially. One must consider the referring agency. Avril was referred to the Brief Psychological Intervention Counselling Service (BPICS) by her GP, the setting for which is in the GP's surgery. Avril was referred for her symptoms of anxiety and depression together with some phobic elements. The GP had prescribed her the antidepressant medication, citalopram and wondered whether Avril might benefit from psychological intervention.

From a systemic point of view, one would argue that Avril's 'problems', while seeming dysfunctional at first, are present for a purpose and maintained by rules that have formed over a period of time. Therefore, the goal would be to change the rule in which Avril's symptomatic behaviour is embedded. This process would require a change in her relationships and how they interacted and would not include interventions specifically targeted at her depressive or anxiety symptoms.

Initial assessment

Avril presented as a well-groomed lady with a seemingly talkative nature. She describes her current difficulties as having problems sleeping suggesting that she lies awake six out of seven nights. She further reports a decrease in energy and appetite and a general feeling of irritability. She also reports some phobic symptoms relating to an incident in 1995, when she was mugged on a train. Although she received six sessions of counselling, she still feels vulnerable, low in confidence and does not like to travel alone. Finally, she reports a decrease in social activity suggesting that she and her husband rarely go out socially. She also finds that she has little time for any pleasurable activities for herself.

Background and family history

Avril has been married for twenty-two years. It is her second marriage. She has one son, aged fifteen, from her present marriage. He was diagnosed with attention deficit hyperactivity disorder (ADHD) in 1995 and appears to be a great strain.

Her first marriage ended after four years when Avril was just twenty-four. She has one son from this marriage. The marriage ended after persistent physical abuse of both her and her young son.

Avril is an only child. Her father died twenty years ago of heart failure. Her mother currently lives with Avril and her family. Her mother is suffering from a dementia, which was also diagnosed in 1995.

Formulation and hypotheses

Hypothesising is an essential process and part of systemic therapy. The hypothesis must be circular and relational, enabling the therapist to organise all the data given by the client. Hoffman (1990) suggests that hypothesising allows the therapist to begin to offer new family scripts.

It appears that the strain of the caring responsibilities caused by the illness of her son and her mother has left Avril with feelings of vulnerability and anhedonia. Due to a lack of support for her in her role as a carer she appears to find little time for her own pleasurable activities. This seems to have had implications for her relationship with her husband.

Furthermore, it would appear that the relationship Avril has with her son at times resembles the relationship she had with her first husband. This has perhaps led to a resurgence of some familiar feelings of inadequacy and vulnerability, a family script that is repeating its pattern.

Contract

- It was agreed that five sessions would allow Avril to explore these relationships and to begin to find ways of changing the family rules and scripts allowing the symptomatic behaviour to reduce.
- It was agreed that the sessions would be taped and a consent form was signed by Avril ensuring confidentiality and anonymity.

Lead into session 3

The section transcribed (which begins at 522 on the tape) comes at the middle–end point of the session. Up to this point Avril has been describing her first marriage, the violence that ensued and how she managed to leave that marriage. At the point where the transcription begins she has just finished describing the incident when she was mugged on a train, which brought back some of these violent memories and images.

Section 3: transcript

CLIENT 1: I tried without . . . but in the end . . . I think I went back to work about twice or three times and I just couldn't cope. The world was going by and I wasn't going with it. It was terrible.

Avril is referring to the experience of being mugged on the train in 1995. She presented with symptoms of post-traumatic stress disorder (PTSD) soon after this incident. The metaphor she has used to describe her feelings appears to indicate how detached and vulnerable she was feeling at this time.

THERAPIST 1: Were those some of the issues you addressed in counselling?

Here I was keen to understand whether any of these symptoms were persisting or whether they had been addressed in her previous counselling experience.

CLIENT 2: Yes . . . she said you better be careful of getting tired . . . because she said then you'll be vulnerable . . . and if you do get tired and a problem hits it'll . . . it'll knock you sideways again . . . .and . . . erm . . . (*pause*) so . . .

Avril has begun to demonstrate a pattern in her life. She appears to be suggesting a pattern of vulnerability through the words of the counsellor although it is perhaps her who is beginning to recognise the family script.

THERAPIST 2: Thinking about what she said . . . and you've brought it up now . . . perhaps there is a connection with how you are at the moment because . . . you are tired and you are finding it difficult to do the day-to-day things . . . you're having difficulty looking after your mother . . . it's very stressful looking after your son, maybe this is another vulnerable period of your life.

Using Avril's previous statement as evidence of a pattern being repeated, I feel it is time to formulate a hypothesis to Avril by suggesting to her that perhaps this is another vulnerable period. I am wondering whether she is beginning to experience the same feelings by acknowledging to herself some of her current difficulties.

CLIENT 3: It is, so, I mean, er, last . . . not last year, the summer before was, must have been, one of the worst years of our life, what with Richard, with the school . . . he was at the school here, which wasn't suitable because of his ADHD . . . it's a terrible condition, it really is a terrible condition, 'cos he's such a lovely boy, he's got such lovely ways . . .

Rather than answer directly, Avril chooses to add further fuel to this hypothesis. She speaks of the difficulties in her relationship with her son but 'blames' the illness rather than choosing to focus on the relationship.

THERAPIST 3: I'm sure he is.

In agreeing with Avril, I have acknowledged to her that I am not interested in 'blaming' but in looking for patterns and relationships.

CLIENT 4: But then he'll turn . . . I mean, like last night, I get such verbal abuse from him. I mean, the things that come out of that child's mouth, I didn't know those words existed when I was his age.

It appears that as I have demonstrated to Avril that I agree with her seeing her boy as lovely, she is able to trust enough to begin to address the nature of his behaviour and the consequent relationships difficulties.

THERAPIST 4: Can you give me an example of something?

In asking this question, I am hoping that Avril will begin to describe this relationship in more detail.

CLIENT 5: You fat bitch, you fat cunt, you fuck . . . I mean, I don't swear . . . and that's what comes out of his mouth . . . if he wants to have a go it's *me* he has a go at, usually.

It appears embarrassing for Avril to give these examples yet in doing so she has been able to identify that the abuse is usually targeted at her.

THERAPIST 5: And how do you respond to him?

In asking this question, I am encouraging Avril to continue the example of the interaction between her and her son, thus enabling us to identify the patterns and processes in the relationship.

CLIENT 6: (*pause*) Erm, it depends how I'm feeling at the time. Er . . . most times I try to ignore him, because if you don't it only exacerbates the situation. He were told by his dad to stop it . . . his dad will tell him that's no way to speak to your mother . . . because half an hour later he'll come and apologise to me . . . but now is that the same scen . . . I've just thought now . . . is that the same scenario as the hus, as the first husband?

By asking Avril to continue the interaction in her mind, she has been able to notice a pattern. Earlier in the session she had reported how her first husband had physically attacked her and then come to apologise. She recognises that the same situation is occurring with her son.

THERAPIST 6: Well, I was just thinking that.

I attempt to confirm that I too had begun to identify this hypothesis.

CLIENT 7: I've just thought that through myself, you see, I don't get much chance to sit and think, to be honest, at home, I think yest . . . last two days was the first time me and Chris have had a reasonable conversation in months . . . without Richard.

Here, Avril has begun to address the benefits of the counselling process. One of the presenting issues is the fact that Avril has little time for herself or her relationship with her husband. It is interesting how she links the experience of being given time to think in the session with the experience of spending time with her husband. Perhaps this indicates that freeing up more time may lead to changes in relationships and thus a decrease in symptomatic behaviour.

THERAPIST 7: And how did that feel?

My response here is with a question. I am allowing space for the client to explore how it felt to give time to her relationship with her husband.

CLIENT 8: It was lovely . . . it was lovely!

In her response the client was smiling broadly and her repeating 'it was lovely' further indicates perhaps how rare and special this situation may have been.

THERAPIST 8: And you, do you feel about, thinking about making that connection there . . . we just skimmed that over . . .

My question here indicates a little anxiety. I am concerned that we have not addressed the identification of a pattern with the client's first husband and her son. It appears that I may be directing the client to think about the situation again. Perhaps she was not ready to address it at this point in the session and it may have been more useful to continuing exploring the relationship with her husband.

CLIENT 9: Oh, wi . . . with . . . with the first husband, yes.

She appears surprised by my change in emphasis, adding weight to my previous thoughts.

THERAPIST 9: That's quite significant.

Now that I have changed the emphasis, I continue to progress, indicating to Avril that there is perhaps a reason why it had not been addressed further.

CLIENT 10: Because he does it, the words that come from him . . . are . . . are very hurtful and he knows he hurts me . . . I think that's probably why . . . and he tries to hurt . . . he doesn't hurt me mum to her face but he says things about my mum to *me*.

This response indicates that it was perhaps too painful for Avril to continue to address the relationship between her and her son. Furthermore, she has brought her mother in to the family interaction. As Avril is an only child, she is extremely close to her mother and they appear to have a somewhat 'enmeshed' relationship, confirmed by the fact that Avril will not access support to help with her mother's dementia.

THERAPIST 10: Which hurts you.

In my response, I indicate that I hypothesise that by her son saying things about her mother to Avril, Avril becomes hurt personally.

CLIENT 11: Whi . . . he . . . he hopes he's gonna hurt me . . .

Avril accepts this hypothesis and takes it further by suggesting that her son wishes to hurt her.

THERAPIST 11: What do you feel towards Richard when he says these things to you? If you're going to make the comparison with your first husband, and, of course, he's your child and you love him, but . . . what, what are your instincts . . . your instinctive feelings?

My question here appears to be rather jumbled. I am trying to explore Avril's feelings towards her son. However, in doing so, I appear to make assumptions, that she loves her child. Perhaps she doesn't.

CLIENT 12: I want to hurt him . . . I want to hurt him . . . to hit . . . to hurt where it's coming from . . .

Avril's response does not address her feelings but rather the actions she would like to take.

THERAPIST 12: What do you want to do?

My response here follows the lead that Avril has taken. I ask a hypothetical question, an example of circular questioning.

CLIENT 13: Smack him across the mouth (*laughing*), sometimes I really do (*very quietly*) . . . because I don't warrant the verbal abuse that I get from him . . . his dad and I are very supportive of him . . . we fought tooth and nail to get him into this school . . . to try and help him . . . and all he seems to do is just . . . just throw it in our faces, shall we say . . . oh well, I don't care . . . and yet he does care, he's just . . . he's such . . . he's just like a split personality, he can be so good, but he can be so (*pause*) bad's not even the right word, evil, sometimes, is a word I would use towards him.

The hypothetical question appears to have evoked a strong response from Avril. Her laughter seems to be nervous laughter, as if ashamed that she feels she would like to exercise some level of violence towards her son. She also seems to be suggesting that this relationship between her and her son is one in which she invests a considerable amount of time and energy, which is not reciprocated but only 'thrown in her face'.

THERAPIST 13: So, I imagine that your son displaying some of these similar characteristics must be quite painful for you?

Although Avril has not explicitly suggested that this behaviour is similar to that of her first husband in her last response, she has suggested earlier in the session that her first husband had a 'split personality'. Therefore, my response is aiming to empathise with Avril and hypothesise how painful it must be for her.

CLIENT 14: Yes, it is. Sometimes I just go out of the room (*pause*) and . . .

THERAPIST 14: Because this time you can't leave and maybe that's . . .

My response has interrupted the client, perhaps neither allowing her the space nor the freedom to continue. However, I have responded with the hypothesis that perhaps she has to leave the room but would like to leave the situation altogether, as she did with her first husband, thus completing the pattern.

CLIENT 15: I've thought about that . . . I've thought of leaving . . .

Her response appears to confirm this hypothesis.

THERAPIST 15: Where would you go?

I respond with another hypothetical question, thus allowing Avril to explore the meaning of leaving.

CLIENT 16: (*pause*) I'd find a . . . I'd probably go back up North, my eldest son lives up there . . . I've got friends up there, still got family up there, his brothers are up there . . . Chris's brothers

THERAPIST 16: And what would happen to Richard if you left?

My response is again a hypothetical question, yet it is also future orientated allowing for an exploration of the change in the relationship that would arise, and allowing Avril to examine the situation from his perspective.

CLIENT 17: The way I feel at the time I want to go, I wouldn't care, that's . . . that's, that's how much he hurts me sometimes.

Avril has established the pain inherent in this relationship by her continuous use of her description of being 'hurt'.

THERAPIST 17: So, what stops you from going?

My response is a sequential question, allowing Avril to explore the reasons why she chooses not to fulfil this hypothetical leaving.

CLIENT 18: My husband . . . and then . . . I'll think, well, you know, this is silly . . . and he can't help it . . . and it . . . it's not his fault he's like he is . . . it's not like it's a bad temper that, er . . . that can be controlled, sometimes he can't control it . . . . . . and I think if I . . . if I give in to him, or let him see . . . I try not to let him see that I'm upset . . .

Here, Avril appears to be acknowledging the support of her husband. She is also moving away from using a blaming language about her son towards using a more acceptant language. Yet it appears that the strain

may be a result of her struggling to hide her feelings in this relationship with her son, perhaps leaving her vulnerable.

THERAPIST 18: Just like you did with your first husband, you covered up your clothes so that your mum can't see the bruises, maybe you're doing the same thing?

My response raises another hypothesis. I seek to question whether the covering up of how she feels is the manifestation of yet another pattern familiar in this family script.

CLIENT 19: That's right . . . my hurt goes inside . . . goes inside (*quietly*).

Again she has addressed her feelings of being hurt. However, on this occasion, rather than discuss her hurt with reference to actions, she describes her hurt as something internal, a feeling.

THERAPIST 19: Maybe that's not helpful to you.

My response indicates another hypothesis, that struggling to maintain the relationship as it stands currently is producing the symptomatic behaviour.

CLIENT 20: No.

Avril appears to accept this hypothesis.

THERAPIST 20: Maybe that's why you're here today?

My question aims to acknowledge further the connection between Avril's relationship with her son and her current behaviour.

CLIENT 21: You see, they always . . . they always think that I'm a strong person because I'm . . . I've always been tall. I've been tall from being about twelve . . . I mean, er, . . . no trouble getting into a pub when I was sixteen (*laughs*) because I looked twenty-something, 'cos I've always been tall. When you're tall and you're big . . . people think you're strong, not only physically but mentally . . . and . . . I'm neither (*laughs*) . . . and . . . I'm good with my hands as regards stitching, I used to make all my own clothes when I was at school and even after school . . . I used to make Chris's slacks . . . till Richard came on the scene and since he's come on the scene I haven't been near a sewing machine . . . but, em . . . so I'm useful in that way and decorating I can do, but lifting no, carrying shopping no . . . like . . . like now my arm's going to sleep . . . I'm . . . I'm . . . seeing the doctor tomorrow and I wanted to see him about getting some neck exercise . . . such trouble . . . I'm not strong . . .

The client indicates here that people have a perception of her as someone who can cope. She has suggested that since Richard was born she has not been able to sew. This perhaps indicates the strength that her relationship with her son has required, a strength that Avril admits she does not have.

THERAPIST 21: People perceive you to be something that you're not.

My response attempts to demonstrate to Avril that I have understood.

CLIENT 22: That's right.

Avril appears to affirm this disparity between the way she feels and the way others view her.

THERAPIST 22: And that's difficult.

I hypothesise that this need to remain strong and keep all the 'hurt' inside is further contributing to the symptomatic behaviour.

CLIENT 23: So, they tend to load me with their problems . . . they don't think I've got problems . . . they think, 'Oh, she's always smiling, she looks well . . . she's fine' . . . the one person who can . . . who can read me is my mother . . . she can tell when I get up in the morning if I'm feeling well . . . if something's bothering me. She knew when I was two weeks pregnant with my first baby (*laughs*) 'cos my face is like a book . . . yeah . . . very much so . . . she, she needs me.

Avril has given further indication of this 'enmeshed' relationship between her and her mother. It is her mother who appears to understand her, even more than her husband. What is becoming apparent is the fact that this relationship between Avril and her mother is changing as her mother's dementia continues to progress. It is now perhaps the case that Avril has nobody who can 'read' her or understand her and this change in relationship is further leading to Avril's symptomatic behaviour as she struggles to conceal her vulnerable feelings.

Section 4: evaluation

Evaluation of session

This session, in particular, appeared to highlight some of the repetitive family interactions in Avril's life. This mainly resulted from the use of circular questioning. This type of questioning allows the therapist to gather information, which in turn instructs their hypothesis. Jenkins and Asen (1992) suggest that, 'The therapist's questioning is intended to help the client view himself as having options for change, examine his beliefs about others imagined beliefs about him, and see himself and others as part of a wider interactional system'.

Tomm (1987) discusses the various ways of conducting circular questioning. I feel that a greater use of the circular questioning technique could perhaps have been made in the session. More future-oriented questions could have been asked in order to look at the possibilities of cultivating goals and exploring anticipated outcomes. Furthermore, observer-perspective questions could have been useful in allowing the client an arena in which to enhance self-awareness, help question others' experiences and focus on interpersonal problems.

Bott (1994) proposes that, in essence, circular questioning is directed towards helping the client actively change the part they play in the family system. The purpose behind choosing this technique with Avril was to help her see different ways of interacting with her family and thereby change the part she plays in family relationships.

Personal reflections

From my experience of working in a systemic way with this client, I sensed how difficult it can be to work systemically with an individual. As the family are not in the therapy room itself, I believe a high degree of creativity and imagination are required in framing the circular questions asked. This is in order to produce the kinds of reactions and feelings in the client 'as if' the rest of the family were actually in the therapy space.

Jones (1993) has pointed to the kinds of problems that may be associated with working systemically with an individual. She suggests that systemic therapy neither has a well-articulated theory of individual functioning nor much background thought about technique in individual systemic work.

At times, I found it frustrating that I could not be privy to the family interactions that might shift as a result of the therapy and was unsure how to proceed in a systemic frame without the presence of the family.

Bott (1994) suggests that in the closing stages of family intervention with an individual, the therapist aims to help the client control and change the part they play in the system of their family of origin.

Therefore, Avril was encouraged to access support and, in addition, to approach certain members of the family and empathically discuss the issues raised during therapy. My experience in this case made me feel that working systemically with an individual can be somewhat restrictive. However, I imagine that with more practice and experience the breadth and depth of the circular questions asked will increase, allowing for a fuller exploration with clients, even when the family is not present.

References

Bott, D. (1994). A family systems framework for intervention with individuals. *Counselling Psychology Quarterly*, 7(2), 102–115.

Burnham, J. (1986). *Family Therapy*. London: Routledge.

Cecchin, G. (1987). Hypothesising, circularity and neutrality revisited: an invitation to curiosity. *Family Process*, 26, 405–413.

Goldenberg, I. and Goldenberg, H. (2000). *Family Therapy: an Overview*. Pacific Grove, CA: Brooks/Cole.

Hoffman, L. (1990). Constructing realities: an art of lenses. *Family Process*, 29(1), 1–12.

Jenkins, H. and Asen, E. (1992). Family therapy without the family: a framework for systemic practice. *Journal of Family Therapy*, 14, 1–14.

Jones, E. (1993). *Family Systems Therapy: Developments in the Milan Systemic Therapy*. Chichester: Wiley.

Selvini Palazzoli, M., Boscolo, L., Cecchin, G. and Prata, G. (1980). Hypothesising, circularity and neutrality: three guidelines for the conductor of the session. *Family Process*, 19, 3–12.

Tomm, K. (1987). Interventive interviewing. Part III: intending to ask lineal, circular, strategic or reflexive questions. *Family Process*, 27, 1–15.

Chapter 9

A case study of an intervention with a client suffering from intrusive thoughts and traumatic grief

with a case study by Jacqui R. Farrants

PRELUDE

We have chosen to include this case study as it is illustrative of a number of themes and challenges that characterise working therapeutically with people and managing their unique experiences in the dynamic and evolving context that is the therapeutic relationship. In particular, this case touches upon the conflicts between external pressures which favour brief, time-limited and symptom-focused therapy and working with clients who present with multiple and unfolding problems throughout the course of therapy.

This case, through its immediate and engaging account of practice, further explodes the myth that sees counsellors and counselling psychologists working at the 'soft' end of the spectrum of psychological disorders. Increasingly, it is the setting and context that determines the nature of the work undertaken by psychotherapeutic professionals. This, combined with the continuing penetration of counselling psychologists into a wide diversity of practice settings, is likely to fuel the rapidly expanding body of knowledge related to the experience of practitioners systematically working to integrate theory and research into their practice. The author of the present case typifies the increasingly sophisticated capacity of the therapist seamlessly to derive action from the interpretation of research and theory.

In the context of the growing dominance of the philosophy of evidence-based practice this case, perhaps surprisingly, discusses the emergence of aspects of the client's historical story within the dynamics of the therapeutic relationship. In particular, the dilemmas and concerns of the client in the world outside the therapy room surface in the context of the helping relationship. Thus, the author reminds us that concepts analogous to transference and countertransference are not the exclusive purview of classically dynamic therapy. Such information serves to remind us that clients will bring with them their worldview, a consideration sometimes omitted from more formulaic and manipulated accounts of practice. We are impressed by the author's sensitivity and capacity to deal with the client's sexual attraction to her and her own struggle to resist 'mothering' the client.

> *Jacqui R. Farrants wrote this case study a number of years ago when completing the requirements for chartership at City University. Her reflective comments were added when she was invited to contribute to the present volume. This work comprises part of her doctoral dissertation.*

Preamble

Why I chose this particular case

Counselling psychology 'adopts a reflective practitioner approach combining understanding both from formal psychological enquiry and from the interpersonal relationship between practitioner and client' (British Psychological Society 2001, p. 4). The work presented here illustrates this approach to working with clients in that it demonstrates the way in which the application of psychological knowledge, together with an understanding of the development of the therapeutic alliance, enhances the outcome of therapy. The work reported here clearly illustrates how dealing with symptoms can be considerably more effective when underlying anxiety about other factors has been worked through. Once underlying anxiety has been addressed the impetus to maintain problematic behaviours no longer exists. I have found this to be the case with many clients whom I have worked with subsequent to this case.

What I think and feel retrospectively about my work

As a result of continual limited resources, particularly in settings such as the UK National Health Service (NHS), the pressure on therapists to use brief, time-limited models in their work with clients appears to be intensifying. There is an increasing expectation that therapists will use a symptom-focused approach and limit their work to a small number of sessions with each client. Working with Jonathan laid the foundation for what has turned out to be an enduring personal belief that brief, purely symptom-focused therapies are not always appropriate, nor indeed efficacious, for some client presentations, and that we need to embrace a range of working methods in order to maximise our effectiveness as therapists. Only then can we help those who have, for example, interpersonal issues that require the development of a strong, trusting relationship with the therapist, which needs to be built up gradually over a longer period of time.

What I have learned through revisiting the case

On reflection, revisiting this case has reinforced the importance of managing the therapeutic alliance with clients who may have a tendency to become dependent upon the therapist. A solid, collaborative, working alliance, in which the therapist genuinely relates to the client as an equal partner in the dyad, allows the client to experience validation of their feelings from a person they respect. This, in turn, increases their perception of self-efficacy as they no longer regard themselves as 'the mental patient'. This shift occurs when therapists are able to validate clients and to encourage them to take responsibility for change themselves. This is consistent with the approach of counselling psychology that promotes the 'working alliance' (Dryden 1992) between psychologist and client, in contrast to more traditional approaches that operate according to the medical model, with the therapist as expert (Cunningham and Davis 1985). The work with Jonathan recounted here, therefore, reminds me of the centrality of the reflective practitioner approach that has become so fundamental to my work with clients. As I continue to practise it is an understanding of psychological enquiry in the context of genuine interpersonal relationships between therapist and client that provides the impetus for my own change and growth.

CASE STUDY

Introduction

Jonathan was referred to me by one of the Community Psychiatric Nurses (CPNs) in the Community Mental Health Team (CMHT) within which I worked. The CPN had supported Jonathan over a period during which he had been admitted to a psychiatric ward as an inpatient following a depressive and suicidal episode six months previously. Jonathan's depression had lifted after a few months of medication and CPN support, however, he was experiencing obsessional, disturbing and graphic thoughts of dismembered bodies and other gruesome images. He reported having suffered from these thoughts since his teens, but that they had reached a peak during his depression. Despite his depression lifting, the images had remained and the CPN felt that Jonathan might benefit from seeing a psychologist.

The initial session

First impressions – appearance and behaviour

Jonathan was a small, casually but neatly dressed, 27-year-old man. Although visibly nervous, he was warm and polite. He was tearful for part of the session and regarded therapy as his final chance of obtaining what he referred to as 'peace of mind'. Although pessimistic that anything would change, he was anxious for reassurance that he was a 'deserving case' for treatment. This led me to believe that he wished me to adopt the role of nurturer and I expected that he might become dependent upon me (Dryden 1989). Jonathan's demeanour did indeed evoke a strong desire in me to take care of him, and so I was careful to monitor this countertransference from the start.

Biographical information and family history

Jonathan was single and shared a house with his mother and older brother. Following a psychiatric illness, his father had died suddenly eight years previously in a mental hospital. Jonathan ran his own roof tiling business. He had a history of adolescent drug and solvent abuse and self-mutilation (cutting his arms with glass), however, he had done none of these things since adolescence.

The client's definition of the problem

Jonathan reported that he felt he was no longer depressed but that he was finding his disturbing thoughts overpowering and difficult to cope with. He was becoming irritable with his family and found it hard to concentrate on his work.

The counsellor's definition of the problem

Initially, I wondered whether Jonathan was suffering from post-traumatic stress disorder (PTSD) following some distressing events actually experienced (American Psychiatric Association 1994). For example, he described witnessing two road accidents during adolescence and seeing dismembered bodies in the wreckage, and also that when he was aged eleven his aunt had been robbed at knife-point. His symptoms shared some of the characteristics of PTSD, for example the vivid images accompanying the thoughts, the fact that they were frequently triggered by news stories relating to death or injury and his irritability with his family (American Psychiatric Association 1994). Following assessment, which included completion of the Impact of Events Scale (Horowitz et al. 1979), it was clear that Jonathan's disturbing thoughts did not relate directly to any of the events that he had witnessed, which would be a requirement for a diagnosis of PTSD (DSM-IV).

Jonathan referred to other obsessional thoughts and behaviour, including positioning of household objects and a fear of contamination leading to excessive hand-washing, and I formed the hypothesis that his disturbing and intrusive thoughts were obsessions. These are defined by DSM-IV as 'persistent thoughts, impulses, or images that are experienced, at least initially, as intrusive and senseless' (p. 245).

Furthermore, Jonathan became distressed and tearful when he spoke of his father who had died eight years previously and I hypothesised that this prolonged grief was a result of some unresolved bereavement tasks (Worden 1995).

It has been suggested (Ehlers and Steil 1995, Wells 1995) that obsessional behaviour is frequently underpinned by extreme underlying anxiety of which the client may not be consciously aware, and I wondered whether there was some further underlying anxiety that Jonathan had not yet articulated. Also, I planned to explore the events surrounding the onset of his depression, which had begun only six months previously.

The approach taken, rationale and goals

The contract and structure of the sessions

We contracted initially for eight further weekly sessions, each of one hour's duration, followed by a review of progress and the option of further sessions to be negotiated. These were to take place within the Community Mental Health Team. Because of Jonathan's tendency for dependence, I was acutely aware of the importance of structure and boundaries and of the need to be consistent and open with him (Dryden 1992).

Goals

The main goals agreed at this stage were to relieve Jonathan of his intrusive thoughts and to begin to work through his feelings about his father's death, with a view to enabling him to function more effectively in his relationships and in his work.

Confidentiality

I explained to Jonathan that what we discussed was between ourselves. However, in order to help him as best as I could, there might be some aspects of what he told me that I would need to discuss with a supervisor within the Department. I informed him that I would contact his GP when we finished seeing each other. In view of his previous suicide attempt, I was careful to explain that I would contact his GP before that time only if I considered him to be at risk of harming himself or others, and that in that event, I should make every effort to let him know of my action before I did so.

The approach taken

In the first session, I adopted what is probably best described as a Rogerian stance, employing the core conditions of empathy, genuineness and unconditional positive regard (Rogers 1990). At this stage, I felt that it was vital for Jonathan to realise that I would continue to accept him, regardless of what he might disclose. In later sessions, I adopted a cognitive-behavioural approach in order to explore the cognitions related to his intrusive thoughts (Beck 1976, Rachman and De Silva 1978) and followed Worden's (1995) approach to the treatment of traumatic grief.

The content and process of the sessions

Bereavement work

Following Worden's (1995) approach to traumatic grief, the early sessions were spent working through Jonathan's confused feelings about the death of his father eight years previously. Jonathan described his father as a distant, shy and withdrawn man, and said that he did not feel as if he had ever had a relationship with him. His father had developed a mental illness two years before his death, which resulted in aggressive, unpredictable, and sometimes violent, outbursts toward the family. Jonathan was tearful when he spoke of his father's death and described relief that his father's terror-isation of the family had ended, while also expressing regret at the lost opportunity of a closer relationship with him. Worden states that 'the most frequent type of relationship that hinders people from adequately grieving is the highly ambivalent one with unexpressed hostility' (Worden 1995, p. 65), and I felt that, as a result of his ambivalence to the death, Jonathan might be suffering from a traumatic grief reaction.

As part of the therapy, I asked him to write a letter to his father expressing his feelings, and this appeared to provoke a cathartic reaction. Following this, Jonathan reported that his intrusive thoughts had been fewer and less intense than at any time since the onset of his depression six months previously, and I felt that we had established a good working relationship. I was encouraged by his early improvement, particularly in view of the fact that client ratings of their counsellor after the third session have been found to be a better predictor of the outcome of therapy than any other variable (Winefield 1992).

The nature and content of the intrusive thoughts

Through a cognitive exploration of the nature and content of Jonathan's intrusive thoughts (Beck 1976) a deep sense of his feelings of worthlessness and self-loathing emerged. There were two themes to the vivid images which accompanied his thoughts. Either images of himself being humili-ated, for example being stamped or spat upon, or of himself carrying out acts of 'depravity' (his word), for example eating the entrails of a dead friend. Jonathan regarded the fact that he had these thoughts as evidence of the fact that he was bad and depraved. He believed himself to be capable of carrying out these actions in reality. This negative view of himself as a result of the thoughts served to perpetuate the thoughts and so maintain a circular feedback loop (Penn 1982) of self-loathing. This is consistent with Salkovskis' (1985, 1989) findings that intrusive thoughts result in distress according to the extent to which their occurrence and/or content is interpreted in a particular type of negative way. This may also account for Jonathan's obsessional behaviour as, according to Salkovskis et al. (1995), obsessional behaviour is likely to occur if the intrusive thoughts are interpreted as an indication that the person may be responsible for harm to others. I explained the difference between fantasy and reality to Jonathan, and reassured him that the thoughts did not mean that he was likely to carry out the actions (Salkovskis et al. 1995). Jonathan found it particularly difficult to talk about the content of his thoughts as he feared that I also might despise and reject him.

However, the act of voicing the thoughts for the first time enabled Jonathan to discover that he could be listened to with warmth and empathy and that I would continue to accept him regardless of his disclosures. The whole issue of acceptance and approval became a theme in itself and underpinned all the work that followed, and I believe that it was the single most important factor in Jonathan's progress. I reflected these themes of worthlessness and self-loathing to Jonathan and used immediacy (Egan 1994) to reflect his desire for approval. Together we explored how he may have come to feel this way and it became clear that as a child he had suffered from emotional neglect by both his mother and father and had never felt loved or approved of. This may account for his low self-esteem, feelings of worthlessness and his dependency, particularly upon older women (Kenward and Hevey 1989). We explored the childhood experiences that had led to his deep sense of worthlessness, in order to identify any negative schemas that he had carried into adulthood (Salkovskis et al. 1995) and their impact on his current relationships.

Relationships with women

From what Jonathan told me of his relationships with women, I formed the impression that he was searching for the care and mothering that he had lacked. He had had only two sexual relationships, both with older women in their fifties. The first relationship lasted over one year and was with a woman who had commissioned him to do some tiling work. The relationship became sexual after he sought sympathy from her following an accidental cut to his finger while working. Jonathan was currently in his second relationship, the onset of which he associated with the onset of his depression six months previously. He had arranged a first date with the woman and she had been over two hours late. He described the time spent waiting for her as 'spiralling into a black depression'. During the session, while exploring his cognitions at this time, it was clear that her lateness had reinforced his notion that he was unimportant, worthless and deeply unlovable. This had mirrored his childhood feelings, and seemed to have precipitated his depressive episode. Although the relationship had continued, he worried about the fact that his partner was over twenty years older than he was, and he felt a sense of the relationship having no future. His partner was inconsistent and conditional in her feelings for him and frequently threatened to end the relationship at some prearranged date. However, when the time came, she would agree to see him for a further period.

The therapeutic relationship

I was aware that my contract with Jonathan very much mirrored the relationship with his partner. We had a fixed contract, following which further sessions would be negotiated. He began to express anxiety at the impending end of our contract, despite my reassurance that we would stagger the ending and that we would not stop suddenly, or without warning, or until he felt ready, as advocated by Ward (1984) for dependent clients. On the penultimate session of our initial contract, Jonathan disclosed that he had strong sexual feelings for me. I was not surprised by this disclosure as I regarded his feelings as an extreme form of transference to the therapist as nurturer (Watkins 1983). I explained to him that his attraction to me was understandable in that our relationship had been the first unconditional relationship that he had experienced with a woman. I explained to Jonathan that I cared about his wellbeing and felt that we had a good working relationship and reinforced the fact that it was to remain on a purely professional footing. He was afraid that I would reject him on account of this disclosure. However, I reassured him that my respect for him was unchanged, which I demonstrated by continuing to behave consistently towards him and by not terminating our contract early, as he had feared. I felt that his disclosure may have been a way to test whether I would continue to accept him unconditionally and seemed to me to be an attempt to elicit a declaration of my feelings for him. Jonathan had clearly become dependent upon our sessions and his need for the love and approval that had so clearly been absent from his early life manifested itself in both the content and process of therapy, namely in his sexual relationships and in his relationship with me. We continued to work on this theme throughout the therapy and I was careful to be consistent, to maintain firm boundaries and to continue to accept him unconditionally. We extended our contract and, having taken this issue to supervision, decided not to have a fixed end date so that Jonathan would continue to feel safe and accepted.

Factors maintaining current anxiety

Jonathan's current living circumstances were a source of anxiety. He was living with his mother, who expressed no emotion towards him, and an out-of-work brother who was becoming reclusive, and occasionally abusive, violent and unpredictable. Jonathan feared that his brother was becoming like his father and he believed that his own intrusive thoughts were evidence that he too was becoming unstable, like his father. Also, his business was not thriving as well as he would have liked and he, therefore, had a sense of a foreshortened future, devoid of hope or happiness.

Having expressed these anxieties during therapy, Jonathan's intrusive thoughts changed from fictional, gruesome and disturbing images to more realistic anxieties concerning his future. He agreed that previously the intrusive thoughts had perhaps been effective in allowing him to avoid responsibility for changing the realities of his present life, which he felt helpless to alter. I suspected that his depression may have served a similar function and that he had become stuck in a negative 'rut' of learned helplessness (Seligman and Maier 1967), believing he was powerless to change his circumstances.

Through therapy Jonathan was able to begin to take responsibility for change. He began working towards moving into a home of his own, he became more relaxed about the future of his relationship with his partner and was able to enjoy the time they spent together on a day-to-day basis. He increased his advertising for his business and began to cycle occasionally instead of driving, as he enjoyed the exercise. He accepted that his mental health was improving and no longer believed that he would degenerate as his father had done. He planned to widen his social circle by joining a conservation action group.

Once Jonathan's sense of helplessness had begun to diminish, we began to work on his specific obsessive-compulsive disorder (OCD) symptoms, using exposure and response prevention (Meyer 1966). Almost as soon as he had begun to monitor his obsessional behaviour he was largely able to resist the compulsion to wash his hands inappropriately and to place objects symmetrically. Similarly, he reported that for many years he had suffered from panic attacks in supermarkets. We were able to deal with these attacks using a biopsychosocial approach (Barlow 1993) after which he was able to control them with relative ease. I was surprised at the speed of these improvements. It appeared that the very fact of gaining mastery over his compulsions and anxieties promoted a sense of control over his life. This, in turn, reduced his need to carry out the compulsions for the illusory sense of control that they had afforded (Reed 1985) and so formed a circular self-reinforcing feedback loop (Penn 1982). As a consequence, Jonathan seemed to attach less importance to his intrusive thoughts which, although still present, were considerably less frequent and, when they occurred, briefer. He took the responsibility himself for beginning to end therapy, suggesting that we change our weekly meetings to fortnightly ones. A few sessions later he suggested that we change this to every three weeks, which indicated that his dependency upon me was diminishing as his sense of control and self-efficacy increased. I reflected this to him, and he was able to see a change from his earlier anxiety about ending. I felt that it was important that it was Jonathan who was able to begin to 'reject' me.

Evaluation

A critical assessment of the effectiveness of the therapy

Jonathan's progress was considerably more extensive and rapid than I had expected at the start. It appeared that my interventions helped him to reframe his situation and to alter his negative beliefs about himself and his life, and to begin to believe that he could change. However, I suspect that most change was caused not so much by the content of the cognitive interventions, but more by the process between us. Jonathan learned that he could feel accepted and cared for unconditionally. I feel that the relationship between us was the most productive factor during therapy.

The client's report of the outcome

Jonathan reported feeling considerably less distressed than he had done for several years, and was able to begin to take action to improve his circumstances, once he overcame his belief that he was helpless. He described feeling that, although he enjoyed our sessions, he no longer felt he *needed* them so frequently as he felt that he was managing well between sessions.

Professional dilemmas and concerns experienced

It was vital to Jonathan's progress that I dealt in an objective and professional manner with regard to the transference and countertransference issues, namely his sexual feelings toward me and my strong caring feelings toward him. I was able to remain warm and accepting without revealing the depth of my feelings and without encouraging his dependency, as is evidenced by his ability to take the initiative to make changes in his life and to take control of reducing the frequency of our sessions.

Summary and conclusion

The work with Jonathan clearly illustrates how dealing with symptoms such as OCD or panic attacks can be considerably more effective when underlying anxiety about other factors has been worked through. For example, once Jonathan had worked on his anxieties concerning his current life and his lack of hope for his future, his obsessional behaviour ceased with relative ease and rapidity. This is not always the case when dealing with clients' symptoms alone. Once the underlying anxiety had been addressed, it seemed as if there was no longer anything to maintain the behaviour. This is something that I have found to be the case with several other clients that I have worked with. Although my findings are admittedly anecdotal, it would be interesting to attempt to quantify these results in some way in future empirical research, as they suggest that a brief, symptom-focused approach may not always be the most effective way of working with some clients.

References

American Psychiatric Association (1994). *Diagnostic and Statistical Manual of Mental Disorders*, 4th edn. Washington, DC: American Psychiatric Association.

Barlow, D.H. (1993). *Clinical Handbook of Psychological Disorders*. New York: Guilford Press.

Beck, A.T. (1976). *Cognitive Therapy and the Emotional Disorders*. New York: International Universities Press.

British Psychological Society (2001). *Regulations and Syllabus for the Diploma in Counselling Psychology* (April 2001 to March 2002). Leicester: British Psychological Society.

Cunningham, C. and Davis, H. (1985). *Working with Parents: Frameworks for Collaboration*. Milton Keynes: Open University Press.

Dryden, W. (ed.) (1992). *Key Issues for Counselling in Action*. London: Sage.

Egan, G. (1994). *The Skilled Helper: a Problem Management Approach to Helping*. California: Wadsworth.

Ehlers, A. and Steil, R. (1995). Maintenance of intrusive memories in post-traumatic stress disorder: a cognitive approach. *Behavioural and Cognitive Psychotherapy*, 23(3), 217–250.

Horowitz, M.J., Wilner, N. and Alvarez, W. (1979). Impact of events scale: a measure of subjective distress. *Psychosomatic Medicine*, 41, 209–218.

Kenward, H. and Hevey, D. (1989). The effects of physical abuse and neglect. In W. Stainton-Rogers, D. Hevey and E. Ash (eds) *Child Abuse and Neglect: Facing the Challenge*, Chapter 23. Buckingham: Open University.

Meyer, V. (1966). Modification of expectations in cases with obsessional rituals. In D.H. Barlow (ed.) *Clinical Handbook of Psychological Disorders*. New York: Guilford Press.

Penn, P. (1982). Circular questioning. *Family Process*, 21(3), 267–279.

Rachman, S. and De Silva, P. (1978). Abnormal and normal obsessions. In D.H. Barlow (ed.) *Clinical Handbook of Psychological Disorders*. New York: Guilford Press.

Reed, G.E. (1985). *Obsessional Experience and Compulsive Behaviour: A Cognitive Structural Approach*. Orlando, FL: Academic Press.

Rogers, C.R. (1990). *On Becoming a Person: A Therapist's View of Psychotherapy*. London: Constable.

Salkovskis, P.M. (1985). Obsessional compulsive problems: a cognitive-behavioural analysis. *Behaviour Research and Therapy*, 23, 571–583.

Salkovskis, P.M. (1989). Cognitive-behavioural factors and the persistence of intrusive thoughts in obsessional problems. *Behaviour Research and Therapy*, 23, 281–299.

Salkovskis, P.M., Richards, H.C. and Forrester, E. (1995). The relationship between obsessional problems and intrusive thoughts. *Behavioural and Cognitive Psychotherapy*, 23, 281–299.

Seligman, M.E.P. and Maier, S.F. (1967). Failure to escape traumatic shock. *Journal of Experimental Psychology*, 75, 1–9.

Stainton-Rogers, W., Hevey, D. and Ash, E. (1989). *Child Abuse and Neglect: Facing the Challenge*. Buckingham: Open University.

Ward, D.E. (1984). Termination of individual counselling: concepts and strategies. In W. Dryden (ed.) *Key Issues for Counselling in Action*. London: Sage.

Watkins, C.E. (1983). Transference phenomena in the counselling situation. *Personnel and Guidance Journal*, 62, 206–210.

Wells, A. (1995). Meta-cognition and worry: a cognitive model of generalized anxiety disorder. *Behavioural and Cognitive Psychotherapy*, 23(3), 301–320.

Winefield, H.R. (1992). Doctor–patient communication: an interpersonal helping process. In S. Maes, H. Levanthal and M. Johnston (eds) *International Review of Health Psychology*, Vol. 1, Chapter 7. Chichester: Wiley.

Worden, J.W. (1995). *Grief Counselling and Grief Therapy: A Handbook for the Mental Health Practitioner*. London: Routlege.

Chapter 10

REBT: the case of Richard

with a case study by Paul Mason

Several factors will influence the way we go about deciding to choose a particular case. Our competence with a particular therapeutic model, the outcome of therapy or even the context within which it was provided are reasons often cited by students. Paul Mason's report encapsulates the 'right' reasons for deciding to present a particular case. The author cites his initial assessment, the client's presenting problems and time restrictions as the core reasons for choosing the case, but more importantly he elaborates on the fact that he choose this case because of what it taught him. Throughout the report Paul reflects on how his expectations of what could be accomplished with his clients were challenged and how he was able to move from the prescribed agenda of reducing rates of recidivism to more complex and challenging mental health issues.

This case also gives the reader a sense of developing along with the therapist. Paul Mason's frank account of the challenges of dealing with co-morbidity in clinical samples and having to learn to work with clients by focusing on their most pressing needs is sensitively and effectively discussed in the text. He makes an effort to provide a detailed account of the therapeutic process and the difficulties encountered across the sessions, thus allowing the reader a glimpse of Paul's own process and professional development over the course of his work.

> *Paul Mason wrote this case study at the beginning of a full-time MSc in Counselling Psychology. The comments were written at the beginning of the first year of a post-MSc Practitioner Diploma in Counselling Psychology.*

Preamble

How did you come to choose this particular topic?

I selected this particular case for two reasons. First, following my assessment of Richard, I felt that he presented for therapy with multiple issues that needed to be addressed in a limited amount of time. My treatment plan required me to draw upon a theoretical model that I felt would suit Richard's needs best. Since the purpose of the case study was to provide an example that illustrated the application of theory to practice, I had to select carefully from my current client work an example that accurately portrayed me working consistently with a client using one theoretical model. When working with clients, I have occasionally found myself drawing from more than one theoretical approach. This was not the case when working with Richard, so it seemed logical to utilise that work when compiling the case study.

Second, although having worked in different mental health settings, I was a novice with respect to the penal system when I first commenced sessions with Richard. I entered the system believing that the amount of help a counsellor could offer clients was mostly rehabilitative, with the main aim being to reduce rates of recidivism. This was not the case, and my experience has been that the setting actually offers counsellors numerous opportunities of working with a variety of adult mental health issues. I saw how counselling was not simply a profession only applicable to settings such as schools and medical practices. I hoped this would be reflected in the report.

How do you think and feel retrospectively about what you have produced?

Retrospectively, I have mixed thoughts and feelings when reviewing this case study. A major hurdle to overcome was in reproducing a case study that illustrated working with a client using a particular theoretical orientation while adhering to a specific word limit. I thought that I had achieved this. However, that achievement was at the expense of including information that I felt had an important impact upon the sessions, for example the barriers encountered when counselling in the penal system. This left me feeling frustrated as I found myself having to choose what aspects of the case study were the important ones to include, and what aspects were irrelevant. Additionally, it was difficult condensing many weeks of client work into a couple of pages while still accurately reflecting what had, and had not, been achieved during my work with Richard. However, finding out that several other students experienced similar frustrations helped allay those fears for the future.

What did you learn from drafting and writing this report?

I learned that it can be difficult getting it right all the time. The act of writing a case study is an art that needs to be practised and improved upon over time. I found myself being forced to confront some of the more annoying habits that I had formed over my years of report writing. Notably, I had to force myself to be more succinct and organised by only selecting the material that I felt was most significant to the assignment. This provided me with a checklist of what I now consider the most pertinent information to include in all future case studies that I might prepare.

CASE STUDY

Introduction

Richard, a male in his late twenties, of average height and weight presented with a history of nightmares that he had experienced frequently for more than fifteen years. He discussed being diagnosed and treated for depression over the last five years. His depression had been treated with desipramine hydrochloride, though this had been recently changed to trazodone during which period he had reported adverse side effects, such as blurred vision, drowsiness, and incoordination, to his physician. He was currently taking a combination of trazodone and nortriptyline. Of additional concern to Richard was the general unease he felt when mixing in crowds. Although he comes from a small family, he has always had a large circle of close friends, and cannot understand why he now experiences episodes of breathlessness, dizziness and nausea when among crowds. These feelings were of recent onset and commenced only after being sentenced.

Theoretical orientation

The case study was approached from a rational emotive behaviour therapy (REBT) framework. Corey (1996a) writes that REBT is a re-educative therapeutic process designed to help individuals gain greater understanding of their own interpretation of events. Clients see how this impacts their behaviour, and this results in a reorganisation of the concepts and statements that are upholding their negative patterns of thinking.

Gordon and Dryden (1997) describe the above idea through the ABC model, where A represents an activating event, B the belief system, and C the consequence. Following a particular event, a consequence occurs based on both one's beliefs and one's interpretation of the activating event. The theory maintains that altering one's perception and belief system after a particular event will alter the eventual consequence. Recently, Dryden and Yankura (1995) have referred to this as the ABCDE approach, where D represents the therapist disputing irrational thought patterns and E represents the effects dependent on whether or not the therapist has successfully disputed the irrational beliefs.

Ellis (1995) explained that the belief system of individuals could be split between rational and irrational beliefs. Rational beliefs are healthy ways of interpreting life events through a preference system, as opposed to the self-imposed demands that are found in the irrational belief system of individuals. According to Nelson-Jones (2000), the therapist's task is to strengthen rational beliefs while dispelling irrational beliefs, which might be disputed either through a didactic teaching style, or through a Socratic questioning style.

Scott and Dryden (1996) state that these inappropriate thought patterns, maintained by a series of irrational commands, set the foundation for resulting pathology. Gordon and Dryden (1997) pointed out how Ellis often called this 'musturbation', since thoughts are controlled by a series of 'must' statements. This is often manifested through depressive and anxious states. High expectations and demands, represented by what Ellis termed 'abso-lutistic' thinking, are the root of a vast variety of behavioural disorders. Therapy, then, has the aim of separating rational from irrational belief systems.

Corey (1996b) emphasises the application of REBT through cognitive, behavioural and/or emotive techniques. Seeking evidence to dispel irrational beliefs, assigning homework to strengthen what has been learned during therapy, altering language from a series of 'must' commands to preferences, and learning how not to take life too seriously are some of the cognitive techniques advanced by Corey (1996b). The use of emotive techniques may include imagery to enable clients to feel better about themselves, role-playing tasks to disturb the irrational belief systems, or self-dialogue to allow the clients to feel better about themselves. Finally, behavioural techniques such as desensitisation or assertiveness training may also be incorporated into therapy (Corey 1996b).

Rationale for applying REBT while working with Richard

Rational emotive behavioural therapy is an approach that might help Richard, because many of its goals are similar to the goals raised by him. Gordon and Dryden (2000) describe the five basic goals of REBT:

The first goal is to survive, exist and remain alive. Richard's top concern was how to cope with prison while living with his depression, anxiety and nightmares. The second goal is to be relatively happy. A history of negative events in Richard's life has left him depressed. The third goal is to live successfully within a social group. Richard is unable to mix with other inmates. The fourth goal, experiencing a meaningful relationship with one or more selected individuals, is of no concern for Richard. Richard has an excellent relationship with many close friends who visit him regularly. The fifth, and final, goal of REBT is to work productively and creatively.

The referral and work context

The client was self-referred. A prior, successful outcome to therapy five years ago motivated Richard into self-referring himself for therapy. He describes how his first encounter literally 'opened me up to discussing my feelings' a process previously alien to him. Realising that he is now able to get in touch with his thoughts and feelings, he identified particular goals that he would like to achieve. These were relief from his nightmares, depression and anxiety.

Therapy was conducted at a prison, meeting for weekly sessions, over a period of six weeks. Richard had just been sentenced. Having just received his sentence, sessions had to be organised around visiting time, and were held on the wing.

Initial assessment, presenting problem and contract

Limits of confidentiality were explained and Richard was allowed to decide whether he wished to continue working with a trainee counselling psychologist.

During this initial assessment, Richard talked about episodes he termed 'nightmares', which he had experienced since the age of fourteen. During these episodes, he screams out, sweats profusely, and appears fearful. He is reported to awaken briefly then fall back into sleep. He is only aware that he experiences these episodes because others tell him so. Many years back, his wife had devised a method of deterring such attacks. She had noticed that Richard's arms and legs would start twitching prior to the onset of the nightmare episode, so she would simply nudge him in his side and that would be sufficient to offset the attack.

In addition to these nightmares, Richard talked about his history of depression. He had been medically diagnosed with this five years before. Richard had reported a desire to die. This was fuelled by guilt for the offence that he had committed, and hence he had been placed on suicide watch. He was currently taking trazadone and nortriptyline. This concerned him deeply, as he had developed blurred vision, drowsiness, and inco-ordination, problems that he had never previously had.

Richard talked about a recent onset of unease and discomfort when in crowds. He felt uneasy leaving the wing for his visits. When mingling in crowds, Richard reported a sense of 'losing control and feeling as if I am going mad . . . feeling dizzy and sweaty'. I pointed out that he had been able to make it across the wing to see me today. He explained that many of the inmates were in the gym, so, since the main corridor was virtually empty, he had managed to get to the counselling room.

Richard was due to be transferred to a low category prison within the next six to eight weeks, so we contracted to meet over six sessions in order to try and address some of the goals that he had laid out.

Therapeutic plan and formulation of problem

Richard was experiencing a disturbance in his sleep, though I was unsure whether this was attributed to nightmares being symptomatic of his depression (or other disorder), or whether he was actually suffering from 'sleep terror disorder' (American Psychiatric Association 2000). In DSM-IV, sleep terror disorder is described as being characterised by repetitive awakening from sleep with abrupt cries and screams, exhibiting signs of fear, with the individual lacking recall of the event the following day. It is important to ascertain the causes of Richard's sleep disorder, since the American Psychiatric Association (2000) notes that a higher incidence of psychopathology is associated with adult incidents of sleep terror disorder.

This might have had implications for my design of a treatment plan since evidence suggests REBT is contra-indicated in some psychopathic individuals. Research from Hogue (2001) suggests that applying cognitive behavioural techniques with moderate to severe forms of antisocial personality disorder might increase the extent of psychopathy. However, neither my initial assessment nor the resident psychiatrist's evaluation suggested that Richard had an antisocial personality disorder.

As part of my intervention with Richard, I ensured that I would check out whether the sleep disturbance was related to traumatic events in the past, notably childhood events, as well as making an assessment as to whether his current imprisonment had increased these episodes of sleep disturbance (Jongsma and Peterson 1999). I would then address Richard's anxiety. Dryden (1999) points out that REBT asserts that anxiety exists when an individual believes an imminent threat will happen. My treatment plan for tackling Richard's anxiety is to challenge the nature of his beliefs when intermingling with crowds. Treatment was then to be directed at dispelling any irrational beliefs Richard might have that reinforced his anxiety when exposed to crowds.

Dryden (1999) further discusses how REBT views depression as an unhealthy emotion that results from loss. The loss need not have happened, and might only be a possibility that could emerge in the future. Depression may also be linked to an individual's self-assessment, and feelings of low worth. During therapy, these issues were addressed with Richard, and will be presented later.

Therapeutic process and difficulties encountered

A three-stage process was followed while working with Richard. Nelson-Jones (2000) discussed how REBT consists of three phases: begin, middle and end. During the 'begin phase' work with Richard, we identified specific issues that he wished to address during the therapeutic process. These were his 'nightmare' disturbances, depression, and anxiety. Over the following weeks, I entered the 'middle phase', which was challenging Richard's irrational beliefs while upholding Richard's rational beliefs. The final 'end phase' of the therapeutic plan had Richard taking the initiative to continue therapy.

Although cognitive-behaviourally-based approaches have been applied to short therapeutic sessions, Palmer (1997) described Ellis' assertion that REBT might fail for some individuals who do not persist in therapy longer than a few sessions. Since my work with Richard only spanned six sessions, the final phase of therapy in our work together emphasised him continuing with a similar therapeutic framework after his transfer and/or release. Prior to his transfer, arrangements had been made for him to enrol in a lengthier cognitive behavioural program at the new correctional facility.

Over the following sessions, Richard showed up punctually and was eager to engage in therapy. Richard had been asked to keep a dream journal next to his bed in an effort to recall dream content. He was able to recall certain dreams in very vivid detail, though he was never able to recall any of the episodes that he termed 'nightmares'. Richard experienced two such 'nightmare' episodes over the six-week period. He was alerted to the episodes by the attending night nurse who had heard 'a series of terrible howls and screams'. His incidence of sleep disturbance had not been increased by his imprisonment.

As the therapy unfolded, Richard expressed a desire to uncover the true cause of the dreams. In his teens he had been placed in a Borstal. He talked about the turbulent environment of the Borstal that he had had to adapt to; an environment that had differed greatly from the protective environment of his own home. It was during that time that his sleep disturbances first appeared. Richard felt that something else 'must' be to blame for the episodes. He reasoned that the impact of being removed from his home coincided with the development of his symptoms, but was baffled as to why the symptoms did not disappear after he had become aware of this associ-ation. As a result, he felt that something else must have accounted for the disturbances. As an adult, Richard found the experiences less anxiety promoting than they had been when he was a teenager.

Ellis (1996) described how individuals who transfer 'musts' into goals and preferences develop self-pity states, rage and self-denigration. Richard continually talked about how, 'something *must* have happened to me that I am unaware of, to explain why I get these nightmares'. Using REBT concepts, I felt that this was an irrational belief since evidence from my initial assessment seemed to suggest that his nightmares were linked to the shock of being removed from his mother (onset occurred simultaneously with this). During supervision, Richard's nightmares had been hypothesised as possibly correlating with his general depressive condition, thus further supporting my suspicions that nothing else had caused them.

I proceeded on the premise that Richard's statement, 'my nightmares *must* have another cause' was an irrational belief. My task was to structure therapy in a manner that would alter this belief system. I attempted to achieve this by applying empirical and logical disputes to challenge Richard's irrational thought pattern. Nelson-Jones (2000) describes empirical disputes as a way of having clients look for evidence that supports their own belief system, while logical disputes point out illogical flaws in a client's reasoning.

To dispute Richard's irrational belief that something else *must* have happened to him, I asked him:

> Do you have any evidence to support that claim?
> Do you have any proof to show that although you remember the separation, it is not still affecting your dreams? and
> Isn't it strange how your sleep disturbance commenced during the time of this separation?

On further examination, Richard agreed that it might have seemed plausible that the separation and sleep disorder went hand in hand. This was based on his own evidence. Several years ago during his first encounter with therapy, while examining the effect that a forced separation from his mother had had upon him, his incidence of 'nightmare' episodes had greatly increased.

I was then challenged by his own rigid belief system and defensiveness, a process Nelson-Jones (2000) describes as occurring to help individuals restrengthen irrational belief systems, possibly as a reaction to a disturbance in maintaining those irrational beliefs. Richard said, 'But I'm now an adult, and do not need my mother. I would clobber anyone who dared lay a finger on me. It doesn't make sense that if I relived the episodes in my dreams, I would not stick up for myself. That's just not me'. Nelson-Jones (2000) suggests that, for clients who are resistant to having their irrational belief system disputed, therapists continually dispute such defensiveness. Consequently, I continued with logical disputes. I asked whether he felt that he might relive his dreams as a child, thus react as a child, and not be able to understand what was happening around him. As sessions progressed, I maintained a similar level of disputing, until the level of defensive responses diminished. At that stage, I was able to address the other issues concerning his depression and anxiety.

It was then that Richard focused on issues surrounding loss in his life. Within a time frame of two years, he had tended his terminally ill mother and father. It was after this time that he became depressed. I wondered whether the depressive feelings he was experiencing in reaction to his previous loss were similar to the feelings he was experiencing with his current imprisonment. That had resulted in being removed from (thus losing) remaining family members (brother and sister). It was during that period that he was placed on a suicide watch after an attempted overdose. As previously discussed, Dryden (1999) described depression as resulting from either an actual or threatened loss.

Further analysis showed how Richard felt that he did not deserve the right to live a healthy life after others so close to him had died such painful deaths. He was evincing a discomfort disturbance, which according to Dryden (1996) REBT recognises as a disturbance that results in an inability to tolerate loss. Nelson-Jones (2000) reports that Ellis viewed this as a form of narcissism, since individuals become uneasy when life doesn't 'cater to *me, me, me, me!*' (p. 192). As well as applying further disputing arguments, I used Corey's (1996b) suggestion and introduced role play, with Richard both expressing his feelings to his mother about losing her, and stating how he felt that she might reply back to him. This technique didn't work as well as anticipated. Richard felt that his mother would have wanted him to 'get on with his life and live it to the fullest'. However, he talked about how those words were not his mother's words, and how he would now never get the chance to hear how his mother really felt, and that the exercise would achieve nothing. I wondered whether events from the session showed exactly how hurt he had been by losing his mother. Since only a few sessions remained, I decided to focus the following session on Richard's anxiety.

When working with Richard's anxiety, I adhered to Dryden's (1999) remarks that REBT views anxiety as a result of imminent threat. As a result, I hypothesised that a jail sentence for Richard might have been the cause of his social anxiety. Dryden (1999) also stated that the very fact that clients feel anxious is enough to make them feel even more anxious. When disputing the belief system that I felt Richard might have been using, I employed a more functional disputing system. Nelson-Jones (2000) describes functional disputing as a way of questioning clients to see how their current belief pattern is affecting their lives. I asked Richard whether avoiding mixing with crowds was really going to help him avoid facing the fact that he had to serve time. I asked him to consider how his behaviour was currently affecting his life, preventing him from even being able to get to the visitors' room to see his friends and family. He agreed that his behaviour was a problem, and wanted to find a way of working around it.

As previously discussed, Corey (1996b) indicates how behavioural techniques of desensitisation and relaxation can be used in REBT sessions. Nelson-Jones (2000) also discusses how irrational beliefs can be challenged by directly enforcing acts to contradict the belief. Therefore, I discussed with Richard whether he was willing to apply behavioural techniques to help him relax prior to entering crowded situations. He agreed, and he asked the psychiatric nurse to train him in relaxation techniques. Further, we discussed ways in which Richard could gradually increase mixing with the inmates. He proposed to work in the gardens. The open space served as an effective 'barrier' to getting too close to inmates, but the fact that he was in the open allowed him an opportunity to mix with passing officers and visitors, and hopefully to reduce his social apprehension.

The sixth session focused on closure and ensuring that Richard continued with treatment after transferring to a different prison.

What I learned from the case

Richard was the first client that I saw in my current placement. The process itself revealed the complexity of the issues that clients within the penal system bring to therapy sessions. The issues are unlike those that I have previously encountered in prior placements. In the penal system, I have found myself working with clients who present with a vast array of co-morbid disorders, many of which are impossible to treat within the time limits that I have been given to work with. Consequently, I have learned how to work with clients by focusing on their most pressing needs. I learned to act under time and room availability constraints, co-operating with other professionals to arrange appropriate timetables to see the clients I needed to see. I was also familiarising myself with the prison system and the strict levels of bureaucracy that operate in any institutional setting.

With regard to theory, I gained greater insight into the application of REBT. This is an approach that I am not too familiar with, having relied mostly on psychodynamic approaches in previous placements.

References

American Psychiatric Association (2000). *Diagnostic and Statistical Manual of Mental Disorders*. DSM-IV-TR, 4th edn. Washington, DC: American Psychiatric Association.

Corey, G. (1996a). *Student Manual for the Theory and Practice of Counselling and Psychotherapy*, 5th edn. Pacific Grove, CA: Brooks/Cole.

Corey, G. (1996b). *Theory and Practice of Counseling and Psychotherapy*, 5th edn. Pacific Grove, CA: Brooks/Cole.

Dryden, W. (1996). Rational emotive behaviour therapy. In W. Dryden (ed.) *Handbook of Individual Therapy*. London: Sage.

Dryden, W. (1999). *Rational Emotive Behavioural Counselling* (Action-Counselling in Action Series), 2nd edn. London: Sage.

Dryden, W. and Yankura, J. (1995). *Developing Rational Emotive Behavioural Counselling* (Sage Developing Counselling Series). London: Sage.

Ellis, A. (1995). Rational emotive behavioral therapy. In R.J. Corsini and D. Wedding (eds) *Current Psychotherapies*, 5th edn. Itasca, IL: F.E. Peacock.

Ellis, A. (1996). Case approach to cognitive-behaviour therapy. A rational emotive behaviour therapist's perspective on Ruth. In G. Corey (ed.) *Case Approach to Counseling and Psychotherapy*, 4th edn. Pacific Grove, CA: Brooks/Cole.

Gordon, J. and Dryden, W. (1997). Rational emotive behaviour therapy. In S. Palmer, S. Dainow and P. Milner (eds) *Counselling – The BAC Counselling Reader*. London: Sage.

Hogue, T.E. (2001). Dangerous and severe personality disorder: where are we at and where are we going? Paper presented at Symposium on Linking Risk, Personality Disorder and Change. Glasgow: British Psychological Society Centenary Conference, March 28–31.

Jongsma, A.E. and Peterson, L.M. (1999). *The Complete Adult Psychotherapy Treatment Planner*, 2nd edn. New York: Wiley.

Nelson-Jones, R. (2000). *Six Key Approaches to Counselling and Therapy*. London: Continuum.

Palmer, S. (1997). In the Counsellor's Chair – Stephen Palmer Interviews Albert Ellis. In S. Palmer, S. Dainow and P. Milner (eds) *Counselling – The BAC Counselling Reader*. London: Sage.

Scott, M.J. and Dryden, W. (1996). The cognitive-behavioural paradigm. In R. Wolfe and W. Dryden (eds) *Handbook of Counselling Psychology*. London: Sage.

Chapter 11

Using CBT to address guilt over sexual fantasies: a process report

with a case study by Litsa Anthis

PRELUDE

Litsa Anthis' account of her work with a man struggling to make sense of his feelings and urges, which he saw as being incongruent with a monogamous relationship, is a wonderful example of how even the simplest problems can result in challenging work. Litsa's remarkable ability to express her ideas and values makes this a model process report. This case takes readers on a journey and allows them to identify key therapeutic moments through the eyes of both the client and the therapist. Litsa's description of cognitive therapy, the approach she adopts for her work with this client, provides testament to her commitment to the scientist practitioner approach. She makes a point of using primary sources as well as more recent critiques and analyses of the approach and makes an effort to draw on the core CBT themes throughout the report in order to justify her interpretations. Her formulation and treatment plan are well thought out and substantiated and she consistently grounds her analysis of her practice within the therapeutic model which she adopts.

A nice feature of this process report is the fact that Litsa spends time focusing on a particular theme, namely, the ethics of counselling. She describes how the development of this case draws on past experiences both clinical and empirical. She concludes that 'there are very few "alwayses" or "nevers" in counselling' and that the realisation of this can evoke as much fear as it can freedom in the therapist. Her way of coping with this challenge in therapy is to turn to alternative sources of guidance not only among the writing of cognitive therapists but also within humanistic and phenomenological paradigms. Her conclusion is that knowledge and personal values cannot be completely separated in any emotive area, and that without self-awareness therapists can not only obstruct client progress but also their own professional development. She shares with the reader how this case, perhaps not surprisingly, re-entered her thoughts following an experience in which she found herself questioning the repercussions of commitment to another person. Litsa Anthis' report once again allows us to acknowledge that paramount to dealing with ethical dilemmas in therapy is the self-examination and reflection that will provide both a value base and guidance for the practising therapist.

> *Litsa Anthis wrote this process report during the last year of her post-MSc in the Practice of Counselling Psychology; the final stage in the process of chartership. Litsa's reflective comments were added to her work twelve months after the original report.*

Preamble

In the course of clinical practice, every counsellor will recollect a handful of clients that remain memorable for different reasons. Usually these clients symbolised a turning point in learning, encapsulated a deeper understanding of the therapeutic process or fostered the development and growth of the therapist in some way. I encountered such a client during my training. His presenting problem was not traumatic – nor horrific, but very human, involving his search to find answers to the notion of commitment within a long-term relationship. His main source of distress centred on his sexual fantasising of women other than his partner, which he deemed incompatible with true devotion. I have chosen this case, and the specific transcript, as the themes and questions it evoked opened up a personal journey that continued long after our sessions ended.

To begin with I reflected on the broader meaning of counselling, which led me to the realm of philosophy that many consider is the birthplace of psychology. The case also invited me to question how 'process', is used in the course of helping. As counsellors we engage with life problems and the internal world of clients. At times we encourage clients to express their feelings about either the therapeutic relationship or us, in order to facilitate learning and insight. Very often this is a reciprocal process and skilled therapists legitimately use this information to deepen the experience of counselling. Most counsellors feel 'comfortable' exploring their own and clients' negative or positive feelings in the alliance. We also answer questions on competency or address clients' interest in our personal backgrounds. These areas are generally familiar and are guided by personal rules and a theoretical framework. Conversations that concern physical attraction between client and counsellor pose a particular challenge and can feel unfamiliar. Consequently, this can lead to the danger of counsellors segregating ideas or feelings just because the content is – or seems to be – sexual. I realised that this is a prejudice, which can stem from either biased training or discomfort with what it may mean 'personally' or 'professionally'. This journey touched my past, as my MSc research explored differences in the ethical beliefs and behaviours of helping professionals. I learnt that there are very few 'alwayses' or 'nevers' in counselling, other than fundamental ethical issues. Capturing my internal 'process' has highlighted, first that self-awareness and the value base of counsellors are tools that can translate counselling into an act of either helping or harming and, second, that every once in a while each of us will come across a case that has to be handled differently to others. Sometimes we may not be able to say why, at the time, but it can become clearer in retrospect if self-examination remains a vital guiding force in our personal and professional development.

PROCESS REPORT

Introduction

In this process report cognitive-behavioural therapy was used as a framework for intervention with a male client who presented difficulties relating to his sexual fantasies. While extensive analysis of the model goes beyond the remit of this report in Section 1, an effort will be made to provide a succinct presentation of the main principles and techniques. Specific emphasis is placed on interventions relevant to the session and in providing the reader with a brief presentation on the area of work relevant to the client. Section 2, outlines the psychological assessment and Section 3, includes a ten-minute transcript, with commentary, from the seventh session. In Section 4, a summary of the work, and an evaluation of both the session and the counsellor are provided, while the development of ideas over time is discussed.

Section 1: theoretical framework

Cognitive behavioural therapy (CBT)

The basic premise of cognitive behavioural therapy (Beck 1976) is that there is an essential interaction between how individuals feel and behave and the way they construe their world, themselves and their future prospects (Freeman 1987). According to the model the tendency to adopt dysfunctional thinking patterns stems from irrational beliefs consisting of assumptions that determine 'a way of being'. Automatic thoughts are the most accessible and identifiable cognitions while core beliefs (or schemata) formed in early childhood lie at the deepest level. Typically, core beliefs consist of absolute statements and exert ongoing influence over the perception of events in fairly fixed ways. Thus, when external events stimulate irrational core beliefs, distortions are observed through patterns of negative automatic thoughts (NATs). For example, dichotomous thinking is the tendency to evaluate personal qualities or performance in extreme all-or-nothing terms, while emotional reasoning uses emotion as evidence for the way things really are, based on the logic 'I feel therefore I am' (Wills and Sanders 1997).

The process of counselling entails working collaboratively with a client in uncovering and challenging dysfunctional thinking, using guided discovery, Socratic questioning, 'thought diaries' and behavioural experiments (Freeman 1987). Guided discovery involves asking questions aimed at understanding the client's framework. It is an investigative process whereby client and counsellor join forces to see if a different way of seeing things is possible (Beck and Young 1985). A key tool in this process is the Socratic method, which uses systematic questioning and inductive reasoning to draw general inferences from experiences within specific events. In turn, this helps clients distinguish between facts, beliefs and opinions (Overholser 1993). Padesky (1993) also stresses the importance of asking synthesising questions to help clients draw conclusions from their explorations. The aim of guided discovery is to help the client learn how to question thoughts and beliefs and 'thought diaries' allow the skill of challenging to become automatic eventually. Specific cognitive strategies include questioning evidence that maintains ideas, looking at the advantages and disadvantages of specific beliefs in order to create a fair perspective, reattribution, labelling distortions, guided association using the downward arrow technique and imagery. Behavioural strategies aimed at facilitating learning, include bibliotherapy, social-skills training and experiments constructed to test beliefs by discerning their relative validity or truth (Beck et al. 1979). Consequently, homework forms a vital part of cognitive therapy because it advocates the idea that counselling is not a weekly occurrence but a process wherein client and counsellor work in partnership to bring about change. Safran and Segal (1990) stress the importance of the 'cognitive interpersonal style' so that in addition to the counsellor's cognitive behavioural conceptualisation an assessment is made of how the client's enduring patterns are replayed in the therapeutic relationship itself. The overall goal of counselling thus aims at building more adaptive and functional skills for responding on an interpersonal and intrapersonal level by endorsing a model of coping and adaptation.

Threats to self-esteem: subjugation and defectiveness

All humans have the capacity for personal evaluation; namely the ability to form an identity and attach value to it. Self-esteem, or personal self-worth, creates a context of freedom and is necessary for psychological survival. Its earliest foundations lie in parental affirmations of worth and in time it depends heavily on the values of others (McKay and Fanning 1992). Humans, however, also have the capacity to distort reality and the perceptions they hold of themselves. This may occur in either a positive or a negative way, but distortions in the latter direction invariably devalue self-esteem and perpetuate emotional problems. Schemata that threaten self-worth include a sense of defectiveness and subjugation (Young 1994). Subjugation relates to self-sacrifice and a conviction that 'others' needs are more important than one's own'. This cognitive style, characterised by an imperative to please other people, leads to feelings of being trapped because it curtails personal freedom by dictating personal choices according to the effect it has on others. Consequently, a clear sense of one's own wants and needs is often missing. Stepping out of the subjugated role leads to guilt and reversion to self-sacrificing behaviour, which over time fosters a passive attitude to life and low self-esteem. Injuries to self-esteem can create feelings of shame; this is particularly evident with defectiveness where the need to hide an inner conviction of 'being inherently flawed and unlovable' leads to a fear of being loved and expectations of rejection. This is based on the idea 'the more deeply someone knows you, the less loveable you are' (Young 1994).

Sexual fantasies

Sexuality is woven deeply into the fabric of human existence. Sex is a motivating force, which brings two people together in intimate contact. Mutual sexual interest may lead either to brief encounters or to a principal relationship. While sexual pleasure may be seen as a potentially uncomplicated positive consequence, the binding effect of sexual intimacy and emotional security is vital. Another important thread in an individual's sexual life is the internal and private world of fantasy, even if it only involves imaginary behaviour (Bancroft 1989). A distinction needs to be made between sexual fantasies that arise during sexual activity and those that occur at other times, such as daydreams. Research shows that men generally have more erotic fantasies than women and devote more of their general daydreaming to sexual topics (Wilson 1980, Kinsey et al. 1953). The content of fantasies also differs. Men tend to lay emphasis on visual aspects, while women accentuate the accompanying emotions (Wagman 1967, Barclay 1973). It has been suggested that male fantasies are often expressions of a sex drive that is not totally fulfilled, whereas women seem to fantasise more when their sex life is going well. Interestingly, research on whether pornography has an undesirable effect on behaviour shows that while erotica induces a degree of sexual arousal there is little evidence that exposure to new types of sexual activity, as depicted in erotica, results in such activity taking place, although it may be incorporated in fantasies (Yaffe 1973, Bancroft 1978). In relationships, mood and its impact on self-perception, i.e. whether we feel desirable, worthy of love or low in self-esteem, also influences sexual desire and intimacy. Interconnected with this, fantasy can act either as a stimulus to sexual pleasure or as a response to an inner emotional state or external circumstance (Bancroft 1989).

Section 2: psychological assessment

Referral

Michael asked his general practitioner to refer him to the Brief Intervention and Counselling Service. The referral stated that he was stressed and was seeking help due to problems with his girlfriend.

Appearance and behaviour

Michael is a 32-year-old, single male. He is of medium build with short black hair and blue eyes. He works as an actor. Wearing a large jersey and jeans his manner was polite and friendly, but on first impression I sensed that he felt burdened. Non-verbal communication indicating this included intense eye contact and a thoughtful facial expression. For most of the session he leaned forward, spoke rapidly and at times, when pausing between thoughts, he sighed heavily and held his head between his hands.

Presenting problem

The client explained that he was in a long-term relationship but was experiencing doubts about getting married. This troubled him as he loved his partner (Donna), but felt strong sexual desires towards other women. His girlfriend wanted marriage, but needed him to make up his mind. This left him feeling guilty, confused and anxious about 'what it was he wanted' and ultimately about what decision to make.

Background and family history

Michael was born in Texas and lived in a small country town, which he portrayed as old-fashioned in its mentality. He was an only child. While growing up he idolised his father, a successful businessman who was often abroad on long trips. His mother is close to him, but was less so when he was a child due to her over-protectiveness and perfectionistic demands. The client came to the UK four years ago, to attend a drama school.

Cognitive behavioural profile

Cognitive factors

Michael demonstrated dichotomous thinking, catastrophisation, e.g. commitment is a 'death sentence', fortune telling, personalisation – 'she is miserable because of me' and strong must–should demands – 'I must make the right decision/I must not fantasise about women'.

Behavioural factors

Fear of upsetting his partner or being pressurised into a decision would lead to his avoidance of conversation on relationship issues or to his spending time away from home.

Emotional factors

Feelings of low self-worth, anxiety and guilt would escalate as the client found himself vacillating between the excitement of his fantasies and not wanting to hurt his girlfriend.

Physical symptoms

Tiredness, physical tension, poor concentration and sleep disturbance.

Social factors

Michael would sometimes talk to this friends about his dilemma and ask for advice or their views on what they would do. He also felt pressure from his family to make up his mind.

Case formulation

Michael's low self-esteem appears to have been triggered by the possibility of marriage. In facing this decision he has become confused over his 'needs' and 'desires' on a personal and interpersonal level. Antecedents, namely his family and social background, may have predisposed him to develop strong moral standards over sexual behaviour. Cognitively, dichotomous and rigid thinking limit communication with his partner due to a fear of being judged unworthy. The client's prerequisite to do the right thing is juxtaposed with vivid sexual fantasies about other women, which fuel feelings of shame. Michael fears that choosing his 'dirty' fantasies at the expense of losing something 'pure' (his partner) even if it brought a sense of personal freedom, would transform his feelings of shame into a factual existence. Yet to deny his fantasies by marrying and thus pleasing his partner leaves him feeling trapped. Michael's frustration seems to stem from his inability to tolerate inconsistency in his thinking around his own sexual values. As such, global negative self-evaluations maintain his emotional upset and lead to behavioural avoidance. In the short-term 'stagnation' prevents him from making a decision on commitment because of his need to find consistency in his thinking. In the long term, however, it has affected his work per-formance, increased his fantasising and stopped him from moving forward in his life.

Contract and counselling plan

Contracting was influenced by the boundaries of the service. It was agreed that hourly meetings would take place weekly, for six sessions and a follow-up. Confidentiality was addressed in terms of self-harm, supervision, taping and correspondence with the client's general practitioner. After assessment it was agreed that client goals would entail increasing understanding of his thinking and improving self-worth. Time was spent educating and socialising Michael into the cognitive model in order to create a language that he could use to label his distress. Identifying and evaluating distorted thinking patterns led to partly normalising his anxiety about fantasising, as a healthy aspect of sexual desire and to developing strategies in challenging NATs. In the middle phase, Michael continued to work hard and focus shifted onto core beliefs about himself and others. These were explored in terms of their meaning and influence over his relationship. After a review in Session 5, counselling was extended to ten fortnightly sessions.

Session 7: aims

1   Review homework from last session.
2   Explore client's core beliefs.
3   Discuss relationship and fantasy issues, in relation to beliefs.
4   Feedback and set homework for next session.

Lead into session

The transcript is taken from Session 7, a few minutes after starting. Prior to this Michael and I were reviewing homework. The client explained that he had attempted to dispute his core beliefs and the idea of 'I'm bad' was now not as strong. However, he reported that 'challenging' was difficult and that he struggled to understand and doubt his belief of being 'selfish'. When Michael mentioned this I recalled past sessions in which we had rigorously explored evidence for and against this belief. I started feeing slightly frustrated and thought, 'We are going round in circles. Has he shifted?' While aware of my inner dialogue I decided to take things slowly, so as to identify possible maintaining factors. I lowered the tone and pace of my voice and asked an open question aimed at inviting Michael to explore his belief. This is where the transcript begins.

Section 3: transcript

COUNSELLOR 1: Let's try and understand what the word selfish means. What does it mean to be one hundred per cent selfish?

Instead of telling Michael he was not selfish, I used questioning to elicit realistic alternatives. This would enable him to think through issues and generate his own evidence, which would also be more convincing.

MICHAEL 1: Hum, it means that you really . . . just think about yourself.

I wondered, after eliciting his automatic thought, whether my question was perceived as patronising, since the answer was obvious. Then again, I felt this was necessary when moving from general to idiosyncratic meanings.

COUNSELLOR 2: Only?

This punctuation checked if Michael believed what he said or whether he was just answering the question.

MICHAEL 2: Mmm . . .

Michael indicated that he believed it but his face expressed doubt. Possibly stronger evidence was needed to challenge his belief. Counselling – came to mind, as the idea of being totally selfish was not quite congruent when he was trying to improve his own life and how he cared for others.

COUNSELLOR 3: Is that what you do?

Narrowing the focus allowed Michael to evaluate whether his definition was a fair and honest view of himself. I hoped that this would start clarifying the distinction between having self-interest and being selfish.

MICHAEL 3: Sometimes, yea . . .

I inferred Michael's belief (M1) had shifted slightly; as before he would have said, 'yes'.

COUNSELLOR 4: Mmm.

My facial expression intimated, 'OK, sometimes he could be selfish', which made him laugh and kept the atmosphere light. It also encouraged him to go on.

MICHAEL 4: And you know sometimes I . . . I don't know . . .

Michael realised that he was thinking in all-or-nothing terms. His pause, signified some confusion about this.

COUNSELLOR 5: So, coming to counselling is also selfish isn't it? . . . 'cos you are just talking about yourself?

I could have explored unselfish behaviours, but I was aware that in the homework he had listed a page on this. So, instead, I used the 'here and now' by offering a distorted and emotive idea aimed at distinguishing facts from ideas. My 'so' may have seemed aggressive but I think my humorous tone averted this.

MICHAEL 5: Well, that's true . . . yes, that's true. It can be regarded as self-centred . . . navel watching or (as well . . .)

Michael reciprocated in a whimsical manner and demonstrated cognitive flexibility as he pondered one possible meaning and moved away from all-or-nothing thinking. To exemplify this, I could have reflected, 'It seems as if you think it is but that you are not sure?', but non-verbally – a sadness came over Michael. As if he believed the above was true. I also thought, after seven sessions, that he was still struggling to make a decision.

COUNSELLOR 6: Mmm . . . well is it?

I pondered over the progress of counselling, as Michael paused to think. My feelings of helplessness mirrored the client's, which increased my anxiety about the quality of helping. This concern detracted from my empathy, maybe because my belief on 'doing my best to help clients change' was triggered.

MICHAEL 6: No . . . no, it's not.

Questioning Michael's perception led to him negating his belief, as his own counselling did not fit his initial hypothesis.

COUNSELLOR 7: Why not?

I kept my questions short, as I knew this was an emotive area for Michael. My aim was not to intrude with words, thus allowing him to consider the impact of his ideas. I also had enough confidence in the alliance to know that this line of 'why questioning' would not be perceived as aggressive.

MICHAEL 7: Because . . . because it's trying to make me a better person and not to be, you know, to actually, to actually try and make a change, to make, you know, try and be a better person, I suppose . . .

Michael provided evidence against his belief. From his lowered tone, I sensed an emotional shift taking place. He didn't finish saying what he did not want to be, which I thought was because even verbalising his beliefs was painful at times. We had now come closer to considering the difference between having self-interest and wanting to improve one-self and being selfish. I should have reflected this back, but I was thinking about how to expand understanding of the client's framework to the outside world as against focusing on using this line of questioning to change his mind.

COUNSELLOR 8: Mmm . . . I'm thinking of this 'unselfish' because I think this is something that came up a lot in terms of how you handled your relationship and this whole notion of commitment, which was a very strong construct in your mind. OK. Um, you often said to me that you felt selfish in the way you reacted or . . . in the fact that you hadn't made up your mind and somebody else's life was on line because of you. Um . . . if you view yourself, as such a selfish person what do you think Donna, lets say, likes about you? . . . Umm because that would also be evidence against . . . 'I'm bad'.

This response was clumsy and verbose. I was clarifying my thoughts instead of checking them out with the client. On a process level, my comment depicted the same conflict that Michael experienced, namely continually trying to hold in my mind the dichotomous nature of his thinking, e.g. instead of saying selfish I said 'unselfish' because of how I perceived him. I should have slowed down and articulated a simple question. My anxiety on confusing him was also evident when, instead of allowing Michael to provide opposing evidence, I justified my intervention to clarify the purpose of my question.

MICHAEL 8: Yes.

Michael said this quite strongly and I felt some relief because, despite my long-winded monologue, he understood my point. His gaze shifted to the floor, and he appeared to be trying to understand.

COUNSELLOR 9: So, given the difficulties in this relationship, what is it that actually keeps it, what is it that she likes about you?

I wanted to contrast Michael's outlook with the qualities that others valued in him, in order to create a more realistic viewpoint.

MICHAEL 9: Um . . . she thinks I'm kind, and um . . . that she can trust me.

Turn 9 enabled the client to recognise that others saw him differently. Acknowledgement of this, I thought, was good progress.

COUNSELLOR 10: OK.

This prompt communicated that there was one piece of evidence and that possibly there were more. I hope that expanding the evidence, using factual data from his relationship, would show how his dichotomy blurred his perception and sustained his core beliefs.

MICHAEL 10: Um . . . and she loves me so . . . you know, she loves me so that's like holding her on, you know . . .

As Michael searched for evidence, I sensed doubt in his voice. The word 'holding' implied, in my mind, that she was uncertain and could still abandon him. Yet in turn 9 he had provided evidence on why she wanted to stay with him. I chose not to explore this further because Michael was making an inference about his girlfriend's behaviour, which would have made it difficult to find evidence either for or against. Instead, I focused on how it contradicted his belief.

COUNSELLOR 11: So, is it possible to be kind? . . . Because kind implies you are kind . . . toward others or kind to yourself. How does that fit in with this notion of selfishness?

This was a good question for leading Michael towards an understanding of how he combined contradictory notions. Although he behaved in a kind and trustworthy way, he still chose to perceive himself as selfish. He agreed non-verbally, as I spoke.

MICHAEL 11: Um . . . mmmm.

Michael became very thoughtful at this point, which indicated that he was thinking about his dichotomy. I found his affirmation hopeful, as it pointed towards a new understanding.

COUNSELLOR 12: It's a completely different perception to what you're seeing yourself.

This reflection confirmed Michael's non-verbal agreement and focused attention on to what he was not noticing.

MICHAEL 12: Yes . . . yes . . . mm . . . I'm sure she doesn't think I'm really that selfish, you know. I spoke to her before about it, you know . . . And she doesn't . . . no . . . no.

Michael was now realising that evidence from his life contradicted his belief. He responded with confirmatory information and his tone when he said 'no' made me think that his girlfriend had substantially verified this point. An important shift had also occurred during the session as Michael was now taking more responsibility for providing evidence against his belief. Moving from a personal to an interpersonal level provided increased insight, therefore I continued with guided exploration.

COUNSELLOR 13: I read that you have started talking to her more about what is going on in counselling.

This was an apt time to link in the homework, as I had noticed that Michael had recorded the above fact in his diary as evidence against being selfish. This was vital as it was new behaviour, which in the past had frightened him.

MICHAEL 13: Yes . . . yes.

Something important seemed to have occurred and Michael wanted to talk about it.

COUNSELLOR 14: What's that been like?

My curiosity prompted the client to expand and assisted in moving the counselling process forward.

MICHAEL 14: It's been, it's been good, I mean, because it felt like . . . um . . . I was saying these shocking things, you know . . . I've said them before in a way, but it was actually met with more kindness, it was met with an openness . . . which maybe, once I can get more, you know . . . 'cos I think, I was thinking the other day, sometimes I'm really petrified of the outcome of saying these things. I'm worried of the attack I'm going to get, so it stops me from opening up but . . . um . . . I really came across something that really made me think about wanting to be closer to Donna. . . . Um . . . it's something I read in the *Feeling Good Handbook*. It was about a man who . . . um, he was married and he didn't want to be married anymore because he . . . wasn't liking what was happening. So, then, eventually he went single and . . . and it made me think that . . . I think I've got another core belief, or I've got something that's stopping me from moving forward. It's just a feeling that you have to have many relationships before you settle down, you know what I mean?

Michael's self-disclosure was illuminating. A dam of information had burst through demonstrating the conflict that he faced. He spoke in a slow and reflective manner, signifying a strong need to understand both his thinking and the possible links with his fantasies. The homework and bibliotherapy had further facilitated this insight. I felt compassion for Michael as I observed him confide his struggle. On a process level, this communication signified for me the safety that he felt in the therapeutic alliance.

COUNSELLOR 15: Mmm . . .

I continued listening without interrupting his thinking.

MICHAEL 15: . . . and that's so rooted in me? It's gone deep you know, deeper than I thought . . .

By identifying the meaning of his fantasies Michael unravelled the dichotomy created in his relationship. This understanding was facilitated by the emotional distress experienced in the session, which provided greater access to his beliefs. It also informed the conceptualisation, as I speculated that fantasising distracted Michael from emotional intimacy. The fantasies also created deep guilt and shame as he was caught in a vicious cycle where they were both a product of his thinking and an activating event for further distress. It dawned on me that I did not know their content, as earlier efforts had been spent on normalising the idea of fantasising.

COUNSELLOR 16: Mmm . . . that notion, I think, came to .. um . . . sort of the first issues we were talking about when you first started coming here about . . . the sexual fantasies . . . you know, and were they normal, were they not normal? And how did they leave you feeling? And it was about your internal battle, about what it is that you want? . . . So, if we revisit that area now, OK?

I now wanted to link this in but, as I embarked into this territory, I got slightly anxious, because I knew where I wanted to go but was not sure what I would find. Asking permission to do this helped reduce my anxiety and reinforced collaboration.

MICHAEL 16: Mmm. (*nodded, several times*)

Non-verbally the client expressed that he also thought that this was an important area to look at.

COUNSELLOR 17: Given that you have probably identified an important belief that, you know, 'I must sleep around with a lot of people before I can get married' . . . um, what are your thoughts of it now, . . . in terms of fantasising, in terms of Donna?

Via a synthesising and more Socratic question, I pursued the 'reality–fantasy' theme and encouraged Michael to draw conclusions. Asking two questions, however, may have confused the client by not allowing him to focus on one area. During the transcript I realised that counter-transference had taken place. Michael disclosed earlier that 'he needed to have many relationships before he settled down', yet when discussing his fantasies (due to his limited sexual experiences) I paraphrased this as 'sleeping around' and instead of saying 'women', I said 'people'. My language was impersonal and objectified his perception of women.

MICHAEL 17: Well, my thoughts . . . are that, um, that if that belief, if . . . I can believe that that is not necessarily true . . . it's a way to actually go forward in a way . . . um . . . 'cos actually saying it to Donna made me feel a lot more . . . I'd said it before anyway, but it was in the way I said it differently to her, this time it was . . . 'I really think its deeper than what I thought it was, . . . this belief, you know . . .'.

Michael drew a conclusion and for the first time offered a solution. I sensed that while he recognised the importance of communicating effectively and exploring self-defeating thinking, he harboured ambivalence as to whether he could do this.

COUNSELLOR 18: Mmm.

I listened, conveying interest and trusting in the client to identify what he wanted. I noticed that Michael felt increasingly safe to share his feelings with a female because they were accepted in a non-judgmental way. I wondered how successful he had been in replicating this quality of communication within his relationship. I also felt relieved that we were closer to making a decision.

MICHAEL 18: . . . and it makes me think that if I can get closer to Donna.

My thoughts were confirmed and I realised this was Michael's first expression of wanting to make a commitment.

COUNSELLOR 19: Mmm.

I wondered if he also wanted to be 'pure'. Were his fantasies like a contamination?

MICHAEL 19: Actually be more open, express myself more easily, I wouldn't, it would be easier not to be so worried about it . . .

I felt hopeful at this point, because our work was engendering cognitive flexibility. Michael was generating his own hypothesis and actively imagining a different reality that involved risk.

COUNSELLOR 20: Mmm . . . could we maybe hypothesise that in actual fact, what it is about, what you are actually trying to improve is the quality of your relationships with people . . . and Donna has been the first person, you know, you fell in love with and considered to share your life with and there have been obstacles there . . . that it's not necessarily about commitment . . . in the way you were looking at it, at first.

A positive reframe ascribed new meaning to Michael's dilemma, namely an interest in relationship quality versus 'damning himself' as defective. I stressed the notion of devotion because he had not faced it before, thus it was normal to be anxious. This was an appropriate time to explore Michael's fantasies, as they represented the most important obstacle to his commitment.

MICHAEL 20: Mmm.

While Michael agreed to this, his manner conveyed a sense of expectation, which made me continue.

COUNSELLOR 21: Remember you were saying you saw this barren land . . . if, if you got married . . . remember when we did that imagery stuff . . . that it felt barren . . . which is interesting, because 'barren' is what you use to perhaps describe a sexuality, you know what I'm saying . . . somebody is barren they cannot give life, they cannot produce.

By focusing on the image Michael placed on commitment (which in itself had a sexual and emotive overtone), I hoped to elicit automatic thoughts on his fantasies. Yet my zeal prevented me from getting feedback and made me insensitive to the impact my thoughts had on Michael. He may have found them confusing and, despite the strength of the alliance, quite threatening.

MICHAEL 21: Mmm . . .

Michael indicated that I should continue. I hoped my next question, which was my point – would make things clearer. The danger in doing this, however, was that I ran the risk of losing the client at the expense of my agenda.

COUNSELLOR 22: I'm going to ask you a difficult question. If you think I'm prying you don't have to answer it but I think, on some level maybe, it will help us understand how you see yourself in this whole situation, OK. We often talked about sexual fantasies, yeah . . . I never asked you directly what they were about. All I knew, really, was they were troubling you and . . . you really didn't want to have them or you felt bad you were having them on some level. What were those fantasies like? I mean, how did you see yourself in those fantasies? . . . Because that might give us a clue into how you see yourself handling this situation.

This was a difficult but important question to ask, as I felt that it would enable Michael to express exactly what he feared that he would get rejected for. My explanation was wordy because my anxiety had risen over the past few minutes and I wanted to remain respectful towards the client. Thus, I provided my inner rationale rather than just saying light-heartedly, 'What are your fantasies about?' Again, my process mirrored the client's as I was trying to bring 'unspeakable' aspects of his world into a forum where they could be spoken about, but, like Michael, I was struggling to ask the question that would do this.

MICHAEL 22: Um . . . it's the . . . well, the fantasies really are just almost, it's, . . . its just very strong, it's almost as if I'm . . . If I see somebody sexually attractive I just want to have sex with them and some days it feels so strong, I'm just looking at women, you know . . . looking . . . you know . . .

Possibly, my long response in turn 22 gently eased Michael into exploring this stream of thought.

COUNSELLOR 23: Mmm . . . .

As Michael related his fantasies I noticed a change in his posture and tone of voice. He became more free, more animated and descriptive on a visual and physical level; almost lustful. His dichotomous thinking re-emerged, through the lack of emotional involvement with the women in his fantasies. I chose not to reflect on this, in order to understand their content.

MICHAEL 23: I even went swimming the other day and there was this really attractive woman just swimming past me and I really wanted to keep looking and then, as soon as I looked, I said to myself, what are you doing? You know she must really be uncomfortable going swimming . . . looking . . . you know . . . but it's really strong, it feels . . . it was that week that I felt, you know, why am I doing this, you know?

Michael's exasperated facial expression revealed that he was disgusted by his reaction. Although he experienced discomfort in relating this event, I hypothesised that it was also a relief to have things out in the open.

COUNSELLOR 24: Mmm.

I kept direct eye contact and non-verbally my facial expression conveyed understanding of the distress that it caused him. Demonstrating acceptance, I felt was crucial when Michael had made himself so vulnerable.

MICHAEL 24: It feels really . . . I just want to have sex with her, I want to . . . almost . . . feel . . . that you could just . . . have sex with them . . . and leave them . . . and then it's finished . . . do you know what I mean?

I felt my stomach tighten when Michael referred to women as 'them'. I thought, 'He is objectifying the whole female population into a sexual commodity'. I realised, however, that I was overgeneralising.

COUNSELLOR 25: Mmm.

I tried to prevent this from obstructing my listening by communicating empathy to Michael on the guilt that these thoughts created.

MICHAEL 25: As if you were just a walking sex machine or something . . . you just . . . see something that you like sexually, you have sex with them, fantastic, and you go away and that's it . . . and you're just constantly doing that, you know . . .

This sexual freedom returned my mind to the conceptualisation. The content of Michael's fantasies seemed to protect him from being vulnerable, because of the assumption that 'he could use women sexually if he was not emotionally connected to them'.

COUNSELLOR 26: Do you think, though, if you challenge your belief about having to sleep with a whole bunch of women before you actually make a commitment . . . Do you think that's going to change the fantasy about women?

I contrasted Michael's idea on intimacy hoping that it would lessen the impact of his fantasies on his defectiveness. In the transcript, I noticed how I had phrased my question 'a whole bunch of women' and wondered if counter-transference was still taking place.

MICHAEL 26: . . . I think I'm . . . just crystallising something . . . it's just . . . its really like . . . a curiosity . . . to actually see lots of different bodies . . .

Michael did not answer my Socratic question, but the contrast helped him to identify a cognition maintaining his fantasies. I wasn't sure whether what he shared was as simple as he presented it or if it would develop into something quite different.

COUNSELLOR 27: Mmmm.

I encouraged him to go on.

MICHAEL 27: It seems to me a curiosity to see different breasts, different legs, different . . . Everything. Do you know what I mean?

This provided evidence of Michael's tendency to objectify women, which in turn made him a 'bad' person.

COUNSELLOR 28: Mmm . . . mmm.

While my body language and facial expression remained neutral, Michael's comments made me feel uneasy again. Sitting before him I wondered if he was doing the same thing to me, looking at my body and fantasising about what I looked like? and I contemplated whether I should ask that? However, despite my irritation, I rationalised that it was not the end of the world even if he did do that and I remained focused on the client. Looking at it now, I may have avoided an area that I felt awkward in because of ethical implications. Also, it was not an easy question to ask because I was not sure if it would have therapeutic value and I did not want to open up an area that would trigger another set of fantasies. With all these thoughts in my mind I wondered if Michael sensed that I was uncomfortable.

MICHAEL 28: . . . and . . . what I sometimes try and do is, I sometimes try and look to prove for me that it's not worth looking at, to look and see. No, I don't want that . . . and I really feel good when I don't . . . you know, and I find a fault in it.

Typically, Michael corrected his thoughts due to feelings of guilt. Was the problem his desire or his inability to act on it?

COUNSELLOR 29: Mmm . . . mmm.

Maintaining an accepting 'open' stance was vital in allowing the client to move closer to aspects of himself that he did not like. Yet Michael was expressing freely in session the very thoughts that frightened him in real life.

MICHAEL 29: You know . . . um . . . it's a curiosity and as it builds up . . . I've even gone, I've gone into a kind . . . into magazine shops with these porno mags. I'd love just to pick . . . that out and just look at bodies . . .

Michael provided a new activating event, but this time based on actual and potential behaviour. It created an image in me of an adolescent boy and I suspected that picking up a magazine would confirm his idea that this type of sexuality was bad.

COUNSELLOR 30: So, why don't you?

I wanted to explore the automatic thoughts that prevented him from carrying this out.

MICHAEL 30: Because I'd feel dreadful in doing that.

Challenging the client was aimed at uncovering the meaning behind this event. I could have asked, 'what would have made it so dreadful?' but I kept my questions short in order to keep our rapport spontaneous.

COUNSELLOR 31: Why?

I hoped that this would allow Michael to become more focused on what his feelings meant.

MICHAEL 31: Because, I'd feel seedy and dirty, and despicable.

Michael's emotional reaction and the emphasis of his words indicated core beliefs of defectiveness had been triggered as negative thoughts, which aided in invalidating his emerging self-esteem.

COUNSELLOR 32: How come?

I wanted to uncover why he believed this.

MICHAEL 32: Because (*laughs*) when I see middle-aged men taking those things down and looking right, I think, God that's really sad . . .

The client communicated something very powerful namely that people who could not have real relationships could only have them through objects or magazines. For Michael to be like those people was more than bad or selfish it was incredibly sad and pathetic. I wondered where he got this meaning from – was there something in his parents' relationship.

COUNSELLOR 33: Mmm.

I followed his train of thought, but had an image of a 'free' father and a 'house-bound' mother.

MICHAEL 33: I know it's not . . . I mean, I'd think 'good luck to you mate' but . . . I view it as that, by me taking that down. What if someone walks in and says 'Hi Michael, how you doing? And I've got this thing in my hand, you know, what are they going to think of me?

It was evident that Michael placed value on external validation of his self-worth. I could have used the downward arrow to explore this meaning further but at that moment, through our guided discovery, I got a child-hood image of an event that he had shared in a past session. It made sense. Michael's views may have been shaped by his conservative upbringing. Growing up in an environment so 'contained and rigid' no wonder he predicted that his own family life would be 'barren' dull and stifling. His fantasies on the other hand encapsulated the exact opposite – an emotional and sexual freedom.

COUNSELLOR 34: You know what you're making me think of?

I wanted to set a new tone in order to share this connection. Looking back, however, I feel it detracted from the client in the 'here and now' and could have been construed as if I had some deeper insight into his life than he had. I was also not sensitive to Michael's last question. Maybe Michael thought that I was going to tell him what I thought of him. This could have been quite frightening.

MICHAEL 34: What?

My question had evoked curiosity. We had moved from changing the client's mind on his beliefs, to identifying meaning.

COUNSELLOR 35: That experience you talked about when you were ten years old . . . with your father . . . when he said have you got a girlfriend? . . . and what are you up to? . . . It was the same type of thing . . . you're saying . . . 'That's disgusting!' . . . 'I would never do that!'

Section 4: summary

Overview of work in session

This session met the aim of exploring Michael's core beliefs 'I'm selfish' and 'I'm bad' and their meanings as they related to his relationship and sexual fantasies. At the start of the session, time was spent reviewing homework and associated difficulties were problem-solved, i.e. listing evidence 'for' and 'against' his belief rather than only 'against' and separating facts from emotional opinions. Identifying these obstacles provided an opportunity for guided discovery and Socratic questioning, which helped Michael to explore the notion of selfishness (turn 1). In particular, by using the milieu of counselling and reasons for seeking help Michael challenged his belief that he was one hundred per cent selfish (turn 7). Generally, because sexual fantasies can, and usually do, remain concealed their frightening significance may continue unchallenged. Consequently, in the middle phase events mentioned by the client, pornographic magazines (turn 29) and looking at women's bodies (turn 27) were used to draw inferences about himself, e.g. 'if I had several relationships then I could settle down' and about others (turns 31 and 32). Examining these ideas led to identifying significant childhood events and to discussing how his fantasies fuelled his belief (turn 33). Furthermore, exploring the advantages and disadvantages of commitment and staying single, revealed the importance that Michael placed on pleasing others. Finally, evidence from a behavioural experiment (turns 12 and 13) and reattribution of his dichotomous thinking enabled the client to offer a potential solution to his problem. Namely, fostering emotional intimacy with his partner could decrease his fantasising. At the end of the session, Michael reflected things that he still felt were 'cloudy'. However, he realised that the process of change was often slow and difficult. Homework for our next session was set.

Evaluation of session and self-assessment of counsellor

Corey et al. (1988) consider the role of the counsellor to be a *person* in the therapeutic relationship who cannot be separated from the practical and theoretical knowledge made available to clients during counselling. In fact they claim

> since counsellors are asking clients to take an honest look at themselves and to make choices concerning how they want to change, it seems critical that counsellors themselves be searchers who hold their own lives and work open to the same level of scrutiny.
>
> (Corey et al. 1988, p. 27)

Reflecting on this session and on the moment-to-moment interactions has been a process filled with a myriad of emotions. At times in the transcript I was filled with anxiety concerning the adequacy of my work and at other times the contents of discussion touched a chord within my own values, yet simultaneously our evident collaboration inspired hope. As a result I recognised how the therapeutic relationship remains a central arena where clients (and counsellors) can practice alternative or new behaviours (Wills and Sanders 1997). Michael's disclosures exemplified our strong therapeutic bond. Not only was he able to share 'hidden' parts of himself that evoked shame, but the non-judgmental atmosphere allowed him to achieve progressively deeper insight. Reflecting on this session required consideration of previous sessions, since they encapsulated an important process that took place. As work with the client moved into his beliefs, my feeling of going around in circles increased despite Michael's progress. I now realise his subjugation schema had influenced counselling. In the same manner that he pleased others, he pleased me by diligently doing all the homework. My irritation was triggered by his ambivalence and interpersonal style of needing me to direct counselling. Within this and other sessions, I strove to understand Michael's idiosyncratic meanings, which only fuelled hope in him that eventually I would tell him what to do or instead – in the next session, that everything would fall miraculously into place. Interpersonally, individuals with subjugation beliefs, often choose partners with a strong sense of self (Young 1994). In our sessions I feel my assertive character perpetuated the above process. Counsellors are also human and they too have 'blind spots' or areas of sensitivity that inevitably interact with client problems (Wills and Sanders 1997). This was evident in the counter-transference (turns 17 and 26), which in cognitive therapy is valuable in providing deeper insight of process issues. A clue to its presence is often 'irritation' and by definition it embodies all of the counsellor's responses to a client, including thoughts, schemas, emotions, actions and intentions (Layden et al. 1993).

Exploring Michael's fantasies was valuable. First, in aiding the conceptualisation by providing a window into his private world and its relation to women, and second, it highlighted my dilemma almost asking if his fantasies influenced our work. Usually when clients say or do something that creates a hunch about the alliance, I use the 'here and now' to address it. Michael stated that he fantasised about sexually attractive women but he did not do or say anything in sessions to make me think or feel he was sexually attracted to me. My thought (turn 28) was based on the fact that I was 'a woman'. To assume that he might be attraced to me, was, I felt, dubious. On the other hand, while very aware of the difference between a therapeutic and personal relationship, if Michael was not offended (based on our bond) and answered 'yes', could that not be used as evidence that he could experience intimacy without his fantasies intruding? If he answered 'no', could that suggest (the alliance as a parallel) that striving to get emotionally closer to Donna could lessen his fantasy, which was devoid of emotion? In retrospect, I could have used another female that he was emotionally close to to test this assumption about me. In the end, I did not ask because on weighing it up, I thought it best not to. I did not want to shame my client or cause him any harm by putting him on 'the spot'. But, most importantly, I could not act irresponsibly by introducing an intervention, whose purpose I was unclear about. If I was prejudiced because it was a sexual issue, maybe it was because I found it difficult to introduce the subject rather than to discuss it. Furthermore, I may have projected my own values on to the features of Michael's fantasies. The morals and conflicting opinions that encase human sexuality reflect the inherent complexity of these issues, which no doubt continue to change in both counsellors and clients as a result of life experience or simply by getting older. Self-awareness and a flexible self-concept enabled me to accept my unease without detracting from the goals of counselling. Evaluating the transcript also highlighted the skills that I need to improve when working with clients. When responding I can gain brevity by following Wills and Sanders' 'three sentence rule'. That is, not saying more than three sentences at any point in time and constantly seeking client feedback. The danger of not doing this (as the transcript shows) is a didactic style that follows the counsellor's pace and is less empathic to client need. Supervision provided a possible way of introducing sexual fantasies that helped put me at ease: 'I assume you have sexual feelings about me, I may be wrong . . . but I guess you have LOTS of feelings about me, both comfortable and uncomfortable. Why wouldn't you? It's all-OK with me. In fact, we'll talk about some of those periodically. It may be uncomfortable for you when we do, and that's OK with me also'. Finally, I was surprised to observe how quickly I spoke, which made me race ahead of the client. This may have contributed to Michael's 'cloudy' feeling, as moving from one area to the next was not always clearly demarcated or brought to a logical conclusion. A slower pace and more use of Socratic and reflecting responses could enhance clarity, empathy, collaboration and the overall delivery of my counselling style.

Development of ideas

Commitment to self-exploration and inspiring self-search in clients is not an easy task. In fact it is often fraught with difficulties and, similarly, so is the self-search of the counsellor. Working with Michael has challenged me theoretically and personally. In terms of the former, it inspired me to search the literature on issues affecting human sexuality, which provided guidance on sexual fantasising (Masters and Johnson 1970, Bancroft 1989). In turn CBT provided a framework for conceptualising this knowledge and its role in emotional disturbance. For example, Bancroft (1989) suggests identifying the discrepancies between the real world, and the ideal fantasised world can be invaluable in helping people with sexual problems. Equally CBT provides the tools for such an exploration. Yet, despite the knowledge that I gained, I still felt something was missing in my understanding. Possibly, because by the end of counselling Michael had not reached a decision. This led me to depart from the 'content' of therapy to contemplating more deeply the 'process' of our sessions in terms of what it signified for the client and my role as helper. An answer came from my reading on existential psychology and in it I found parallels to the humanistic underpinning of counselling psychology, which essentially involves helping clients fulfil their potential. The centrality of this value-base is emphasised by Duffy (1990) who suggests that the way counselling psychologists think about what they do is very important. Clients' crises and problems are not seen as evidence of pathology but as normal human experiences, which pose a challenge for developmental adaptation. Cognitive-behavioural therapy, as a method of working upholds this tenet by promoting change through adoption of meanings that foster personal growth. Yet Viktor Frankl makes the important claim (which CBT possibly neglects) that what characterises human beings is a 'will to meaning' (Frankl 1967). By this he essentially means that the striving to find meaning in life is a primary motivational force in all mankind and also needs to be understood as an existential phenomenon. The client's request for counselling signified this need and over and above the contents of his thoughts, Michael used sessions to explore his *freedom of will* through his sexual values. Namely, the stance he would take towards himself and his conscience. A tension or 'existential angst' had been created between a relationship that required the responsibility of commitment and freedom to explore, or act on, his sexual desires. For Michael choosing the relationship ultimately meant acting in 'bad faith' a self-deception that restricted his freedom and escaped the responsibility of being an individual. However, not to choose it meant selecting an existence that he deemed had no essence. Eventually his decision would determine his meaning, which in turn was indispensable to his mental health. Understanding the meta-communication of 'essence and existence' and identifying its paradoxes helped me realise the phenomenology of human experience present in all counselling. Spinelli (1994) writes that in addition to sound theoretical knowledge – counselling psychologists should also demonstrate suitable maturity and life experience that infuses their ability to confront and deal with their own existential dilemmas. A complex interaction exists between knowledge and personal values and in any emotive area these cannot be completely separated (Bancroft 1989). On a personal level, not surprisingly, this case re-entered my thoughts following my own life experience of questioning the repercussions of commitment to another person. Through this work I cultivated understanding of my strengths, vulnerability and enhanced my belief that without self-awareness and a deep curiosity in the human condition, psychologists can obstruct client progress and their own professional development. Above all, I now sense that the 'will to meaning' is inextricably linked to the therapeutic relationship and emerges existentially through the steps that lead to a process of change.

References

Bancroft, J. (1978). Psychological and physiological responses to sexual stimuli in men and women. In L. Levi (ed.) *Society, Stress and Disease, Vol. 3. The Productive and Reproductive Age*. Oxford: Oxford University Press.

Bancroft, J. (1989). *Human Sexuality and its Problems*. New York: Churchill Livingstone.

Barclay, A.M. (1973). Sexual fantasies in men and women. *Medical Aspects of Sexuality*, 7, 205–216.

Beck, A.T. (1976). *Cognitive Therapy and the Emotional Disorders*. New York: International Universities.

Beck, A.T. and Young J.E. (1985). Depression. In D.H. Barlow (ed.) *Clinical Handbook of Psychological Disorders*. New York: Guilford Press, pp. 206–244.

Beck, A.T., Rush, A.J., Shaw, B.F. and Emery, G. (1979). *Cognitive Therapy of Depression*. New York: Guilford Press.

Corey, G., Corey, S.C. and Callanan, P. (1988). *Issues and Ethics in the Helping Professions*. California: Brooks/Cole.

Duffy, M. (1990). Counselling Psychology USA, patterns of continuity and change. *Counselling Psychology Review*, 5(3), 9–18.

Frankl, V.E. (1967). *Psychotherapy and Existentialism: Selected papers on Logotherapy*. Middlesex: Penguin Books.

Freeman, A. (1987). *Cognitive Therapy*. New York: Human Sciences Press.

Kinsey, A.C., Pomeroy, W.B., Martin, C.F. and Gebhard, P.H. (1953). *Sexual Behaviour in the Human Female*. Philadelphia: Saunders, pp. 759–763.

Layden, M.A., Newman C.F., Freeman, A. and Morse, S.B. (1993). *Cognitive Therapy of Borderline Personality Disorder*. Boston: Allyn and Bacon.

Masters, W.H. and Johnson, V.E. (1970). *Human Sexual Inadequacy*. London: Churchill Livingstone.

McKay, M. and Fanning, P. (1992). *Self-Esteem*. Oakland: New Harbinger Publications.

Overholser, J.C. (1993). Elements of the Socratic method: II inductive reasoning. *Psychotherapy*, 30(1), 75–85.

Padesky, C.A. (1993). Schema as self-prejudice. *International Cognitive Therapy Newsletter*, 5/6, 16–17.

Safran, J.D. and Segal Z.V. (1990). *Interpersonal Processes in Cognitive Therapy*. New York: Basic Books.

Spinelli, E. (1994). *Demystifying Therapy*. London: Constable.

Wagman, M. (1967). Sex differences in types of daydreams. *Journal of Personality and Social Psychology*, 7, 329–332.

Wills, F. and Sanders, D. (1997). *Cognitive Therapy Transforming the Image*. London: Sage.

Wilson, G.D. (1980). Sex differences in sexual fantasy patterns. In R. Forleo and W. Pasini (eds) *Medical Sexology*. Amsterdam: Elsevier.

Yaffe, M. (1972). Research survey. In F. Longford (ed.) *Pornography: the Longford Report*. London: Coronet.

Young, J.E. (1994). *Cognitive Therapy for Personality Disorders: a Schema Focused Approach*, 2nd edn. Sarasota, FL: Personal Resource Exchange.

Chapter 12

Treating co-morbidity in an NHS context: a CBT approach

with a case study by Christine Haworth-Staines

PRELUDE

As therapists, we are on an imaginary personal and professional trajectory that is characterised by growth and change in how we may view or experience things. When we come to revisit an experience we seldom see things in the same way as we did the first time. This is true of our experience of therapy. Christine Haworth-Staines started working with this client a year before she submitted the case study for assessment and her initial drafts were subjected to several revisions over a number of months. She describes how therapy need not be a single, seamless process, but may instead be characterised by different phases during which a series of problems are dealt with. Further-more, trainees and experienced therapists alike are challenged to grapple with ethical and professional issues, as illustrated in this case. Christine also recognised that, while therapy unfolded, the task of writing it up for assessment required her to organise and present her experience and ideas in a readable, clear and coherent format. This client study is included because it illustrates both 'good' therapy and a clear written account thereof.

> *Christine Haworth-Staines wrote this case study between the first and second year of a part-time MSc in Counselling Psychology. The comments were written after the MSc course in a year of deferral before starting the post-MSc practitioner diploma.*

Preamble

At the outset of my two-year MSc I was aware that two case studies had to be prepared, in addition to a number of other assignments. This client was seen more than twelve months prior to the submission date and I made a first draft of the case during the summer break at the end of the first year. Later I went back to it and refined, reflected and prepared a final draft just prior to the submission deadline. My reason for working in this way was not only to spread the course workload more effectively over the two years, but also because I saw this case as a particularly good one to write up. I felt that it was important to get down the main features while the information was still fresh in my mind.

I believed this to be a good case for several reasons. First, it reflected, for the most part, one particular theoretical orientation, i.e. cognitive-behavioural therapy. The number of sessions, eight in all, made it a concise piece of work which was relatively easy to write up. There was enough material to prepare a written report but not too much to have to work through in terms of determining what must be left out. Second, the outcome was good and the number of sessions was a reflection of this. I also felt that it was a fairly unique case with some interesting features. One of the features that I found interesting was the way in which the case had been approached as two discreet pieces of work. The first, an almost problem-solving, practical piece which once resolved allowed the move to a second stage of more typical cognitive-behavioural work. The case also allowed me to demonstrate my understanding of ethical and professional issues, use of supervision and liaison with other professionals.

Although the outcome was positive I had certain doubts over the way therapy had proceeded, particularly from a theoretical perspective. Writing up the study allowed me to reflect on this and take a 'macro' view of the whole intervention. During my sessions with this client I was aware that the assessment stage was lengthy and the client's need to relate her history in detail particularly her childhood, was not typical of a cognitive-behavioural approach. At the time my justification for this was that it led to the development of a good therapeutic relationship, particularly in view of the fact that the client had concerns about confidentiality and trust. In retrospect, another important feature to emerge from this process was the identification of the root of her anxious behaviour together with material that later allowed me to challenge her negative automatic thoughts. In summary, writing this report, raised my awareness of the importance of history taking, at least for some clients, no matter which theoretical perspective is employed.

My final comment is that this case study was prepared with the marker in mind. I had read, several times, the course guidelines and identified precisely what would be assessed. This study formed part of the assessment for 'Practice and Skills in Counselling Psychology'. The choice of case, the extraction of relevant material and the linking of theory to practice was undertaken with this information always at the forefront of my mind.

CASE STUDY

Part 1: introduction and the beginning of therapy

Introduction

This case study is an example of a piece of work with a client referred to an outpatient psychology service in a National Health Service (NHS) Trust.

The client was referred with both a depressive and an anxiety disorder. The therapeutic intervention involved cognitive-behaviour therapy, this is discussed briefly in the sections that follow together with a brief client history and the assessment process. Part 2 of the study focuses on the therapeutic plan, the techniques employed and the use of supervision. Part 3 offers a critique of the content and process of therapy and concluding comments.

Theoretical orientation

Cognitive-behaviour therapy (CBT) is based on the notion that our behaviour is driven by our thought processes and these in turn are driven by the schema we develop from childhood experiences. This model has been derived primarily from the work of Aaron Beck (Beck et al. 1979) and encompasses the work of the early behaviourists, together with cognitive theories acquired in the mid-twentieth century.

The approach can be applied to a number of disorders (Hawton et al. 1989), and is typically goal orientated, with a fixed number of time-limited sessions. To encourage the process of therapy, techniques from other perspectives were employed, i.e. systemic and person-centred therapy, but they did not detract from the overall framework of CBT.

Context and referral

The placement in which this client was seen, was the adult mental health psychology service of an NHS Trust. This service accepts referrals for clients aged between sixteen and seventy-five years, from within a specific catchment area. The client discussed in this case study, Sarah, was referred by her GP in December 1998 for an episode of severe depression and anxiety. Reference was also made to marital problems. The GP described some improvement with medication (seroxat) but felt that further improvement could be made, and future relapse prevented, with a course of CTB.

In February 1999, Sarah was seen for screening by an assistant psychologist in the department. During this screening a number of psychological questionnaires were administered. These indicated moderate levels of depression and slightly elevated scores measuring somatic anxiety and obsessional traits. As a result of this screening, Sarah was placed on the routine waiting list for individual treatment. In January 2000, the client's name reached the top of the waiting list and she was offered an appointment with me, as a Counselling Psychologist in Training, working under the supervision of a Chartered Counselling Psychologist.

Client biographical details and recent history

Sarah is a 30-year-old, female medical student. She has been married for four years. Her husband is the same age and is a solicitor with a small legal company. Sarah described a happy childhood and continues to have a close relationship with her parents and two sisters (for a genogram see Figure 4, Appendix A).

Sarah left school and gained a place to study medicine at university in Scotland. During her first year she suffered her first major depressive episode. She was asked to leave at the end of that year. She took some time off from studying, then reapplied to medical school, but was unsuccessful. She made a decision to undertake another degree and apply to medical school later. She obtained her first degree in biochemistry from a university in the north of England then went on to achieve a PhD from Oxford University.

Following this she was accepted to study medicine at a London medical school. She was in her final year when therapy commenced. She had not had psychological therapy in the past.

Initial assessment

Sessions 1 and 2

At her first appointment, Sarah presented as pleasant and co-operative, but anxious. She was visibly perspiring and quite fidgety. I began the session by introducing myself and explaining my status in the department and the supervision arrangements. She claimed to be familiar with this and comfortable with my position as a trainee. We discussed issues of confidentiality and it was clear that this was important and of some concern to her. She was, however, reassured by the fact that breach of confidentiality would only be necessary if it was considered that a life was in danger. And that in this event every effort would be made to discuss the matter with her first.

We discussed the most likely course of therapy and it was agreed that she would be offered eight to ten bi-weekly sessions followed by a review.

The history taking was lengthy and detailed and there was an element of obsessionality in her need to relate the story in accurate detail. I felt, however, that to gain her confidence and trust it was important to allow this. I placed particular emphasis on employing the Rogerian skills used by client-centred therapists (Rogers 1951) to establish the core conditions, which would assist in the development of the therapeutic relationship.

Sarah described her childhood as 'perfect' and 'wonderful'. However, as she related her history chronologically a number of quite traumatic events emerged:

- When she was 9 years old her father had a heart attack and was hospitalised.
- When she was 13 years old, soon after the death of her grandfather, she witnessed her uncle having a heart attack.

- When she was 16 years old she learned that both her parents were taking benzodiazepines and, on reflection, suspects they were probably addicted.
- In the same year it emerged that her father was having an affair with his secretary at work. Sarah, her mother and sisters were very distressed.

It was clear, therefore, that there were events in childhood that may have contributed to her current anxiety. Adopting a cognitive model of anxiety these events could be viewed in terms of contributing to the development of unhelpful schemata, for example about uncertainty, trust and lack of control in her world (Emmelkamp et al. 1992). Sarah was able, in this first appointment, to acknowledge her parents' difficulties and the effect this may have had on her, without criticism or blame.

During this and the next session she continued with her story and described the difficulties she had faced at medical school.

Sarah felt that she took bad advice when going to university. She had been offered a place at a university in the north of England, close to her home town, and would have preferred this but accepted an offer at a Scottish university instead because her parents were moving to the area. She also chose not to live in halls of residence but to share a flat with other students. She became isolated from the students on her course and struggled to adapt socially to university life. She believed that this was the trigger to her first depressive episode. Following this depression she was unable to study effectively and failed her first-year exams. She did, however, pass the resits but failed a viva examined by her personal tutor, who was aware of her depression and recommended that she leave the course. She described this experience as creating a great deal of mistrust with feelings of anger and frustration on her part.

Her degree in biochemistry went very well and she described herself as being popular among her peers. At Oxford University she also thrived academically and socially. It was during this period that she met her husband. She reported having regained her confidence and self-esteem during this positive period.

Sarah entered medical school for the second time in 1995. Initially she enjoyed the course and gained good grades. However, she became increasingly anxious and depressed during the second half of the course. She attributed this to feelings of guilt about her application. Sarah had not informed the medical school that she had started a medical degree previously. The application form asked for the last two educational establishments attended and it was, therefore, not necessary to mention this fact. She also lied during the interview when asked why she had not applied to medical school earlier. Sarah now saw the omission and lie as totally unacceptable. The anxiety about this appeared to be triggered by a series of lectures on law and ethics presented by a female professor of whom Sarah thought very highly.

Since the screening appointment Sarah's husband had raised the issue of children and was quite keen to start a family once Sarah had qualified. Although she had always wanted children, the responsibility associated with this prospect had added to her current anxiety. She was particularly concerned that if she lost her place at medical school, she would be unable to help provide for a new family.

At the end of the first session I asked Sarah to complete the Beck Depression Inventory (BDI) (Beck 1996) and the Brief Symptom Inventory (BSI) (Derogatis 1975). I was interested to see her score on the BDI because she described symptoms of depression that appeared to have intensified since the screening appointment. For example she was not sleeping well, had poor appetite and weight loss, and was withdrawing from social contact. The BSI, which was a useful tool to measure a number of psychological factors, had been introduced to our department after her original screening.

Her BDI score had increased from twenty-four to thirty-one points, indicating a move from moderate to severe depression during the eleven months that she had been on the waiting list. Her BSI also suggested elevated levels of anxiety, obsessive-compulsive traits and interpersonal sensitivity. There was no evidence of suicidal ideation. In view of the severity of her depression I suggested that Sarah return to her GP and discuss the possibility of a further course of antidepressant medication. She informed me that she had stopped taking seroxat approximately six months ago and since then her symptoms had worsened.

Part 2: the development of a therapeutic intervention

Problem formulation and therapeutic plan

It was evident from the initial assessment that Sarah was experiencing the symptoms of both a severe depressive disorder and an anxiety disorder, which fulfilled the criteria of DSM-1V (American Psychiatric Association 1994). Subjectively, she described feeling low in mood, guilty and pessimistic about the future. She described feelings of panic about exams and performing medical procedures, which were excessive in comparison to her usual frame of mind. She also described obsessional thoughts about her medical school application and was beginning to catastrophise the consequences of 'being found out'. She described images of being humiliated and exposed as a 'fake' in the tabloid press and her family being hounded by journalists.

Following supervision it was agreed that the first stage in the therapeutic plan was to help Sarah reach a decision as to whether she would reveal her concerns to staff at the medical school. I felt that she would be unable to make progress until this decision was taken, as she was spending a great deal of time ruminating on the issue and the possible consequences. If Sarah made the decision not to discuss the matter with the university then my role would be to assist her to develop strategies to control her obsessional thoughts. Should Sarah agree to disclose the information then my role would be to support her through this process.

Sarah agreed with the plan and at the end of Session 2 I suggested that she discuss her difficulties further with her GP, in order to gain the opinion of another member of the medical profession. Information gathering and use of resources in this manner is an important step in the decision-making process (Johnson 1997). I also sought Sarah's approval to discuss the matter with her GP myself. I felt that it was important to determine his opinion of the professional and ethical implications.

The initial problem formulation also included the hypothesis that the maintenance of Sarah's depression and anxiety may have been exacerbated by unhelpful core beliefs about perfection and failure and the impossibly high standards that she sets herself.

In summary the following plan was agreed:

- A decision-making process would be encouraged in respect of her disclosure to the medical school. I would support Sarah, assisting her to develop strategies to overcome her anxiety, whatever the outcome of this decision.
- Following this process, we would look at her underlying core beliefs, with a view to challenging those which resulted in automatic negative thoughts and unhelpful behaviours.

The content of therapy and techniques employed

Session 3

Sarah had visited her GP and begun a course of antidepressant medication. She had asked for his opinion on the consequences of disclosing her academic history to her medical school and was told that he felt this would be dealt with as a 'welfare' matter and would be unlikely, in his opinion, to result in exclusion from the course. Sarah did not feel reassured by this. When I asked her to rate the likelihood of a negative outcome, she rated it as 9/10. I asked her to rate the outcome in the eyes of her GP, which she scored as 1/10. She was unable to explain the discrepancy in opinion and remained fairly convinced that she would lose her place.

With this in mind we drew up a decisional balance chart (Butler and Hope 1995). This involved looking at the advantages and disadvantages of disclosing or not disclosing the information. Ultimately, Sarah came to the conclusion that she could not continue with the anxiety of not disclosing.

She decided that even if the outcome were negative she would feel no worse than she did at the moment. On the other hand should the outcome be positive she felt that this would, in her own words, 'allow me to get on with my life and career plan'. We examined the feelings that Sarah experienced on making this decision and these were feelings of relief. This reinforced her decision further.

At the end of the session we briefly examined her relationship with her husband. This had been mentioned in the referral letter as a source of some difficulty. Sarah was of the opinion that since the initial screening appointment their relationship had improved and she saw her husband's feelings about starting a family as positive in this respect. She did, however, describe feeling disappointed that he did not show her much physical affection. It appeared that lack of communication was an issue here and Sarah agreed to discuss this with him further.

Session 4

Sarah had discussed her worries with staff at the medical school. She had received reassurance that she would not be asked to leave the course. The medical school would, however, have to investigate the matter further and this involved checking that the information she had included in her application was correct, i.e. that she had attended the universities listed and received the qualifications described.

Sarah described the past two weeks as extremely difficult. She had not been attending lectures and for two days had been unable to get out of bed. She described feelings of panic and terror. She had talked to her husband about her feelings and felt that he had been making an effort to show affection. She also described her father as a source of strength. I used this opportunity to examine what strategies Sarah found helpful when she was feeling anxious. We identified that distraction techniques had been most successful and made a note to return to this later in therapy.

In view of the fact that Sarah had made her decision and acted upon it, we were ready to move to stage two of the therapeutic plan. In her own words, her goal for treatment had now become 'to modify my personality so that I do not worry excessively'.

Session 5

The transition to the next stage of therapy was not smooth. Sarah had not received details of the outcome of the medical school investigation. She had been provided with reassurance verbally, but could not accept the matter was over until she received a formal notice. We focused on anxiety management and relaxation techniques. Sarah was given a tape to practise a tense-and-release method of muscle relaxation (Payne 1995). The benefits were explained and she was educated about the cycle of anxiety. Despite her medical background Sarah had not fully appreciated the effectiveness of such techniques in breaking into this cycle at a physiological level.

During this session, it also became apparent that Sarah's tendency towards obsessive behaviour went beyond obsessive ruminations. She described having not played golf, for example, for the past two years for fear of injuring someone with a golf ball. She also described checking behaviour at home and when out driving the car. I suggested to Sarah that this behaviour could be explained in terms of providing a release from anxiety; although the root of the anxiety may not be directly relevant to the behaviour.

Sarah appeared to relate to this model and on that basis I was able to inform her of useful techniques such as distraction, which she had previously found effective, thought stopping and other methods typically used in cases of obsessive-compulsive disorder (Emmelkamp et al. 1992). She was encouraged to reinforce her own confidence when doing things by making deliberate statements such as 'I am now turning off the gas' and 'I have turned off the gas', or consciously forming a distinctive image of herself undertaking the task (Tallis 1995). She was also encouraged to practise relaxation techniques when avoiding the compulsion to check, as an alternative way of reducing anxiety.

Session 6

Sarah reported feeling in a better mood and more positive about the future. She was still awaiting a formal letter regarding the investigation, however interim reports had been good. In the recent past Sarah had felt a 'fake' at medical school and undeserving of her place. I asked her to rate this feeling, to which she replied that two months ago she would have said she felt one per cent like a 'real' doctor and now she felt ninety-five per cent a 'real' doctor.

She had also managed to increase her activity levels, resuming some of her past interests and hobbies. In addition she felt that her relationship with her husband was stronger. They were both looking forward to a holiday that they had booked and to moving to a bigger house.

It was acknowledged that despite her current more positive mood, Sarah had a predisposition to anxious and depressive episodes, and that there was a need to re-evaluate some of her beliefs in order to prevent relapse. This session was spent looking at some of her negative automatic thoughts, which were then challenged and reappraised. For example, Sarah held a strong belief that she should always maintain the highest moral standards and that anything else was unforgivable. She was asked to consider whether she held these standards for others and her father was used as an example. Sarah has great respect for her father, however she is able to accept that her father's behaviour had been 'less than perfect' when he had an affair during Sarah's teens, without this respect being diminished. In addition, using circular questioning techniques from systemic therapy (Burham 1986), I asked Sarah to imagine what other significant people in her life would say about her own actions. The aim here was to encourage Sarah to be less critical of herself and more accepting of her own human fallibility.

Session 7

Sarah had received a letter from the medical school stating that the matter had been investigated and no further action would be taken. She described feeling extremely happy with this outcome and much more positive about the future. We reviewed the work of the last few sessions and Sarah reported using distraction techniques to prevent obsessional thoughts and behaviours. She had practised, and was able to apply, muscle relaxation when feeling anxious. She also reported having reappraised her standards and had decided that it was important to have a balance in her life between home, work and socialising. She stated that this was ultimately the best for her patients too, indicating a cognitive shift in her beliefs about perfection.

Sarah had not sat her final exams and felt that she would like the option of another appointment, in six weeks' time, to review progress and discuss any difficulties that might have arisen. This appointment was made with a view to discharge.

Session 8

Sarah arrived at the appointment a little late having been caught in traffic. Nevertheless she looked relaxed and happy. She informed me that she had passed her final exams at medical school and had taken up her new House Officer post, which she thoroughly enjoyed. She had also become an aunt recently and was enjoying this new role and looking forward to having a family of her own. Her relationship with her husband was stronger than ever.

We reviewed, once again, the strategies for overcoming anxiety and obsessional behaviour. We also identified the major changes that she had been able to make in her thinking. Sarah was encouraged to monitor her mood and anxiety levels carefully and apply the appropriate techniques that she had developed in order to manage her distress. She was also encouraged to request a rereferral should this be necessary in the future. Finally, Sarah completed the BDI, which was now scored within the normal range.

The use of supervision

Supervision was very important in the work with this client, as there were, potentially, ethical and professional issues involved. When Sarah described her omission from the medical school application form, and the fabrication at her interview, it was important to determine whether or not withholding this information had ethical implications. I sought the advice of my supervisor, who in turn spoke to the head of our department. I also spoke to Sarah's GP, with her permission. The consensus of opinion was that this issue was fairly trivial and that the most important factor was her current ability to perform her professional duties. It was agreed that it was essential that Sarah developed the strategies necessary to manage her anxiety and depression.

Part 3: review and conclusions

Review of therapy

The content

The content of therapy, from a cognitive-behavioural perspective, is driven by the view that unhelpful cognitions, which have developed over many years, are triggered by an event. The resulting behaviour causes distress and further unhelpful cognitions (Beck 1967).

In this case it is likely that Sarah had developed core beliefs which were rigid, with elements of black-and-white thinking (Burns 1980). Her drive for perfection resulted in obsessive behaviour and unrealistic standards. It is also likely that she learnt her anxious behaviour in childhood, which was evident from the history taking. The matter of disclosing her omission to medical school may have appeared trivial to others but for Sarah, with her rigid beliefs and obsessional nature, this was of enormous significance and had to be addressed.

As a result the content of therapy was divided into two discreet pieces of work. The first was to help Sarah with the decision-making process concerning medical school issue. The outcome of the decision was almost irrelevant but a decision had to be taken in order to move on. The second stage involved a typical cognitive-behavioural approach to anxiety, depression and obsessive-compulsive traits.

A difficulty that arose was my own initial reluctance to 'state the obvious'. It is a necessary part of CBT to educate the client into the model but, as I was acutely aware of Sarah's own medical background, I was cautious about pitching information at the right level. I now see, with hindsight, that I could have made this easier for myself by being more open, with statements such as 'please stop me if you know this already'. The tendency on my part was to avoid.

The process

Sarah worked well within the cognitive-behavioural framework. It was particularly interesting to observe her initial lack of insight into her own anxiety. She felt that she did not 'deserve' to be depressed or anxious because, as she stated, her life was 'quite perfect'. The reality that emerged during the history taking was, however, very different and Sarah had, in fact, experienced a number of traumatic events. The realisation of this and the powerful effects the traumas must have had was almost reassuring for her. She was somehow able to reattribute the blame to events out of her control. This view can be supported by theories of attribution that differentiate external and internal control (Bem 1972).

It is possible that this was the turning point for Sarah. The ability to recognise that she cannot control everything, allowed her the freedom to be less than perfect. Hopefully this shift in perspective will reduce her obsessional drive for perfection and consequently reduce the resultant anxiety that such obsessive behaviour brings.

It was noticeable during the sessions that Sarah had an appeasing nature. She was very reluctant to accept praise for her positive attributes and behaviours. It was a little disappointing that at the end of therapy she felt that progress had been made because of the input of her GP, me and seroxat. I felt that my attempts to reassure her, that we had supported and guided her but that the decisions and changes were her own, were futile. Without this realisation I am concerned that she may well still lack the confidence to be able to deal with new, anxiety-provoking situations that might arise in the future. In other words, she may be unable to generalise what she has learnt in therapy.

Conclusion

The use of standardised questionnaires is one method of measuring the success of a therapeutic intervention. In this case there was strong evidence that Sarah's levels of psychological distress had been significantly reduced. Subjectively, Sarah reported feeling more confident and happy with herself.

The concern that remains is whether, given the number of sessions, Sarah can generalise what was achieved. In the final session we had spent time reviewing the strategies that had worked best. It is to be hoped that she can continue to utilise what she has learnt beyond therapy. It may be that 'top-up' sessions will be required in the future. I feel quite strongly that for clients who have had time-limited therapy the option of rereferral should be made explicit. In CBT books, this is recommended as good practice for ending therapy (Hawton et al. 1989).

In summary, I feel that this case study was an example of how therapy can assist individuals to deal with immediate problems and avoid crises. Such help can then be followed by an attempt to challenge and shift unhelpful core beliefs for long-term positive change.

References

American Psychiatric Association (1994). *Diagnostic and Statistical Manual of Mental Disorders*, 4th edn (DSM-1V). Washington DC: APA.

Beck, A.T. (1967). *Depression: Clinical, Experimental and Theoretical Aspects*. New York: Harper Row.

Beck, A.T. (1996). *Beck Depression Inventory II*. The Psychological Corporation. San Antonio: Harcourt Brace.

Beck, A.T., Rush, A.J., Shaw, B.F. and Emery, G. (1979). *Cognitive Therapy of Depression*. New York: Guilford Press.

Bem, D.J. (1972). Self-perception theory. In L. Berkowitz (ed.) *Advances in Experimental Social Psychology*, vol. 6. New York: Academic Press.

Burnham, J.B. (1986). *Family Therapy*. London: Routledge.

Burns, D. (1980). *Feeling Good: the New Mood Therapy*. New York: New American Library.

Butler, G. and Hope, T. (1995). *Manage Your Mind*. Oxford: Oxford University Press.

Derogatis, L.R. (1975). *Brief Symptom Inventory*. Minneapolis: National Computer Systems, Inc.

Emmelkamp, P., Bouman, T. and Scholing, A. (1992). *Anxiety Disorders – A Practitioner's Guide*. Chichester: Wiley.

Hawton K., Salkovskis, J. and Clark, D.M. (1989). *Cognitive Behaviour Therapy for Psychiatric Problems*. Oxford: Oxford Medical Publications.

Johnson, S.L. (1997). *Therapist's Guide to Clinical Intervention*. San Diego: Academic Press.

Payne, R.A. (1995). *Relaxation Techniques, a Practical Handbook for the Health Care Professional*. London: Churchill Livingstone.

Rogers, C.R. (1951). *Client-centred Therapy*. London: Constable.

Tallis, F. (1995). *Obsessive Compulsive Disorder: a Cognitive and Neuropsychological Perspective*. Chichester: Wiley.

Appendix A

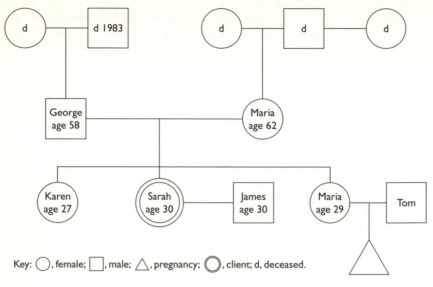

Key: ◯, female; ▢, male; △, pregnancy; ◎, client; d, deceased.

Figure 4   Genogram of family members discussed by Sarah.

Chapter 13

Historical truths versus a sense of integrity: developing a frame of mind to enable letting go

with a case study by Jo Ploszajski

PRELUDE

Our work as therapists entails making choices. There are always costs and benefits to all the decisions we take and the experienced therapist will entertain a range of foreseeable implications of the options available. This case reflects something of this psychotherapeutic inevitability, as the author intentionally validates the client's reality, in the understanding that such an intervention may be seen as antithetical and contraindicated by alternative conceptualisations of the problem. The author's account is illustrative of the therapeutic axiom, 'everything our clients do, they do for good reason'. Counsellors do well to remember this proposition as it implores the discovery of cause, rather than the deft elimination of the troublesome aspects of the client's cognitive, emotional and behavioural repertoire.

Indeed, symptoms are often solutions to problems that have their origins in a time and place where the alternatives that may be available today were well out of reach. Therapy conducted with the purpose of understanding the complex intentionality of seemingly problematic behaviour moves at a measured pace. This case illustrates the importance of evaluating the protective function of defensive behaviour and ensuring viable alternatives are available before questions relating to the desirability of known ways of being are tackled therapeutically.

The author's work with her client explores her own process of risk-taking in therapy. In every therapy session, therapists are faced with a set of circumstances not encountered before and so constantly have to synthesise interventions based on probability rather than certainty. In brief therapy the potential need for risk-taking is high when clients present with deep-rooted problems and the time available to help is short. As a novice therapist Jo Ploszajski suggests that she probably erred on the side of caution, and frequently let opportunities to work with core aspects of her client's psyche go unexploited. This case, in contrast, captures the risk of pushing historical limits of practice and illustrates the tensions involved in taking therapeutic responsibility. This case study provides us with a unique opportunity to catch a glimpse of the process of my risk-taking, in order to prompt us to think about the potential value for both client and therapist that may be imbued in the therapist moving out of the comfort of the known, familiar and routine.

> *Jo Ploszajski wrote this client study in the last stage of her training prior to chartership as a Counselling Psychologist at City University. Her reflective comments were added, for the purposes of this publication, within a month or two of her writing the original report.*

Preamble

Reflection on constructing the case study

In constructing the case study, it was inevitable that I had to present a selection of material from the sixteen sessions. I aimed to show how therapy progressed from exploration and early partial resolutions, during which I learned about my client's ability to manage distress, to seizing an opportunity precipitated by the anxiety produced by the proximity of ending (and thus to facing what is feared), followed by the process of reconstruction. I selected material to illustrate both the general pattern and the detail of my thoughts relating to key interventions. Inevitably, some material is left out and I do have a feeling of regret that only part of the story has been told. In some ways, the need to be selective left me with a feeling that I have not done justice to the quality of my client's input. However, I am also aware of the need to achieve a balance between preparing an academic document for assessment and doing justice to the precious, real-life experiences of both me and my client.

Learning

As I reflect upon my work now, I feel surprised by how much information we, as therapists, process. In my own experience, much of the information is not fully articulated, unless reconstructed in the form of a case study. Seeing it laid out in this way, I realise how the articulation of case formulations helps to provide therapists with greater assurance in their work. From this case, it seems to me that risk-taking requires having a very clear grasp of the case formulation with accompanying hypotheses of the client's fears and needs. Then, when an opportunity presents, indicating readiness to move behind a particular defence, the therapist is able to act within the moment. This analysis has alerted me to the need to become increasingly sensitive to how and when clients do provide these 'windows of opportunity', which all too quickly close again if not taken up.

CASE STUDY

Introduction

This case study was chosen as an illustration of how the client's experience of being believed in therapy may enable them to let go of destructive behaviour patterns without the need for an objective appraisal of historical truth. In this case, I shall describe how it seemed that even though this client had been treated for paranoid delusions, the ego strength he gained from having his story heard and believed, seemed to enable him to accept past injustice, let go of his anger and begin to rebuild his life. During the therapy, I was aware that I took a risk in stating my belief in the objective truth of my client's narrative, as it could be construed as colluding in a delusion and potentially antitherapeutic. Perhaps, therefore, this publication of how and when counsellors take risks will provide greater insights into the appropriate circumstances for risk-taking in therapy.

The setting

I met John as part of my work as a counsellor in a clinic for people with substance abuse problems (the clinic). The clinic provides a four-month, residential, therapeutic programme, plus six months', non-residential, after-care for eight clients. The aim of the clinic is to enable clients to learn to manage their lives without the need for drugs or alcohol. As one part of this learning process, counselling is offered for one hour, once per week, while clients are resident at the clinic.

John had been referred to the clinic for alcohol dependence by the Substance Abuse Unit of the Health Service, having undergone a successful home 'detox' six weeks prior to admission and remained abstinent. He appeared, therefore, to be in a promising state of physical and psychological readiness to begin therapeutic work.

Theoretical orientation

Clients arrive at the clinic at different points in the cycle of change (Prochaska and Di Clementi 1982), so that the programme aims to provide a range of information, social-skills training and opportunities for insight. On the whole the more cognitive and behavioural aspects of change are addressed in group work, while the exploration of self and relationships tends to be addressed more during individual counselling. The brief supportive psychodynamic counselling model that I use is based on Rockland (1989). This model was chosen because it takes a flexible approach to the extent to which a more exploratory or supportive emphasis may be adopted to accommodate individual needs. The model aims to strengthen ego function by developing a more 'realistic' sense of self in a more 'realistic' world, largely through clarification of the details of clients' accounts of experience and confrontation with any internal conflicts revealed (Rockland 1989, see his Appendix 1 for an outline of the theory and techniques). Because the work is brief and clients' ego strength is known to be weak through their poor impulse control, regression is minimised.

In addition to the structure provided by Rockland, it is sometimes helpful to follow Malan (1995) in linking hidden feeling, defence and anxiety, but this is rarely shared overtly with clients. However, issues of dependency, which generally seem to underlie clients' needs for alcohol, are addressed directly, using attachment theory and the techniques which focus on present patterns of behaviour recommended by Bowlby (1979). My own experience of people with alcohol problems accords with Liebeskind's (1991) view that the work of therapy is largely about re-establishing clients' need for people, and Holmes' (1996) work on autonomy versus intimate attachment styles provides a helpful, if sometimes over simplified, backdrop.

Towards the end of therapy, work shifts towards a more conscious appraisal of learning and the development of relapse prevention strategies, in order to create a coherent whole and a structure for ending. This approach fits with Prochaska and Di Clementi's transtheoretical analysis that exploratory work is followed by more cognitive work towards the action and maintenance phases of change (Prochaska and Di Clementi 1982). At this stage, I aim to create a balance of imagery and verbal cognitions, drawing on the strategies identified by Marlatt and Gordon (1985) and a balance of autonomous and shared strategies for coping with emotional arousal (Holmes 1996). The flexibility of Rockland's approach means that relapse-prevention strategies are incorporated as supportive work and remain congruent with the overall model.

Initial meeting

John arrived at the first session with a 'bright and breezy' air; his fleeting eye contact and quick 'matter-of-fact' speech suggested to me that he felt anxious about the intimacy of the counselling relationship and that sharing personal experience may not be too easy for him. He appeared casually dressed in jeans and a football shirt. He was clean but untidy and his curly hair falling over his eyes and ears gave the impression of some adolescent personal neglect.

As with all clients, I began by outlining what I thought I could offer in the time we had together, which was likely to be about fifteen sessions. I also explained the limits of confidentiality and gained John's permission to use material from our work together for training assessment.

John, who was now 37 years old, described a series of misfortunes during the past twelve years, which seemed to start when his three-year relationship with his girlfriend began to go wrong shortly after their son was born and she developed some mental-health problems. John spoke about how he gave up his work as a computer programmer to care for his son, but his girlfriend became more and more unstable and had a number of affairs, one of which John believed was with his brother. Their relationship ended when John's son was four; his girlfriend was awarded custody of their child and the family home.

John also described how, at around this time, his mother had died and his father had developed senile dementia. When he lost his home, he returned to live with his father and care for him, struggling to cope with his father's increasing dependence and the demands of his own work. John was the fifth of seven children and he bitterly resented the fact that his brothers and sisters, several of whom lived locally, didn't offer to help with his father's care. He also began to feel that the legal fraternity, mortgage company, local housing authority and medical services were against him and he was treated for paranoid delusions (he was currently taking medication for depression and psychotic symptoms). He became angry and violent about the injustice of the loss of his son and what he saw as his family's cover-up of his brother's behaviour. John further explained that as a consequence of his feelings of rage, he had behaved recklessly and had received convictions for criminal damage and drink-driving. Shortly after these events, John suffered a spinal injury which led to surgery and the need to give up his sports and fitness regime. As John became more socially isolated and depressed, his drinking escalated. Approximately eighteen months ago, his father's mental and physical health deteriorated and John was no longer able to care for him at home. Against John's will, he was taken into residential care and John moved to live alone. From that time, he became very isolated, drinking around ten to fifteen units of alcohol daily, well above the safe limit of three to four units.

John spoke about these events without showing emotion but recognised that his anger was a consequence of feeling unable to make people listen to him and acknowledge his view of events. He felt that he could accept that he had been wrong to act aggressively, but he wanted the other parties involved to take some responsibility for the damage which he felt had been done to him. John also explained that, what he wanted to achieve through counselling was to be able to draw a line under these experiences and to move on.

Initial hypothesis and formulation

John's present manner and the indications that he had been alienated from his friends and family suggested that he may have some difficulty with closeness in relationships and that he may have used alcohol in an attempt to blot out the painful feelings of helplessness and rejection. His attachment style seemed characteristic of the 'avoidant person' described by Holmes (1996), who is: '. . . detached but not autonomous. He longs for intimacy but fears he will be rejected: he hovers on the shores of intimacy ever fearful of taking the plunge' (p. 20).

It also seemed that the disinhibiting effect of alcohol had allowed John's anger to surface. In John's case, Malan's triangle of anxiety, defensive behaviour and hidden feeling may be interpreted thus:

> John felt powerless or weak in his relationships with his girlfriend and siblings and perhaps felt that authority figures were either self-interested or indifferent to his needs. This defensively led him to avoid contact, or, when disinhibited through alcohol, to act aggressively in an attempt to protect his ego from the insult of rejection. The implication of this hypothesis could suggest that John's hidden impulse might be to seek protective nurturence and indeed, later in therapy, John indicated that to be seen as weak, hurt or self-nurturent would be scorned in his social group.

Rockland (1989) advises that all defences should be evaluated for their protective function and only undermined if the anticipated advantages clearly outweigh the disadvantages. It seemed that John's intellectual ability may be helpful in facilitating being able to think about his experience, but his intellectual distance from his feelings, although a mature defence, may have contributed to his difficulties in forming close relationships and meaningful communications with others. Within the therapeutic relationship, I was aware that John's emotional inhibition created a sense of his autonomy, which might be misleading if it disguised his feeling of vulnerability. However, I was also aware that John's inhibition could also be a consequence of his medication and/or the fact that he lacked strategies for self-regulation. I thought, therefore, that although it might be helpful to John to develop more ability to express feelings, it would be wise to proceed cautiously with expressive work until the extent to which he had developed strategies for managing his feelings was clear.

Although John was being treated for paranoid delusions, it seemed possible that his perception of events was fairly accurate and that his anger could be proportionate, if inappropriately expressed (O'Neill 1999). However, it appeared that his behaviour had resulted in further losses and that it might be helpful to him to recognise this and explore alternative behaviours (Bowlby 1979). From my formulation, it appeared that Rockland's combination of clarification and confrontation within a supportive framework would be appropriate to my work with John.

Consequently, my strategy for proceeding was to begin by trying to establish what might be salvaged from the past (relationship with siblings, home, work, friends, hobbies, a sense of justice, etc.), and also discover which of these might need to be mourned as losses. It also seemed likely that John would need the support of some problem-solving and interpersonal-skills training, much of which would be supplied within the clinic group work.

The development of the therapy

Therapy began with John considering whether he could take any action to restore his sense of justice. What seemed important to John was that his siblings should acknowledge the damage they had done to him through denying and distorting, although John was ready to acknowledge his wrongdoing too. However, as he prepared a letter to send to his siblings explaining his views, he began to have doubts about whether his family would listen to him, as there seemed to be a family pattern of avoiding. We spent some time too, talking about whether John's memory of familial closeness prior to the start of his problems was perhaps a fantasy. Over the course of a few sessions, it seemed that John's feeling of hopelessness over being understood was, on another level, also an acknowledgment of the apparent reality that his brothers and sisters tended to be self-interested. Through the process of clarification and confrontation, John began to accept loss of hope for familial closeness, and these feelings were accompanied by sadness as he let go of his fantasy.

John also became aware that his anger had fuelled a desire for revenge, which seemed to have resulted in him being further hurt, and we talked about the possibility of converting the feelings of anger into feelings of determination to construct a more satisfying future (O'Neill 1999). With anger, I have often felt that expressive work alone is unhelpful, even when traced back to its historical roots in the family. If there is no present focus through which to address the anger, it can leave the client as frustrated as before. Consequently, I have found that after acknowledging the source of anger and its justification, encouraging clients to consider the consequences of their behaviour, together with its advantages and disadvantages (Bowlby 1979), seems to lead to a greater sense of 'mastery' and resolution.

These first steps towards greater ego strength through acceptance of reality were followed by discussions of human limitations, and John observed that he may have been naive in assuming that everyone should abide by the same very high moral standards that he set for himself. John also spoke of his feeling of internal fragility and his sadness at the death of his mother, which I thought might indicate a willingness to risk letting me see his vulnerability. During this stage of acceptance and readjustment, we talked about the reality of injustice within broad bands of justice, and John's own thought that many people, such as ambassadors, negotiate with regimes that they dislike for the sake of wider peace of mind. With this thought, John began to see a way of maintaining his own integrity, without the need for those to whom he attributed wrongdoing, either family or acquaintances, to agree with him. Speaking to them did not necessarily mean acquiescence. This strategy was probably appealing to John, because it drew on his strength of autonomy and allowed him to give up hope of intimacy where it appeared to be hopeless; it did not require the more anxiety-provoking need to attempt greater intimacy (Holmes 1996).

This phase of therapy was characterised by John oscillating between looking forward to glimpses of possible egosyntonic future ways of living, and opening up the painful feelings of being his forced out of the family and neighbourhood. We explored the possibility of reconstruing feelings of rejection more egosyntonically, as John choosing to leave in order to protect himself (Rockland 1989). We noticed, too, how John, in coping with present problems, tended to overgeneralise and split perceptions into all good and all bad, and to take things personally, suggesting a somewhat immature egocentricity (Klein 1987). We were able to address this splitting and projection fairly successfully, simply by looking at the real details of the circumstances (Rockland 1989).

Resolution and confrontation

By Session 10, it seemed that John was still struggling with the idea of letting go of the past. It was likely that we only had about six sessions remaining and, since John showed a number of obsessional traits characteristic of avoidant attachment style (Holmes 1996) and could fear letting go, I felt that something different was needed to move him on. In supervision I had discussed the strategies that I might adopt to help John decide whether he wanted to confront his siblings or not and we talked through what else might need to be different for him to be able to let go of the past; we also discussed my feeling that for John, talking therapy could reinforce his intellectual vacillations and could collude with his avoidance of confronting his feelings.

As session ten began to unfold, however, something in John's demeanour indicated that he seemed more emotionally expressive and, I hypothesised, more prepared to entertain change. I thought that it might be helpful to take a risk in confronting him with his hidden feeling, the fear of being weak. I judged that John had gained ego strength through his experience at the clinic, which seemed to have facilitated greater intimacy in therapy. I therefore decided to reinforce both trust and intimacy, by stating that I believed that John had been treated unjustly but perhaps realistically there was no hope of justice. I put to John the possibility that letting go of the past might mean facing up to not having been able to protect himself, that the battle was over and perhaps he had lost. Maybe the hope of justice had gone.

While we talked, our seats were at an angle of about 120 degrees. John's body was turned away from me, but he repeatedly glanced back at me over his shoulder, which I thought indicated a wish both to face and to avoid. He also appeared to have tears in his eyes. I spoke very gently and acknowledged how painful it must feel to let go of hope and accept that you were vulnerable, but also I acknowledged the courage that it took to face the fear and reminded John of the strength and stability of the clinic, which he could draw on to help him cope. As this was a moment for mourning the loss of hope, my aim was to share John's sense of loss and to offer care in the form of acceptance and concern for his feelings (Bowlby 1980), rather than to attempt reconstruction.

At the end of this session, I encouraged John to ask for help from the staff if he felt unduly distressed, and I alerted the staff to the possibility that he may need extra attention to work through some of his feelings.

In confronting John in this way, I took two risks. First, that he had the ego strength to cope and second, that expressing unconditional belief in John's story would be experienced as validating and ego strengthening, rather than reinforcing a delusion, the consequence of which might have been to strengthen his anger and undermine the possibility of taking a different approach to regaining a sense of self-efficacy.

It appeared that the risk I took paid off, as during the next session John described how he'd begun to realise that he needed to listen to feedback from the other residents and to adapt, as he sometimes got lost in ruminations about the past. This seemed to be an indication of a move towards a new, viable intimacy. I was also aware of a transference from John that I was somehow holding him back. This might have reflected John's childhood experience of being held back by limiting parents, or it may have been a projection of John's own anxiety which itself was holding him back. Rather than make the transference/projection explicit, as this is often confusing in brief therapy, and our time was running out, I chose instead to refuse to engage with the transference/projection and was both supportive and encouraging of his thoughts towards the future. Together we developed the metaphor of the journey to recovery, and accepted that the steps along the way could be enjoyed without necessarily having a clear picture of where the journey was leading (Wanigaratne et al. 1990). This also seemed to symbolise a way for John to tolerate the anxiety of not knowing what his eventual destination might be.

Conclusion of the therapy and review

Ending

In the remaining four sessions, we focused on strategies for coping with setbacks and self-soothing behaviours that could replace drinking. We also reviewed learning and awareness of high-risk situations. In line with Marlatt and Gordon's relapse prevention strategies (1985), John developed an image of his recovery as like driving a car up hill. He envisaged that it was when the car stalled and began to slide back that he would feel overwhelmed, lose hope and feel in need of a drink. Consequently, we developed other images of ropes and cables to hold the car if it stalled, These represented the staff at the clinic, fellow residents and other sources of help and advice. Having a number of interests, for example getting a pet, starting a college course, decorating his home, etc., was also seen as a collection of 'ropes', so if one broke there were others to turn to. John also had the idea that the information I had provided for him on future sources of counselling, was like a grappling hook that he could throw out if he felt that he was really sliding back!

As we discussed coping strategies, I repeatedly fed in questions to elicit John's thoughts on his need for other people and the role that they might play in the future. Although John seemed aware that people might be called upon for help, he didn't seem to see forming relationships as prophylactic, and I concluded inwardly that he was not yet ready to address the possibly still deeply hidden impulse for nurturence, care and intimacy. Furthermore, although I opened up the issue for discussion, as John showed little awareness of a sense of loss of our counselling relationship, I did not labour the issue of our ending, as I felt that despite signs of change, John's avoidant attachment style (Holmes 1996) would probably make it difficult for him to be aware of a sense of need at this stage. I was surprised, therefore, by the importance with which John viewed our follow-up sessions, perhaps indicating a preconscious awareness of a need for others, which might be expressed more consciously in time.

Some evidence of the extent of John's greater ego strength occurred in his final week at the clinic, when he marginally failed a random alcohol test. Rather than feeling unjustly accused and responding destructively, he calmly worked back over all of his contacts and realised that he had come into contact with someone who had used an alcohol based perfume, which he had absorbed through his skin. John had clearly learned new strategies for coping with distress and was gaining in self-esteem through their successful application (Marlatt and Gordon 1985).

Follow up

After John left the clinic as a resident, he continued to attend group sessions as a non-resident, and we met for two follow-up sessions, two weeks and six weeks after his leaving. The main themes in these sessions were ensuring a sense of balance between keeping busy and self-care through relaxation, 'time-off' and rewards (Marlatt and Gordon 1985). John commented that he had been surprised by how well he had coped, which led to some discussion of whether he might underestimate his ability. Overall, John felt that the most important thing that he had learned about himself was that by listening to others and listening to 'feedback' within himself, he was able to regulate his feelings of angry arousal. This was interesting, as his initial complaint had been that others didn't listen to him! I wondered whether his experience of being heard and accepted in therapy was a catalyst to his own ability to listen and accept, forming the first steps towards intimacy with others. Our last counselling session was three months prior to the time of writing this case study and John had remained abstinent from alcohol, reporting that he felt his confidence growing by the day.

Evaluation of the therapy

I found working with John very rewarding. Despite his fears of internal disintegration, it seemed that he felt sufficiently 'held' by the supportive environment at the clinic, to enable him to accept some unconscious fears, learn new skills for coping with the fears and let go of some of his fantasies about past ways of relating and thus adjust to a more realistic relationship with his social world. I believe that the risk that I took in creating 'reality' from the 'unknown' with respect to the degree to which John had been unjustly treated was justified, in that my belief in his judgement seemed to provide the ego strength to allow him to acknowledge those parts of his story which were wishful thinking, and therefore create better adjustment to reality. The risk was that I might have appeared to 'side' with John in his feelings of injustice and thus fuel his feelings of anger. However, I think that my stance of supporting his feelings, while holding out the possibility of finding a way to restore a feeling of integrity without redress, seemed to show John a way that he could regain a sense of control over his circumstances, which enabled letting go and reintegration.

Mollon (1998) has provided guidelines on the risks of creating false memories in therapy and the internal experience of belief, even when the 'true' events were different, and this is certainly something that therapists need to take into account in working with historical material. What seems important is how one reconstructs stories and how the client then acts as a consequence of re-storying. I am aware of a number of anecdotal accounts from mothers of how their children have reconstructed their memories of events to make them more egosyntonic, so that it appears that this kind of reconstruction may occur as a natural prophylactic. However, more research is needed into how similar reconstructions occur in therapy, when access to 'the truth' is unattainable.

In my work with John, I was also able to explore my skills in using imagery and metaphor as a way of gaining objectivity. Interest in this area seems to be developing and through my work I have observed that methods for obtaining a more objective view of self are valuable in developing clients' ability to control impulsive behaviour. In this case, I realised that sharing my imagery seemed to help John to develop his own images and metaphor, however, I would like to develop my skills in this further, perhaps through training in the techniques of hypnosis.

References

Bowlby, J. (1979). *The Making and Breaking of Affectional Bonds*. London: Tavistock.

Bowlby, J. (1980). *Loss: Sadness and Depression*. London: Pimlico.

Holmes, J. (1996). *Attachment Intimacy Autonomy: Using Attachment Theory in Adult Psychotherapy*. London: Jason Aronson.

Klein, J. (1987). *Our Need for Others and its Roots in Infancy*. London: Routledge.

Liebeskind, A.S. (1991). Chemical dependency and the denial of the need for intimacy. In A. Smaldine (ed.) *Psychoanalytic Approaches to Addiction*. New York: Brunner Mazel.

Malan, D.H. (1995). *Individual Psychotherapy and the Science of Psychodynamics*, 2nd edn. Oxford: Butterworth-Heinemann.

Marlatt, G.A. and Gordon, J.R. (1985). *Relapse Prevention: Maintenance Strategies in the Treatment of Addictive Behaviours*. London: Guilford Press.

Mollon, P. (1998). *Remembering Trauma: a Psychotherapists Guide to Memory and Illusion*. Chichester: Wiley.

O'Neill, H. (1999). *Managing Anger*. London: Whurr.

Prochaska, J.O. and Di Clementi, C.C. (1982). Transtheoretical therapy: towards a more integrative model of change. *Psychotherapy: Theory, Research & Practice*, 19, 276–288.

Rockland, L. (1989). *Supportive Therapy a Psychodynamic Approach*. New York: Basic Books.

Wanigaratne, S., Pullin, J., Wallace, W., Keaney, F. and Farmer, R. (1990). *Relapse Prevention for Addictive Behaviours: a Manual for Therapists*. London: Blackwell.

Chapter 14

Depression: a case study

with a case study by Amanda Evans

PRELUDE

Trainees sometimes tell us that they mostly find it easier to choose to present client case studies from within the client-centred or cognitive behavioural therapeutic approaches. This may, in part, be due to the perception that the core skills required appear straightforward and that there is a standard literature and series of references available to support the trainees' interpretations. This is not always the case. Amanda Evans describes her therapy with a client, using a cognitive behavioural approach, but gives due consideration to three issues that make this a more complex case. First, the therapy takes place within a medical setting. Second, the therapy is required to be brief or time-limited. Third, the client has HIV infection. This case study provides extensive insight into the 'mind of the therapist' who must recognise and address her own feelings and conflicts when working with this client. It also demonstrates that our ability to recall what actually happened in sessions is seldom an objective or neutral account of the process. When preparing case studies, the description of what the therapist believed was transacted in the therapy sessions is usually the less contentious section for trainees. The appraisal of the effectiveness of the interventions used and outcomes invites the trainees to reflect on their confidence and competence as a therapists. In this case, Amanda gives an enlightening account of her therapy with this client which, in turn, makes the reader think, 'I wonder how I would have dealt with a similar case or reacted to this situation?'

> *Amanda Evans wrote this case study at the end of the second year of a part-time MSc course. The comments were written during the first year of her post-MSc practitioner diploma.*

Premable

In this case study, cognitive behavioural therapy (CBT) was used as the theoretical basis for intervention with a client who presented with some of the cognitive, emotional and behavioural symptoms associated with depression. I chose this case because it represented an example of short-duration therapy in a medical setting, where the client was able to use the therapeutic relationship and CBT methodology to tackle some of the automatic thoughts that were contributing to her distress. The case provided me with an opportunity to learn more about the application of CBT in the context of HIV infection, and to use supervision as a means of dealing with the feelings raised by working with HIV-positive clients.

This case gave me the opportunity to reflect on many aspects of the counselling process, the application of theory to practice, the development of the therapeutic relationship and the influence of the thoughts, feelings and inner conflicts of the therapist. Drafting and writing the case study was an interesting exercise in that it challenged me to try to distinguish between what actually happened and my subsequent memory and reconstruction of it. It underlined the value of cogent case notes made soon after a session. Writing a case study is a reflective process and, on this occasion, it allowed me to re-examine my own feelings about working with women of a similar age to me who are infected with HIV. Such reflection is all too often squeezed aside during the busy working day and yet is vital if we are to bring our own responses to clients into consciousness.

On reviewing this report I am aware that it reflects only a selected proportion of what occurred in the therapy, and I now think that I could have included more examples of how the client examined negative automatic thoughts and core beliefs. There is a balance to be drawn between focusing on the particular and providing an overview of the work done.

CASE STUDY

Theoretical framework

The cognitive model holds that cognitions are an important mediator of feelings and behaviour and that the interrelationship of the three types of experience plays an important role in the development and maintenance of psychological problems, including depression (Hawton et al. 1989).

The cognitive model of depression involves a two-tier model in which core assumptions, or schemata, formed in childhood, subsequently influence how individuals perceive and evaluate later experience (Beck et al. 1979). These assumptions are necessary for making sense of the world but, when overly rigid, erroneous or too extreme, can lead to depression after a precipitating critical event in later life. For example, the diagnosis of a life-threatening disease in someone making the assumption 'I must be perfect in order to be loved' may give rise to negative automatic thoughts (NATs) such as 'I'm not good enough to be in a relationship' or 'no-one will want me now'. NATs are thought to lead to the various symptoms of depression in the modalities of behaviour (withdrawal), emotion (guilt, anxiety), soma (lethargy, weight gain) and cognition (concentration). These, in turn, lead to more NATs that serve to maintain and intensify the experience of depression in a cyclical way. Beck (1967) recognises the presence of the 'cognitive triad' in depression where the individual manifests distorted thinking in the areas of the self, the world and the future. These cognitions are usually associated with the themes of loss, failure and lack of worth.

CBT aims to reduce symptoms in an enduring way by breaking the cycle of NATs leading to symptoms. This is undertaken by means of the identification and modification of NATs and the assumptions that underlie them. A variety of cognitive and behavioural methods are used including questioning of NATs, behavioural experiments and homework tasks, e.g. pleasure and mastery. Therapy occurs within the context of a therapeutic relationship characterised by 'collaborative empiricism'. Here, a client's thoughts, feelings and behaviour are seen as open to exploration and modification via discourse and experiment (Beck et al. 1979). The therapy also emphasises the learning of cognitive-behavioural skills that the client can utilise outside sessions and once the therapy has ended (Scott and Dryden 1996).

Organisational setting

The HIV Counselling Unit is based at a teaching hospital in London that offers comprehensive care to HIV-positive patients. A brief, focused counselling service is available to patients attending the HIV medical service. Patients may be at any stage of HIV infection from asymptomatic to advanced disease. Referrals are accepted from medical, nursing and other professional groups. Patients are also able to self-refer.

Client profile

Susan is a 40-year-old Afro-Caribbean woman living with HIV infection. She works as a teacher in a secondary school and is undergoing a specialist study programme. She is a single parent, living with her 10-year-old daughter, Sophie, and is in a six-year relationship with a male partner, Derek, who is HIV negative. Susan's parents moved to the UK from Trinidad in the 1950s and she is the youngest of four children. All the children live in the UK, the parents returned to the West Indies in the 1990s, where her father died in 1996.

Susan was diagnosed as HIV positive just before her father's death in 1996 after donating blood. The routine screening of donated blood by the

National Blood Transfusion Service detected her infection; she had no reason to suspect that she might be HIV positive before then. Her health is good and, at present, she doesn't need to take any medication. She attends the out-patient clinic for regular follow up. She was referred to the counselling unit at the time of her diagnosis when she saw another counsellor. She had used the service during her initial adjustment to the diagnosis and subsequent bereavement. Before the current referral she had disclosed her HIV status only to her partner and to two friends.

The referral

Susan rereferred herself to the counselling service as she felt she wasn't coping well with her life. She felt irritable towards her daughter, had taken a break from her studies, as she found them stressful, and had broken off the sexual side of her relationship with Derek. She doubted her abilities as a worker and mother and felt that she was unworthy in some way. She had also failed to attend a medical appointment, as she feared the outcome of her latest blood tests. As her status was secret within the family, Susan felt that she needed to talk to an outsider who might be able to facilitate her dealing with her emotional state before it became a bigger problem. She had found counselling helpful four years before and agreed to meet the counsellor for an assessment session.

Assessment and formulation

The assessment session involved evaluating Susan's symptoms, coping strategies and the suitability of using a cognitive-behavioural approach. Another aim was to attempt to establish a good therapeutic alliance, as this would be essential for the satisfactory progress and conclusion of therapy. I wanted to build an atmosphere of trust, through demonstrating a willingness to listen, empathy and non-judgemental concern. In this session I also hoped to establish some specific goals for therapy by which we could assess its effectiveness.

Susan presented as open and sophisticated in her use of counselling and saw herself as an active participant in the process. She readily identified NATs and was willing to share the emotional content of her experience. She felt that her current difficulties had developed gradually and had not followed a discrete event, although she did believe that her father's death 'blotted out' her response to her HIV diagnosis. She demonstrated no suicidal ideation or intent. She also reported that she felt poorly motivated and got less pleasure from her life than previously. She continued to attend to her daughter's needs, go to work and attend some social events.

Summary

Cognitive factors

All or nothing thinking, 'I can't cope with *everything* so I'm no good'; self-judgement, 'I'm a bad person for getting infected'; negative thoughts about herself, 'It's my own fault', the current situation, 'I'm not worthy of people's good opinion' and the future, 'Who'd want me now unless out of pity?', 'There's no point as I'm going to get ill anyway'.

Emotional factors

Shame, guilt, fear of rejection, fear of illness, sadness.

Behavioural factors

Withdrawal from sex in her relationship, withdrawal from career development, avoidance of medical results, irritability.

Physical factors

Disturbed sleep, physical tension.

Social factors

Perceived need for secrecy removed her usual coping strategy of talking to her sisters. Otherwise good social support.

It seemed that Susan was experiencing mildly depressive symptoms (she demonstrated few physical features, no suicidal thoughts, and the ability to maintain much of normal functioning). It is possible that the diagnosis of her HIV infection might have triggered dysfunctional assumptions about responsibility, worthiness and blame. These may then have led to the occurrence of NATs, which affected her perception of herself, the current situation and the future; the cognitive triad associated with depression (Beck et al. 1979). Self-blame and feelings of guilt associated with being HIV positive may then have contributed to NATs associated with worthiness and acceptability. It is possible that fears of rejection could lead to the avoidance of sexual intimacy as a protective coping strategy. Selective thinking may then have lead to a discounting of evidence that contradicted NATs, further contributing to the maintenance of her distress.

The issue of self-blame seemed central to her poor view of herself, her withdrawal from Derek and her continued secrecy with her sisters (normally a great source of support). It also seemed that Susan's coping mechanism, of avoiding the examination of the physical and social consequences of her HIV infection, contributed to the maintenance of depressive thoughts and feelings.

Susan showed an interest in the CBT approach and saw herself as an active participant in the counselling process. It appeared, then, that she might be able to utilise the collaborative nature of CBT and might be able to benefit from a short, focused therapy (Fennell 1989). Susan demonstrated the use of effective coping strategies in the past, had good social support and was optimistic about her capacity for change, further good prognostic indicators for this approach (Wills and Saunders 1997).

Contract

Susan and I agreed to meet for a further five sessions. She was amenable to the concept of homework tasks and her goals were to stop blaming herself for becoming HIV positive and to explore the possibility of further disclosure of her HIV status to her sisters and daughter. She agreed to monitor her NATs during the following week and read relevant photocopied material on depression and thinking errors from the *Mental Health Handbook* (Powell 1992).

Subsequent sessions

During subsequent sessions Susan identified and challenged several of her NATs around the issue of becoming HIV infected. We used the method of asking the questions, 'What is the evidence?', 'What alternative views are there?' and 'What logical errors am I making?'

We went through the narrative of how Susan had become infected via unprotected sex with a former boyfriend, and discussed what she could reasonably have been expected to know, and what precautions she should have taken. She was able to accept that, when she had slept with her ex-boyfriend, HIV was uncommon and unexpected within the Afro-Caribbean community and that she'd behaved in a way consistent with the behaviour of her contemporaries. It was interesting to note that the only family member that Susan had disclosed her status to so far was a 20-year-old niece with the primary objective of warning her to take heed of prevention initiatives. Thus, at some level, she believed that it could have happened to anyone and that she wasn't unusually to blame.

After session three, Susan did a homework task of 'talking' to her younger self who had become infected with HIV, appreciating her valuable qualities. She reported that she'd valued her former ambition, resilience and taste for life. Over the weeks of therapy she reported a decline in self-blaming NATs and an improvement in mood. She reported that she was focusing more on the future rather than ruminating about the past. She felt that she was finding a way of challenging her more harsh estimations of herself. This was reinforced with homework tasks that challenged her to itemise the achievements and abilities that she was proud of in her life, such as raising her daughter, being successful at work and being a valued family member and friend.

Another aspect of looking at the impact of HIV in her life involved Susan airing her fears about having a potentially life-threatening illness. Many people with asymptomatic disease have reported anxiety about the uncertainty of their future duration and quality of life (Gallego et al. 2000). Susan's avoidance of her recent blood-test results reflected her anxiety about becoming unwell, being exposed as HIV positive and seeing treatment as 'the thin end of the wedge' leading to inevitable decline. Through projecting forward and looking at realistic possibilities with the aid of current HIV-related educational materials, Susan was able to desensitise to her fear of treatment and to contemplate a future where treatment may be useful. Avoidance had been such an important strategy for Susan that it was challenging for her to contemplate the realities of her condition. I was constantly aware of the need to balance reality against a desire to reassure her falsely. I used supervision to help with this dilemma. Susan did decide to return for her results and felt more able to live with whatever consequences arose. Her results indicated that she didn't need to contemplate treatment at the present time.

Before Susan received her encouraging results, she had been considering the pros and cons of disclosing to her family, particularly to her closest sister. She felt a great need to preserve a strong, capable image within her family and feared that she would lose this if they knew about her status. Two of her sisters were religious and had a poor view of what they classed as 'promiscuity' and Susan feared that they would respond judgementally to any revelation of hers about HIV. However, she also valued honesty and felt that her secrecy about HIV was a painful anomaly in her family life. After receiving her good results she decided to postpone her exploration of this issue. I noticed that I felt some conflict at this point as I wondered whether Susan was cutting herself off from what might turn out to be a great source of supports both now and in the future. Again, at this point I turned to supervision and to our team's peer supervision group for help in exploring my conflict.

At the end of our sessions, Susan reported that she felt less distressed, less irritable, was sleeping better and was less aware of NATs in her daily life. She had returned to attending routine appointments in the outpatient clinic and felt she had more realistic views about HIV treatment. She had decided not to disclose her status to any of her family until she did start treatment and felt content with this decision for the time being. She reported that she felt warmer towards Derek but that she wasn't sure about resuming the sexual side of their relationship. She said that she had found the counselling approach helpful and might make use of it again in the future should the need arise.

Effectiveness of interventions and professional development

CBT appeared to provide an effective framework for intervention with this HIV-positive woman who was experiencing negative cognitions that contributed to her lowered mood, lowered self-esteem and behavioural withdrawal.

It seems that a diagnosis of HIV infection can affect the thinking, mood and behaviour of an individual at any stage after the initial diagnosis. Perhaps this is because the diagnosis of a chronic condition is not a discrete event but rather a lifelong adjustment process (Rolland 1994).

It may also be that the shock of initial diagnosis and following bereavement masked or delayed the adjustment process in this client. Awareness of, and previous use of, the counselling service facilitated Susan's access to counselling. This availability, I believe, played a useful role in preventing the exacerbation of symptoms. Further, the paradigm used helped her to gain some skills in dealing with NATs, which she was able to use outside the therapy sessions.

Susan is clearly a resourceful woman but, for her, the nature of her diagnosis separated her from her accustomed way of accessing emotional and problem-solving support, i.e. her relationship with her sisters. Unable to use these relationships due to a number of factors, including protecting them from discomfort, fear of judgmental attitudes and wanting to maintain her own view of herself as a 'coper', she had had difficulty in dealing with her thoughts and feelings. This is a common feature in HIV infection and, for me, underlined the value of counselling services in a setting where stigmatisation (or fear of it) is widespread and individuals are more susceptible to mental health problems than the general population (Gallego et al. 2000). I experienced some difficulties in working with Susan around the issue of disclosure. I am well aware that disclosure can lead to the loss of relationships, one's sense of belonging and even to violence. However, after looking at the possible outcomes of disclosure to each family member with her, I believed that Susan's fears of rejection might have been unfounded. At times, I think I saw her reluctance to disclose as something to overcome. At such times I might have been in danger of trying to persuade her to disclose, thus infringing her autonomy and practising unethically (Cohen and Spieler Cohen 1999). Supervision was invaluable at this point and my supervisor was able to postulate reasons for her choice. It is clear that Susan's sense of herself as a successful career woman and mother and her family's perception of this are important to her sense of self efficacy and it may be that secretiveness in this area of her life was important to her during her current difficulties. Susan has found other ways of receiving emotional support from friends, her partner and counselling. I believe that her relationship with disclosure is dynamic and conflicted and will be resolved differently at different times. I think counselling enabled her to re-examine the issue of disclosure and come to a decision that she felt happy with at the time.

HIV infection is a long-term process both medically and psychologically, it will present different challenges at different times depending upon the individual's personality, level of social support, progression of disease and life-stage (Miller and Bor 1988). Events may trigger NATs at any stage and, for this reason, counselling within the CBT model offered a useful strategy, in this case.

As HIV encompasses many emotive issues it is a challenging and interesting field within which to work. However, for this reason, it can be emotionally demanding and supervision and personal therapy have been essential in exploring and dealing with my own attitudes and feelings about sex, expression of sexuality, disease, infection and disfigurement and parent-hood. In this case, I felt a great sense of identification with this woman and so keenly wanted the best for her that, at times, it may have affected my conduct had I not been able to explore my own response in supervision and through the less formal support of my colleagues. This case enabled me to appreciate the value of teamwork and supervision. My experience of empathy for Susan brought home to me the essentially human nature of counselling for both client and therapist, I feel privileged to have been a facilitator in this woman's exploration of her relationship with HIV infection and her struggle to lead a fulfilling life.

References

Beck, A. (1967). *Depression: Clinical, Experimental and Theoretical Aspects*. New York: Harper Row.

Beck, A., Rush, A., Shaw, B. and Emery, G. (1979). *Cognitive Therapy for Depression*. New York: Guilford Press.

Cohen, E. and Spieler Cohen, G. (1999). *The Virtuous Therapist*. Pacific Grove, CA: Brooks/Cole.

Gallego, L., Gordillo V. and Catalan, J. (2000). Psychiatric and psychological disorders associated to HIV infection. *AIDS Review 2000*, no. 2, 48–59.

Fennell, M.J.V. (1989). Depression. In K. Hawton, P. Salkovskis, J. Kirk and D. Clark (1989). *Cognitive Behaviour Therapy for Psychiatric Problems. A Practical Guide*. Oxford: Oxford Medical Publications, pp. 169–234.

Hawton, K., Salkovskis, P., Kirk, J. and Clark, D. (1989). *Cognitive Behaviour Therapy for Psychiatric Problems. A Practical Guide*. Oxford: Oxford Medical Publications.

Miller, R. and Bor, R. (1988). *AIDS: A Guide to Clinical Counselling*. London: Science Press.

Powell, T. (1992). *The Mental Health Handbook*. Bicester: Winslow Press.
Rolland, J.S. (1994). *Families, Illness and Disability: An Integrative Treatment Model*. New York: Basic Books.
Scott, M. and Dryden, W. (1996). The Cognitive-Behavioural Paradigm. In R. Woolfe and W. Dryden (eds) *Handbook of Counselling Psychology*. London: Sage.
Wills, F. and Saunders, D. (1997). *Cognitive Therapy: Transforming the Image*. London: Sage.

Chapter 15

Working with children: a communicative approach

with a case study by Janet Penny

When writing a case study, one of the most difficult things to decide is how to integrate the most relevant aspects of the client's experience without minimising the importance of the therapist's own process. This is what I think Janet Penny does very well. In her discussion of her work with a 10-year-old boy, Kieran, she makes reference to the fact that our clients often elicit incongruent feelings within us and that the recognition of those feelings is an important part of both the establishment of the working alliance and our development as therapists.

This case also highlights how different cultural and demographic issues need to be taken into account when working with clients. Kieran's age dictates the way that Janet is able to work with him both developmentally and cognitively. As such, both the language she uses and her interpretations of Kieran's behaviour take this into account.

The final point that makes this case study worthy of discussion is that Janet makes it clear that there is not always necessarily a clear end point to therapy. Rather, it is a progressive dynamic process in which the client and therapist construct and deconstruct interpretations and perceptions of different issues and through this are able to move towards a healthier and more comfortable place for the client.

> *Janet Penny wrote this case study at the beginning of a full-time MSc in Counselling Psychology. The comments were written at the beginning of the second year of a post-MSc practitioner diploma.*

Preamble

Working with this particular client presented a number of challenges, and it was for this reason that I chose to include him in a case study. Kieran evoked a number of strong feelings in me, such as respect, sadness about his experiences – being left by therapists and his father leaving home –

curiosity, and, sometimes, great exasperation. I was left wondering at times how I, as a female, would relate to a 10-year-old boy who was much more interested in football and Pokemon. He could be unruly and aggressive, and was often reluctant to leave the sessions. At the time, having to write a case study presented a useful opportunity to reflect on sessions with him, and my feelings towards him. It was hoped that this would help me in my work with him. Thus, the case is an unfinished story for the reader.

Writing the case study helped me to gain more of an appreciation of the communicative approach, particularly the idea that the therapist needs to be attentive to the client's unconscious understanding in the sessions. Some clients do not find it easy to be at odds with a therapist and so may communicate their needs or displeasure in an oblique, unconscious way (Casement 1985). This may be particularly true for a young client where the difference in power is apparent, probably more so in a school setting. It helped me be mindful of the fact that Kieran had been passed from therapist to therapist, and made me more ready to acknowledge his distress and anger, which was sometimes seen in his destructive play. However, with the emphasis of the model on addressing what is happening in the session, I struggled to know how to deal with the external difficulties that Kieran faced, such as his father being arrested.

On reflection, the case study lacks some of the warmth of the relationship with Kieran and the vitality of the sessions. As a trainee, I was keen to be seen adhering to the theoretical framework correctly. I had slightly missed the point that part of the learning experience wasn't in always 'getting it right', but developing the ability to think about the process. There also seems to be little discussion of either Kieran's feelings or my own, yet as the sessions developed, more feelings were expressed by him, and many evoked in me. It would have helped to reflect on these more, to understand both what Kieran might be feeling and my own reactions. Nevertheless, the case study does show the increasing interaction Kieran and I developed despite our obvious differences in age, gender, and background.

CASE STUDY

Introduction

This report presents the case of a 10-year-old boy being seen in a primary-school setting, using the communicative psychoanalytic approach. It focuses on the client's anxieties, which centre on issues of separation, and the therapist's attempts to deal with these. A summary of the main assumptions of communicative psychoanalysis is given, followed by the content of the sessions, the difficulties encountered in working with the client and, finally, an evaluation of the therapeutic work.

Theoretical orientation

The framework adopted was the communicative psychoanalytic approach which has been developed mainly by Robert Langs (e.g. 1978, 1988; cited in Myers 1997). This approach focuses on the spontaneous stories or narratives told by clients, which convey unconscious communications about what is going on between the client and therapist in the here and now (Smith 1999a). Langs argues that there are two forms of verbal communication: the narrative mode and the non-narrative mode. The latter is more abstract, whereas the former involves story telling that provides concrete descriptions or easily visualised accounts. It is the narrative mode that conveys latent meaning. Communicative psychotherapy is based on the following premises: that in social situations, we spontaneously tell stories to unconsciously convey something about that situation, and that these unconscious views are perceptive and subtle readings of the situation. In therapy, clients' narratives, or 'derivatives' (Bonac 2000), analogously reflect the clients' perceptions about the therapeutic situation. For example, a client who gives consent to have the session taped and then goes on to recount a negatively-toned story involving an intrusive third party may be expressing a negative evaluation about the taping.

The main therapeutic interventions employed in communicative psychoanalysis are: silence, interpretation and 'frame management' (e.g. Thorpe 1999). Silence serves a number of functions, such as acting as a 'holding' intervention to encourage communication (Smith 1999b) and demonstrates the therapist's faith in the client's ability to take the significant role in therapy (Langs 1992, in Oaten 1999). The frame is the contract, or ground rules, between therapist and client, which outlines what each will do in therapy, and frame management is the handling of the therapeutic situation in order to adhere to the contract. The concept of the frame is given great importance in this approach and the structuring and management of the frame is seen as the 'real business of psychoanalysis' (Smith 1991, p. 164). Interpretations are the therapist's attempts to 'decode' the latent meaning in the client's derivatives, and, if correct, they bring symptom relief and insight to the client (Bonac 2000). Interpretations are validated by clients as correct, if followed by positively-toned narratives, or incorrect, if not. The aim of communicative psychoanalysis is to be guided by the client's unconscious communications and provide a secure frame within which the client can experience its 'inherent healing properties' (Smith, 1999a, p. 203).

The communicative approach was employed in this case, not least because it was the perspective used in the charitable organisation, and communicative supervision was provided as part of the placement. However, it was an appropriate model for working with this client for a number of reasons. Masson's insistence that the 'therapeutic relationship *always* involves an imbalance of power' (1988, p. 290) is particularly pertinent when the client is a child and the therapist is an adult. Langs developed the communicative approach to address the inequality of power (Langs 1982, cited in Holmes 1999) and the approach attempts to do so in a number of ways. For example, by insisting that therapists be utterly guided by clients' deep unconscious communications, and considering interpretations to be validated only when this is done by the client. This approach also acknowledges the potential harmful effects of the therapist. Given Kieran's silence, shyness, age and past experience of therapists unilaterally terminating therapy, a more directive approach might have caused him to withdraw further, thus impeding the development of a therapeutic relationship. This approach provided a useful starting point for work with this particular client, because of the emphasis on silence and being guided by the client's concerns as expressed in concrete narratives. Also, the model argues that clients are able to communicate unconscious perceptions regardless of their age, cognitive abilities or mental health status (Bonac 2000).

Organisational setting

The client received individual therapy from a Counselling Psychologist in Training working voluntarily for a charitable organisation, which offers psychotherapy to children in schools. Therapy took place in a designated play therapy room in the client's primary school. The client was collected by the therapist from his class and taken out of lessons for the sessions. On occasions, treating the client in this setting compromised his therapeutic frame. One notable difficulty of working in this setting was that when collecting the client from class, his teacher commented to the therapist about the child in front of the whole class, and was sometimes reluctant to let Kieran go to therapy.

Referral

The client was originally referred for therapy by his teacher three years ago and has since seen a number of therapists. He was referred to the present therapist by the organisation's team leader who also works at the school. In keeping with the communicative approach, little information was available regarding Kieran's history or initial referral. Referrals and assessment by others are viewed as one might view a third party that threatens the trust and confidentiality of the therapeutic relationship (Smith 1999a, 1991). However, Kieran was described by the team leader as 'the most deprived child in the school, and silent'.

Client profile

The client, Kieran, was a 10-year-old boy in his penultimate year of primary-school education. He had an older brother and younger sister at the same school who were also receiving sessions with therapists from the same organisation. Kieran lived with his mother who was described by the team leader as 'an alcoholic, friendly but sometimes unable to cope'. Based on his play, and reading and writing abilities during the therapy sessions, Kieran appeared to have below average intelligence. He was sometimes collected from a class for 8-year-old children, rather than his own class, which supported this impression. Kieran's appearance was frequently untidy and his clothes and face were often a little dirty. He did not wear the required school uniform, but was usually dressed in casual clothes, such as sweat shirts or T-shirts, trousers and trainers. His hair was always kept cut very short and he was physically small for his age. Initially, Kieran was very silent and avoided engaging in much eye contact.

The therapeutic frame

During the first session, the boundaries and rules of therapy were outlined to Kieran. The rules were that he was not allowed to hurt himself, to hurt the therapist, to take items from the room, or to intentionally break the items in the room. Also, Kieran was told that he would come to the room once a week at the same time, have fifty minutes with the therapist, and, during that time, it was his time when he could do anything he liked or talk about anything he liked. The issue of confidentiality was conveyed by saying that the therapist would not talk about what happened in the room to other children or teachers unless there was risk of harm to someone. Another rule was explained in a later session, which related to Kieran taking his artwork out of the room. This rule is that children are only allowed to take their artwork from the room at half terms and at the end of terms. Otherwise, children's work is kept in individual folders in another part of the school and brought to the room for the children's sessions.

Given the setting in which therapy occurred, the therapeutic frame differed in certain aspects from the ideal or 'secured frame' advocated by Langs (1982, cited in Warburton 1999). Fee paying would normally be part of a secured frame (e.g. Bonac 2000, Smith 1991). However, this did not occur in this setting. According to the communicative approach, this may make it hard for the client to express negative emotions towards the therapist and the gift of free therapy may be seen as harmful by the client (Smith 1991). An important component of the secured frame is total confidentiality and this was not always possible in this setting. For example, the children had to be escorted to and from the sessions for safety reasons. Being collected from class occurred in front of the other pupils and their teacher, and so the child had to 'run the gauntlet' from class to the therapy room in front of others, which afforded the child little confidentiality. Privacy in the therapy room was also sometimes compromised as sounds from the adjacent therapy room could occasionally be heard during sessions. Therefore, the client might have inferred that people in that room could hear him during his sessions. However, there was consistency in the location, timing and duration of the sessions. Other aspects of the secured frame, such as the therapist's neutrality and anonymity were conveyed implicitly by the therapist's behaviour. For example, neutrality was communicated by avoiding verbal interventions other than interpretations and, particularly, by avoiding evaluative statements or comments about the client's activities. Anonymity was conveyed by keeping self-disclosure to a minimum, which is in accordance with the communicative aim of patient-centred therapy (Smith 1991). Also, in keeping with the approach, one of the main aims of therapy was to maintain the therapeutic frame.

Initial assessment

Assessment was not carried out by asking questions in the conventional way for two main reasons. First, communicative therapists avoid asking questions as they are usually 'technically incorrect'; they do not address the client's unconscious communications and may suggest that the therapist is avoiding the client's derivatives (Raney 1999). Verbal interventions are limited to interpretations. Second, the fact that the client was a child, and a particularly quiet child at that, also influenced the manner in which assessment was made. Putting a large number of questions to a child could seem threatening and Kieran's silence made it almost impossible to elicit information from him on the few occasions when this was attempted. Continuous assessment was therefore based on Kieran's behaviour in the sessions over time.

At the outset, Kieran was very silent, and a little slow to interact with the therapist. Given the paucity of social interaction between Kieran and the therapist in the earlier sessions, it seemed appropriate to quickly rule out disorders such as autism and Asperger's disorder, which are of higher incidence in males. However, Kieran did start to engage in eye contact, talk and play games over time, and did not shown any evidence of repetitive or inflexible behaviours. Therefore, it seemed unlikely that he had any disorders of that kind. He did not communicate any clear or strong derivatives initially. However, his play did have themes of being dropped or discarded. For example, a lot of play involved Kieran throwing objects, sometimes aggressively. This suggested that Kieran had concerns over being 'discarded', i.e. being dropped by the therapist leaving, which is something that he had experienced in the past with previous therapists.

Content and interventions of sessions

Session 1

The therapist introduced herself to Kieran and the rules of therapy were outlined. Kieran spent the whole session in silence and sat at a small table drawing. While the therapist was sitting on a chair next to the table, Kieran sat turned away from her, shielding his drawing from her with his arms. The therapist moved away and sat on the floor to one side of him. After this non-verbal intervention, Kieran visibly relaxed and carried on drawing. Kieran's initial non-verbal behaviour may have been a 'model of recti-fication', i.e. a hint about how the frame should be (Bonac 2000). One could infer that the intervention was validated by him, based on his subsequent relaxation.

Sessions 2–6

The client engaged in more interaction with the therapist by inviting her to play catch with various toys. In the earlier sessions, Kieran spoke only one or two words, commenting on the toys and directing play. The throwing games suggested unconscious communication concerning Kieran being 'dropped' by the previous therapist. However, there were no clear themes, and the client showed no signs of distress. Therefore, no interpretations were given, as interpretations are only offered when there is some indication the client wants one, i.e. when in distress (Smith 1991). Verbal interventions were limited to the therapist occasionally reflecting back some of Kieran's words in order to elicit possible communications. This is an additional intervention advocated by Langs, according to Thorpe (1999). In sessions five and six Kieran started to explore the room more and use a greater variety of the items in the room than in previous sessions. His interaction with the therapist continued to increase. Kieran spoke more about the activities that he was engaged in and gave instructions about what to do in play. Kieran involved the therapist more fully in the activities he was doing. In session six, Kieran was the most vocal he had been. He spent most of the session completing a jigsaw, constantly talking to the therapist about it, and asking for her help and involvement. This level of conversation more or less carried on in subsequent sessions. Again, there were no negatively-toned themes in his play or words, and so no verbal interpretation was given.

Session 7

Kieran's play was particularly rich in meaning in this session. It was the penultimate session before the Christmas break and this had not yet been addressed by the therapist. While playing the 'Frustration' game with the therapist, Kieran openly cheated and won. This may have been communi-cating that Kieran feels things aren't 'fair', or he is redressing the inequality that he perceives, in which the therapist can just leave any time she wishes. Kieran then spent a significant portion of the session dumping puppets in and out of a dumper truck and trying to get rid of them by putting them in the oven. This derivative was triggered by his concern over the forthcoming

Christmas break, and his being 'dumped' by the therapist. Vacations are a time when therapists traditionally leave and do not return. An intervention regarding the break was given, confirming that there would be a number of weeks' break and then, on a specific date, Kieran and the therapist would meet again. The intervention may not have been fully validated as Kieran then carried on playing with some toys in a neutral way, although he did not express any negative themes.

Sessions 8–9

In session eight, there were no clear unconscious communications or signs of distress from Kieran in this session. Most of the session was spent playing football. However, in session nine, which was the first session after the Christmas break, Kieran showed concerns over third parties, which presented a threat to the confidential secured frame. On entering the room, Kieran asked where some new balls had come from. The therapist replied that she did not know, but thought that someone had put them in the room over the vacation. This trigger probably led to the derivatives about third parties. Kieran spoke more than usual about specific friends, his teacher and class while making cards for them. In retrospect, an interpretation may have addressed this and secured the frame, thus alleviating Kieran's anxieties.

Sessions 10–13

Kieran's play seemed to become increasingly chaotic during these sessions. That is, he would start one activity and then say that he wanted to start another. He did not seem settled in any one activity. His play was also quite boisterous, items were thrown or knocked down during games of catch, etc., but there seemed to be no intention to break anything, nor any aggression directed at the therapist. Notably, Kieran was very reluctant to leave the sessions at the appropriate time, and refused to go back to class. There seemed to be no break in the frame or trigger, that the therapist was aware of, to account for the symptoms and so no interpretation was given. However, the distress did coincide with Kieran revealing, just as he went back to class in session ten, that his father had been arrested by the police. This may have caused the distress, rather than something in the here and now of the therapeutic situation. This incident brought to mind one of the criticisms directed towards communicative psychoanalysis; that the approach is over concerned with the therapeutic frame almost as if it were in treatment rather than the client (Bonac 1998). Kieran chose not to talk further about the family situation.

Sessions 14–16

The sense of chaos in Kieran's play seemed to subside slightly during these sessions. He appeared more content and absorbed in his activities. During these weeks, there was a half-term break and this was addressed in advance by the therapist warning Kieran of the break, and confirming when she and Kieran would next meet. There were few signs of anxiety relating to this issue before the break. However, Kieran was still a little reluctant to leave the sessions, though less so than before. The therapist maintained the frame by reminding Kieran of the rules of therapy.

Session 17

At the start of the session Kieran repeatedly threw a ball at a doll's head saying, 'I've got to try and hit her head'. He asked the therapist to try and hit the doll also. The trigger for this derivative may have been explained by the fact that on the way to the room, Kieran said that he had seen the therapist with another child earlier in the day. An interpretation was given to the effect that Kieran felt angry with the therapist because she was with someone else earlier. This was validated by Kieran as he then ceased his aggressive throwing and played more quietly.

Session 18 and 19

An activity common to these two sessions was the game of hide-and-seek which Kieran initiated. This was the first time that he had played this game. The therapist had recently decided to terminate therapy unilaterally in four months' time, and had decided to tell Kieran in session eighteen. The hide and seek communicated Kieran's concerns about termination and so this needed to be addressed. Kieran was warned about the forthcoming Easter break and told about the therapist leaving in July. However, Kieran did not seem ready to hear the latter and carried on playing and talking as if he had not heard. His latent and manifest communications seemed to deny this piece of information. He carried on playing, showing no distress or reference to her leaving. At the end of session nineteen, Kieran was again reluctant to leave the session, indicating concerns about being separated from the therapist. He was again told about the holidays and termination and this time did listen to and understand the intervention. His response was to ask immediately who would be seeing him after the therapist was gone, and he commented on how it was only a 'few days' until then.

The client continued to be seen for therapy.

Main psychological interventions used in sessions

The main interventions employed were those advocated by the communicative approach. Silence was used to allow the client freedom to associate and initiate topics of conversation or activities. This proved to be particularly useful in earlier sessions in which Kieran himself was silent. It allowed him to invite interaction on his terms rather than the therapist's. Frame management was an often used intervention, mainly because of Kieran's attempts to break the frame, e.g. Kieran was often reluctant to leave and wanted to take items from the room with him. The frame was preserved by reminding Kieran of the rules of therapy. Interpretations were given in response to Kieran's unconscious communications. Many of his narratives showed themes of termination and separation anxiety, and concerns over third parties. On the whole, these concerns could have been addressed more thoroughly by interpreting more of his derivatives.

The therapeutic process

Over time, Kieran had increasingly expressed himself, talking more, showing emotions such as aggression, frustration and happiness and interacting in various activities. The therapist had attempted to keep literally to the rule that Kieran was allowed to do or say whatever he liked (within the boundaries). This included things like making a mess and being silent if he wished. This stood in contrast to school and family life where one cannot do whatever one wants. At times it had been hard to maintain this attitude, for example owing to the time pressure of having to clean up afterwards before the next session. Kieran's reluctance to return to class had similarly led to some frustration. As Kieran may have sensed and been affected by this, the therapist had attempted to keep focused on doing what was therapeutically appropriate at the time, rather than what was merely convenient for her.

Difficulties encountered in working with the client

The main difficulty faced in working with Kieran was his reluctance to leave the session. Also, Kieran would sometimes leave the session, but refuse to return to his class. This presented a problem, as the client could neither be forced to return and nor be left on his own. This was dealt with in a number of ways. Primarily, the therapist reminded Kieran that he had to go back to class as part of the rules of therapy. On the basis that his reluctance indicated a desire to be with the therapist, the therapist also tried leaving the room at the end of sessions and waiting just outside the door for Kieran to come out. This did have the desired effect on most occasions, which suggested that the inference was correct. Time was allowed for

Kieran to talk about his not wanting to go back to class, while also trying to maintain the boundaries. Another notable difficulty was Kieran's inclination to take items out of the room, both surreptitiously and openly. To address this, interpretations were given to the effect that Kieran wanted to take something of the session and the therapist with him. Kieran stopped stealing, but continued to express a desire to take items with him.

Making use of supervision

An intrinsic part of the communicative approach is the notion of 'client-centred supervision' (Smith 1996, p. 427), in which the client validates or otherwise the therapist's interventions. For example, positively toned play after an intervention would indicate that the intervention had been validated by the client, i.e. it is correct. Kieran's play offered the therapist 'supervision' on occasions. His constant narratives regarding termination and being left alone point to his concerns over these issues and so future sessions will need to address these more thoroughly. This is particularly important now that the therapist has given notice of terminating therapy. More attention to these concerns may have reduced the distress seen in later sessions. Clinical supervision by a communicative psychotherapist also helped the therapist to learn to look for and decode the unconscious communications in Kieran's play. Supervision was useful in thinking through any issues of guilt that the therapist experienced owing to ending therapy, and in coming to terms with the possible iatrogenic effects of termination.

Evaluation of practice

This case was presented because it provided the therapist with a number of challenges and opportunities to learn, both from the client and the communicative approach. The client was very silent initially and, in later sessions, showed considerable resistance by attempting to break the frame on numerous occasions. Kieran also communicated many narratives concerning termination, perhaps because of being left by previous therapists. This was a challenge. Some headway was made regarding Kieran taking items from the room. However, more work needs to be done to explore why Kieran wants to do this.

The model of therapy is also a challenge to the therapist. It can be unnerving, and leads one to develop an appreciation of one's potential for harmfully affecting clients (Smith 1996). It also challenges therapists' notions of themselves as healers (Smith 1991, Bowers 2000). As Smith states, the approach also provides the client with the 'deep unconscious experience of being truly heard' (1991, p. 217). For this to occur, the therapist must interpret in such a way as to recognise their own impact on the dyad. In this case, such communicative interpretations have begun to be made. For example, when Kieran hit the female doll, and on the occasions when he was reluctant to leave the session because of anxiety about the therapist leaving during breaks, communicative interpretations were made. However, future interpretations will need to address the client's anxieties more fully, particularly as the therapist has now said she will be leaving in four months. A therapist leaving is one of the most fundamental breaks in the frame. The challenge of the communicative model for the therapist is to 'come face to face with one's own destructiveness' (Smith 1991, p. 215) and then clients can have the experience of being fully understood.

References

Bonac, V.A. (1998). Perception or fantasy? A new clinical theory of transference. *Electronic Journal of Communicative Psychoanalysis*, Vol. 1, No. 1. http://www. mortimer.com.psychoanalysiscom/articles

Bonac, V.A. (2000). *Communicative Psychoanalysis with Children*. London: Whurr Publishers.

Bowers, P. (2000). The terminator. In V.A. Bonac (ed.) *Communicative Psychoanalysis with Children*. London: Whurr Publishers.

Casement, P. (1985). *On Learning from the Patient*. London: Routledge.

Holmes, C. (1999). Confessions of a communicative psychotherapist. In E.M. Sullivan (ed.) *Unconscious Communication in Practice*. Buckingham: Open University Press.

Langs, R. (1978). *The Listening Process*. Northvale: Jason Aronson.

Langs, R. (1982). *The Psychotherapeutic Conspiracy*. New York: Jason Aronson.

Langs, R. (1988). *A Primer of Psychotherapy*. New York: Gardner Press.

Langs, R. (1992). *A Clinical Workbook for Psychotherapists*. London and New York: Karnac.

Masson, J.M. (1988). *Against Therapy*. London: HarperCollins.

Myers, P. (1997). Reconsidering communicative psychoanalysis. *Electronic Journal of Communicative Psychoanalysis*, Vol. 1, No. 1. http://www.mortimer.com. psychoanalysiscom/articles

Oaten, G. (1999). Brief communicative psychotherapy and the fixed altered frame. In E.M. Sullivan (ed.) *Unconscious Communication in Practice*. Buckingham: Open University Press.

Raney, J.O. (1999). The informative value of erroneous questions. In E.M. Sullivan (ed.) *Unconscious Communication in Practice*. Buckingham: Open University Press.

Smith, D.L. (1991). *Hidden Conversations: An Introduction to Communicative Psychoanalysis*. London: Rebus Press.

Smith, D.L. (1996). The communicative approach to supervision. In S. Palmer, S. Dainow and P. Milner (eds) *Counselling: The BAC Reader*. London: Sage Publications.

Smith, D.L. (1999a). *Approaching Psychoanalysis: An Introductory Course*. London: Karnac Books.

Smith, D.L. (1999b). Communicative psychotherapy without tears. In E.M. Sullivan (ed.) *Unconscious Communication in Practice*. Buckingham: Open University Press.

Thorpe, I. (1999). The two parts of myself: decoding a video-recorded session between 'Kathy' and Rogers. In E.M. Sullivan (ed.) *Unconscious Communication in Practice*. Buckingham: Open University Press.

Warburton, K. (1999). Student counselling: a consideration of ethical and framework issues. In E.M. Sullivan (ed.) *Unconscious Communication in Practice*. Buckingham: Open University Press, pp. 109–122.

Chapter 16

Substance abuse: treatment using personal construct psychology

with a case study by Ian Mallandain

PRELUDE

We are pleased that Ian Mallandain accepted our invitation to publish his process report from a session of work with his client. This is an interesting and informative piece of work utilising a Kellian approach to therapy (Kelly 1955). Kelly's personal construct psychology, although often over-shadowed by more dominant mainstream models such as CBT and psychodynamic ways of working, continues to offer intellectually fascinating and empirically validated alternative to more routine approaches to working with people (Winter 1992). The report that follows utilises techniques such as the role construct repertory test or 'rep grid' of Kelly and the laddering technique of Hinkle (1965) operationalised in a fluid, conversational mode. As such, this work is at once quintessentially Kellian, while reflecting the personal style of the therapist.

Questions play an important role in Kellian therapy and Ian's work is illustrative of the importance of not assuming that one understands the client's experience until the opposite is elicited. For Kelly, the constructs that people use to make sense of their world are bipolar. In asking what might appear on first sight to be a redundant question, 'what for you is the opposite of that?' the therapist seeks to exploit Kelly's notion that in order genuinely to know what something is, you must know what it is not. Ian's work with his client gives real insight into the process of hypothesis development and iterative formulation that is so much a part of the Kellian approach to working with people.

The reader is given intimate access to the thinking of the therapist and his experience of being in the therapeutic relationship. In particular, we are struck with Ian's modesty in self-appraisal. Indeed, in our roles as trainers and supervisors, we regularly note the propensity of reflective practitioners to discount their competency for fear of overshadowing their client's authority and understanding of their unique experience. Kellians assume that their clients are experts in the content of their construct system, i.e. *what* they see, while the therapist is expert in the process of construing, i.e. *how* they see. Thus together, with their distinct areas of competency, Ian and his client reflect the synergistic collaboration that is crucial to the development of insight and, ultimately, change.

> *Ian Mallandain wrote this process report during his MSc in Counselling Psychology at City University. There were some three years between the first writing of this work and the revised report that follows.*

Preamble

Why I chose this particular case

At the time of writing this process report, I had been working as a trainee counselling psychologist in the substance-misuse field for about three years. This was a challenging area to be working in, as substance misusers were most usually ambivalent towards change. They knew that they wanted to stop taking drugs, but at the same time they still had a need to continue using them, which could not be solely explained by physical dependency alone.

During this period of work, I soon learnt that the reasons people chose to abuse substances were many and varied and therefore unique to the individual. Despite considerable health implications for some clients, many users still made a decision to return to a way of life that was either familiar to them, or enabled them to cope in some way. I therefore needed an approach that would enable me to explore and understand the clients' idiosyncratic reasons for their substance misuse problem, as well as enable me to help the person change. It is for this reason that I found personal construct psychology (PCP) particularly helpful (Kelly 1955). With its abstract theory and broad application, PCP enabled me to work in a flexible way, with a client group that is generally regarded as difficult to engage with.

To carry out an assessment within this approach, I would usually administer Kelly's role construct repertory grid (Kelly 1955), which is a quick and systematic technique for exploring the client's repertoire of constructs (*see below under* theoretical framework), and the relationships between them. To apply the rep grid, I would present the client with approximately seventeen role titles (such as mother, father, best friend, etc.), to which I would ask him/her to attach names (elements) of people known personally to him/her. To elicit constructs, dimensions for classifying and understanding the world, I would use the minimum context form of construct elicitation (Fransella and Bannister 1977). This involves presenting the client with a random triad of elements and asking him/her to identify one way in which two elements are similar but different from the third. I would ensure that one role title related to how the client saw him/

herself as a substance misuser and then include one role title, which related to how the client would ideally like to see him/herself in an abstinent role.

The client described in this report is a woman called Sarah who was in recovery from alcohol abuse. The main construct that differentiated Sarah as a problem drinker from how she ideally wanted to be in an abstinent role, was someone who was 'subservient as opposed to assertive'. Ideally, Sarah wanted to be assertive, but as a problem drinker she had found herself to be compromised with regard to this construct. In her abstinent role, Sarah continued to have difficulties in asserting herself and this was most evident in her relationship with her husband, which at times could be a source of unhappiness to her. It was in this context that her problem drinking had started.

To demonstrate the clinical utility of Kelly's rep grid (Kelly 1955), as an aid to counselling substance misusers, I decided to write-up this case example as course work for an MSc in counselling psychology that I was undertaking at the time. Furthermore, using the rep grid with Sarah proved to be rather revealing, by identifying the construct 'subservient–assertive', which we subsequently explored. It is for this reason that I opted to write this up as a process report rather than a client study, in order to illustrate the qualitative Kellian techniques that I had used.

What I think and feel retrospectively about what I produced

It is now just over two years ago since I wrote this process report and while I feel mostly happy with it, I nevertheless regret not discussing the therapeutic relationship itself. During the time that I saw Sarah, I found her to be a most propositional client (Kelly 1955). Propositional in this context refers to Sarah being prepared to experiment with new ideas. Sarah also seemed comfortable in working with me and on one occasion mentioned that she was not afraid of me. 'Afraid–not afraid of others' represented a construct of Sarah's, which seemed to affect her relationships. I mention this here, because the fact that I had established a good rapport with Sarah is an important part of the process that could have been commented on in the report.

What I learned from writing-up this and other client studies and process reports

A final comment should be made concerning what I learnt most from writing this report. To answer this truthfully, I should have to say that I found drafting and writing this report hard work. As with client work, report writing involves reflection and it can be difficult to find time to do this. The process report presented here, is the end product of three years of training and represents (I hope) a progression in my work. During those three years, there were occasions when I did not make the grade, but I think what has helped me most is Kelly's notion of sociality (Kelly 1955). In other words, when writing a process report/case study, I have always tried to put myself in the shoes of the person marking the report and imagined what I would have been looking for if I were that person. I cannot say that it has always worked, but it got me there in the end!

PROCESS REPORT

Theoretical framework

The theoretical framework used in the following transcribed session is personal construct psychology (PCP). The rationale for choosing PCP has been discussed above.

Kelly (1955) provided a model of the person as man the scientist, whereby the individual is testing out his/her view of the world, represented by personal constructs (bipolar discriminations), through engaging in experiments (his/her behaviour) with others.

Although Kelly believed there to be a reality, he nevertheless considered no one to have direct access to it. According to Kelly, one person's interpretations of his/her world are as valid as the next. This concept is known as constructive alternativism in PCP and represents the philosophical foundation of this approach. What is important in PCP is the usefulness of the individual's interpretations and most of the time they will serve him/her well. However, there will be occasions where the individual continues to maintain a personal construction of themselves or others, despite subsequent experience failing to validate it. The aim of the Kellian therapist is to suspend his/her own beliefs and subsume the client's constructs in terms of professional constructs (which describe process taking place in the individual's personal construct system). Furthermore, where the client is continuing to use constructs despite their constant invalidation, the counsellor will help the client to see an alternative construction of events. Therefore, in this case, my aims were to:

1   Listen credulously (Kelly 1955) to my client, i.e. to make sense of what he/she was telling me, through endeavouring to suspend my own beliefs and identify his/her constructs.
2   Make use of professional constructs to describe process in my client's personal construct system. This included revealing the relationships between my client's constructs, including hierarchical organisation and finding where the potential for change lies. Also, to look for evidence of construing in transition, e.g. guilt, threat, and anxiety. Kelly integrated emotional experience within his theory by seeing these different

emotions as an awareness that our construing system is in a state of transition, or an awareness that it is inadequate for construing the events with which we are confronted (Bannister and Fransella 1971).

3   Treat my client as a co-worker. Kelly viewed the relationship between the Kellian therapist and the client to be analogous to that between research supervisor and student (Kelly 1955).

By adhering to these three aims, my purpose was to provide a collaborative therapeutic relationship – one, which my client would hopefully perceive as a secure base from which to explore his/her emotional life and identity.

Personal details

My client, Sarah, is a 44-year-old woman. She is married and lives with her husband and is not employed outside the home.

Presenting problem

Sarah mentioned that she had been a problem drinker for the past eight years. Although now in recovery, Sarah felt that psychological therapy could help her understand the reasons behind her drinking.

Contract and assessment

After standard preliminaries were discussed (duration of session and confidentiality, etc.), time-limited therapy was offered.

Given that Sarah wanted to do some exploratory work to understand her problem drinking, I decided to make use of a PCP theoretical perspective (Kelly 1955). From this perspective, behaviour can be seen as an experiment, a way in which the individual attempts to validate his/her notions (constructs) of others and him/herself. This theoretical perspective considers that there are constructs, which the individual will not necessarily be aware of. In PCP such constructs are considered to operate at a low level of awareness (Fransella and Dalton 1990). As Sarah seemed unaware of what psychological factors had maintained her problem drinking, I hypothesised that constructs which related to her alcohol problem, may have been operating at a low level of awareness (Kelly 1955). I discussed the PCP approach with Sarah in broad terms and she agreed to proceed with the therapy contract.

During the assessment, Sarah reported that she had started drinking around the time that she was going through a particular marital difficulty. While this issue had now passed, Sarah continued to drink at a level indicative of alcohol dependency. She said that she had recently stopped drinking and had made this decision, when a friend told her that he had sensed something was wrong. She mentioned that he had been very supportive.

For the assessment, I was mostly informed by the output from Kelly's rep grid (Kelly 1955). The output showed that as someone with a drink problem, Sarah saw herself as someone who was 'subservient', whereas if she could be different, she wanted to be 'assertive'. This was the main construct, which differentiated her as a problem drinker, to how she ideally wanted to be in her abstinent role. The remainder of the sessions primarily related to this issue.

Lead-in to the session

The session reported was our sixth session together. We had completed Kelly's rep grid (Kelly 1955) during sessions three and four. During the last session, I provided Sarah with feedback. However, there was no time to explore why Sarah wanted to be assertive and whether being subservient was implicated in her problem drinking.

Transcript and commentary

COUNSELLOR 1: What I thought might be interesting to do today, is to come back to the grid again, that we did, and explore a couple of relationships on the grid, because what I thought might be useful to look at was assertiveness, as that is the only one area, if you like, that you wanted to change.

Sarah had indicated on the grid that she wanted to be 'assertive' as opposed to being 'subservient' and yet the grid output revealed that this conflicted with being 'soft' which is how she saw herself and wanted to be.

CLIENT 1: Yes.

COUNSELLOR 2: But also, there seemed to be some conflict there in the sense that being subservient was more in tune, if you like, with the rest of these qualities. So, sometimes when we want to change an area in a particular way, it can be difficult to negotiate that quality with other things we might not want to change.

I was attempting to explain Hinkle's notion of implicative dilemmas (Hinkle 1965). Hinkle's argument was that constructs which are super-ordinate (more representative of self), would be most resistant to change. If being 'assertive' conflicted strongly with a self-concept of being 'soft', assuming this is superordinate for Sarah, then by definition being 'sub-servient', the opposite of assertive, will also be resistant to change. For Sarah to be assertive, may cause her to reconstrue herself in a more fundamental way, which could be uncomfortable and too threatening a change for her to undertake.

CLIENT 2: It's strange you should say this because the other day I was talking to Ben (*friend*) and he said something about my being afraid of people, something he had picked up and it was funny, I don't, I can't remember how it arose. I shall pursue it with him next time I see him.

COUNSELLOR 3: It would be interesting to know.

On reflection, I'm not sure why I made this response and whether it was particularly helpful to Sarah. Nevertheless, knowing why Ben thinks this of Sarah, could confirm what she already knows or could make her aware of other ways in which her fear of others is expressed.

CLIENT 3: Yes.

COUNSELLOR 4: Why.

CLIENT 4: Why he said it, yes.

COUNSELLOR 5: What is he basing that on.

CLIENT 5: Yes, I will try and mention it. Looking at this chart thing again (*grid output*), I was wondering, erm, had I misjudged him on the 'hard and softness' (*construct*), I think I put him quite high up on the hard side, but then I ought to think about it a bit more, because with regard to me he has been helpful as you know, but I would still put him as hard with regard to other people as I can see he is with his family.

COUNSELLOR 6: Yes, because with these things, obviously they're not set in stone, it's a picture of where you're at now.

I wanted to share theory with Sarah. Within PCP, the rep grid provides an understanding of how we currently see others and ourselves, which may change in the course of events.

CLIENT 6: Well this is it, and every day can change can't it?

COUNSELLOR 7: Of course, yes.

Validating her acceptance of what I was proposing.

CLIENT 7: Yes.

COUNSELLOR 8: Absolutely, and that's quite right. Just focusing on this assertiveness for the moment. The opposite of assertiveness is sub-servient. Can you think why it is important to be assertive?

Here I used my influence as a practitioner to guide the session. Exploring the importance of a construct is referred to as laddering (Hinkle 1965). The idea is that by exploring the importance of a construct, one moves into more core areas (those constructs which are representative of our identity).

CLIENT 8: I suppose we all need to be to some degree don't we, otherwise we will get trodden on by other people. Whereas being subservient, I suppose, is doing what you think other people want you to do. Or being afraid to show what you would want to do yourself, I suppose. It's so difficult these definitions.

COUNSELLOR 9: Yes, being afraid of showing?

I wondered what the fear represented.

CLIENT 9: Yes, being afraid of showing that you disagree with them. Perhaps even being afraid of letting it be seen that you want to do something, although there again you see I'm a mixture because, I always say of everybody, 'don't know' is 'no', if you ask someone something and they say 'I don't know' that means 'no', because 'yes' is 'yes', 'don't know' and 'no' are 'no'. So, I suppose I say 'no' more than I should, because I won't let myself say 'I don't know' and so I rarely say 'yes' if I think. Perhaps do I say what I think the other person wants to hear in a way I don't assert myself? But on the other hand, I mean I, I'm not unhappy about any of this as you know. I still do largely what I want to do. I think I am better since I've spoken to you.

COUNSELLOR 10: That's interesting.

In hindsight, I regret not exploring in what way she felt better since she had spoken to me and what it was in particular that left her feeling this.

CLIENT 10: I think I am, I am, Yes.

COUNSELLOR 11: Sarah, just returning to that theme about the reason why it's important to be assertive is to avoid being trodden on by other people. Can you think why it's important not to be trodden on by other people?

Here again, I was trying to explore further superordinate implications of why Sarah wanted to be assertive, as well as trying to understand what in particular she wanted to avoid (where did the potential for invalidation lie?)

CLIENT 11: There again, that is selfish, isn't it? Because if you don't want to be trodden on by them. Now is that selfish? How do you define being trodden on by other people? Letting them have their own way, when you disagree with it at heart, but you let them have it? No, you shouldn't do that. You should stick up for yourself more, without hurting them of course. If that's possible.

Was Sarah trying to avoid being selfish? Was this a negative implication of being assertive? Here she was considering the importance of 'sticking up for oneself'. A particular concern of Sarah's was 'hurting others'.

COUNSELLOR 12: It's about respecting your own rights as well as respecting others.

As I was striving to operate from a Kellian frame of reference, it would have been more appropriate to propose a definition of assertiveness, rather than to provide my own idiosyncratic meaning, or to provide an assumed truth.

CLIENT 12: That's right, a form of mutual respect really.
COUNSELLOR 13: Yes, which is what assertiveness is about.
CLIENT 13: It is, and you should be able to discuss it with people.
COUNSELLOR 14: Yes.
CLIENT 14: With whom you don't agree, necessarily.
COUNSELLOR 15: Of course, it isn't always possible.

I am not sure why I said this, other than perhaps I was aware that Sarah was afraid of certain others. The question comes across in a way as validating a personal belief in both Sarah and me.

CLIENT 15: No, this is the thing, and so then I back down, I suppose. Yes I do, I would back down and then I wouldn't complain, but I moan to myself afterwards and say to myself I wish I had the guts to say so and so. So, that's what I mean, but then of course in those situations where it occurs, I don't say anything, or even later, because I feel I would hurt them and I don't want to do that.

It was interesting that Sarah returned to a concern almost hurting others, a further implication of being assertive.

COUNSELLOR 16: Right, so it would be the fear, is that what you are saying?

I thought it important to stay with this issue and explore further.

CLIENT 16: It is, you see, it goes to my being frightened of people again a little bit.
COUNSELLOR 17: Yes, because, I wonder if it is also the fact that you don't want to disagree with someone.

I returned to an earlier theme Sarah mentioned under turn 9. On reflection, I would have liked to have stayed with the 'being frightened of people' and explored this further. What is she afraid of? How does this make it difficult for her to assert herself? What are the implicative dilemmas? (Hinkle 1965, Tschudi 1977).

CLIENT 17: Yes, I don't like disagreeing, although we all, I mean we all disagree with people at times don't we and even have sort of rows about it, if you like.

COUNSELLOR 18: So, Sarah can you think why it's important not to disagree with someone?

Again, exploring the implicative dilemmas (Hinkle 1965, Tschudi 1977).

CLIENT 18: It's in me not to disagree, really, I suppose. But then, that comes back to my personality again.

It was interesting that Sarah saw it in herself not to disagree, with this being a function of her personality.

Summary

The session began with exploring the construct 'assertiveness' as opposed to being 'subservient', with Sarah wanting to be assertive as opposed to the bipolar opposite. This was the main construct, which differentiated her as a problem drinker as opposed to an ideal abstinent role. We began exploring the importance of this construct to establish superordinate qualities (what she was trying to validate on a higher abstract level) and she mentioned that, 'you should stick up for yourself'. Themes emerged which I hypothesised as being implicative dilemmas (Hinkle 1965, Tschudi 1977) and therefore preventive of change. They were: *fear of disagreeing, not wanting to disagree, being afraid of people, not wanting to hurt others*, and possibly the *fear of being selfish*. Such dilemmas could be theoretically understood in respect of the choice corollary (Kelly 1955). This proposes that an individual chooses those alternatives from his/her own construct poles, which are more meaningful and coherent with his/her construct system, thereby protecting his/her identity from invalidation. It certainly seemed that to reconstrue herself as 'assertive', rather than 'subservient' could be too threatening a change for Sarah to make, requiring a radical reconstruction of self. Finally, at the end of the transcript, Sarah described her lack of assertiveness as being a function of her personality. Further exploration would have been useful to understand Sarah's view of what personality means. For example, did she regard her personality as fixed and therefore resistant to change? Such a view could act as a barrier to change and would effectively contrast with Kellian construct psychology, where personal constructions are considered to be the primary factor governing personality (Engler 1991).

At the beginning of this report, I made reference to three broad aims. The first aim referred to was credulous listening. I feel that the transcript illustrates the difficulty I experienced in achieving this consistently. In particular with reference to the theme of *being afraid of other people*, Sarah mentioned this on more than one occasion and it could have been useful to have explored this. Why was she afraid of others? Had she suffered some trauma in the past, for example? This was never mentioned. However, exploratory work could have been carried out to understand the impact of early experience on her construing (a concept known as time binding in PCP). Sarah also made reference to being better since having spoken to me. It could have been useful to explore in what way she felt better and what was it in particular that made her feel this.

The second point concerns the conceptualisation of the client's problem. During the session I attempted to elaborate the construct 'assertive – being subservient', to understand why Sarah wanted to become more assertive and how this construct pole would fit with her other construing. I attempted to do this through laddering (Hinkle 1965) and searching for implicative dilemmas (Hinkle 1965, Tschudi 1977). The session was exploratory, which is essentially what we had collaboratively established as a therapeutic contract.

In relation to the third point, overall the relationship felt collaborative, although I am conscious that I started off this session launching in with the aim of elaborating 'assertiveness – being subservient'. Although we had discussed this during the last session, it may have been more collaborative to have allowed Sarah space to discuss any concerns that she had, reflections of the last session and also to have checked out whether she still wanted to explore this particular construct during this session.

A final criticism relates to my providing a definition of assertiveness to Sarah during the session. The sharing of knowledge of assumed truths contrasts with a constructivist epistemology (Fransella 1995, Neimeyer and Mahoney 1995). As I was working from a Kellian perspective, it would have been more appropriate for me to propose a definition, which Sarah could then have entertained, refined or rejected.

Considering the assessment overall, Sarah came into therapy wanting to understand her problem drinking. She described the onset of her problem drinking as occurring eight years ago. At the time she was going through a particular marital issue. Although this had now passed, she had continued to abuse alcohol and seemed unaware of the reasons why. I hypothesised that constructs relating to this were operating at a low level of awareness.

I mentioned from the outset that Kelly's rep grid (Kelly 1955), had been a useful assessment tool for substance misusers and had chosen this case example to illustrate this. When using the rep grid with Sarah, this revealed that as a substance misuser, Sarah was 'subservient', whereas in an ideal abstinent role, she wanted to be 'assertive'. This information proved useful, as it transpired that Sarah's husband could often be quite hurtful in terms of the remarks that he directed at her. It seemed that she largely left these remarks unchallenged and while just a conjecture, it is possible that alcohol had enabled Sarah to cope in such situations, due to her difficulty in asserting herself.

An interesting turn of events occurred in a subsequent session, when Sarah reported that she had threatened to leave her husband, with the intention of following this through. After her threat to leave, her husband changed his behaviour towards her and appeared to be more considerate, based on her descriptions, with this leading to an improvement in their relationship. Sarah mentioned feeling able to respond in the same fashion again, should the need arise.

By the final session, Sarah had remained abstinent, although continued to maintain a view of herself as someone who is 'subservient'. However, my sharing of theory, not to mention her own experimentation (through threatening to leave her husband), may at the very least, have planted the idea that her relationship with others could be different.

References

Bannister, D. and Fransella, F. (1971). *Inquiring Man: The Psychology of Personal Constructs*. London: Croom Helm. (Reprinted by Routledge, 1993.)

Engler, B. (1991). *Personality Theories: An Introduction*. Boston: Houghton Mifflin.

Fransella, F. (1995). *George Kelly*. London: Sage.

Fransella, F. and Bannister, D. (1977). *A Manual for Repertory Grid Techniques*. London: Academic Press.

Fransella, F. and Dalton, P. (1990). *Personal Construct Counselling in Action*. London: Sage.

Hinkle, D. (1965). *The Change of Personal Constructs from the View Point of a Theory of Construct Implications*. Unpublished doctoral dissertation, Ohio State University.

Kelly, G.A. (1955). *The Psychology of Personal Constructs*. New York: Norton. (Reprinted by Routledge, 1990.)

Neimeyer, R.A. and Mahoney, M.J. (eds) (1995). *Constructivism in Psychotherapy*. Washington: American Psychological Association.

Tschudi, F. (1977). Loaded and honest questions: a construct theory view of symptoms and therapy. In D. Bannister (ed.) *New Perspectives in Personal Construct Theory*. London: Academic Press.

Winter, D.A. (1992). *Personal Construct Psychology in Clinical Practice. Theory, Research and Applications*. London: Routledge.

Chapter 17

When things go the therapist's way: the case of Sarah

with a case study by Felix Economakis

PRELUDE

This case study is probably every trainee therapist's dream. The patient responds well to the treatment, symptom reduction is immediately apparent during treatment and the therapist's use of the therapeutic model is clear, concise and works like a dream. The reason we selected this case, however, is not because it seemed to work well, but rather because Felix, through his own process, was able to recognise that (1) this is rarely the case and (2) that several factors, both internal and external, contributed to this outcome. In his summary and self-evaluation section, Felix reflects upon the importance of being able to demonstrate the efficacy of a particular therapeutic approach and the rarity of being able to use an approach effectively in its purist form.

This case study also highlights that fact that working briefly with clients can be a daunting task but at the same time exciting and rewarding. Felix refers to his own anxieties about the 'ease' with which he was able to apply this new approach and constantly questions other possible explanations or reasons for the outcome.

Finally, this case illustrates that progress in therapy can be time limited and that one should not be afraid to go at the pace that the client sets and make use of the powerful nature that comes from the simplicity of the brief therapy model.

> *Felix Economakis wrote this case study at the beginning of his first year of the post-MSc practitioner diploma and the comments were written half-way through the second year of the post-MSc practitioner diploma.*

Preamble

How did you come to choose this particular case? What did you learn?

There's a saying that 'when the pupil is ready the master appears'. Every so often in my clinical experience I find this to be the case. The 'master' that provides the lesson often tends to materialise in a timely manner in the form of a client who brings with them to the session seemingly 'tailor made' situations to test my newly emerging psychological muscles. Such was the case with Sarah. On my very first day in my placement in primary care, I had barely finished reading the last pages on systemic and brief therapy over the holidays, when in walked Sarah; one of the first clients that had been booked in for me. The situation almost cried out for the exercise of my new learning.

Afterwards, I was rather impressed by the apparent ease with which therapy seemed to unfold with this model, there appeared to be a natural, orderly progression until resolution was reached in just one session.

Rather naively, I believed that this was the shape of things to come with other clients, and looked forward to similar outcomes of therapy that could be relatively content-free yet, nonetheless, remain rapid and impactful. Since then I have learnt that it's rarely that simple. Even when the 'solution' is staring us both in the face, the client is not always after mere solutions at first. Often they have recently taken an emotional battering and just want to be 'held', so to speak, nursing a broken heart or expressing and processing their rollercoaster-ride of feelings, before it is possible to begin goal setting.

Nevertheless, when the client has come to terms with their emotions sufficiently, then brief therapy begins to show its power. Brief therapy's effectiveness lies in its simplicity, which makes it easier for the therapist to keep it in mind and translate it into practice.

CASE STUDY

Introduction

The present case study refers to a 30-year-old female client, seen for a total of two sessions in my capacity as a counsellor in a group practice. A brief-therapy approach was used for the presenting issues relating to panic attacks and anxiety brought about by the client's stressful work environment. A summary of the overall approach and interventions used as well as critical evaluations are provided at the end of the report.

Biographical details

Sarah is a 30-year-old strategic director of a major credit-card company. She was recently married. Her husband, Robert, is a lawyer and they are an upper-middle-class couple. Her father was a successful artist, her mother the manager of her own business. She describes her parents as very supportive but 'possibly overly so'. Life was 'too easy, there were not enough upsets, the path was always clear-cut'.

Sarah is clearly a very high achiever who has never 'failed' in her life. She graduated with a first-class degree from Cambridge University, had a meteoric rise through several high-profile companies, and also obtained an MBA. She is doing a very stressful job in the management division of her present company. Her siblings and husband have similar high-profile careers.

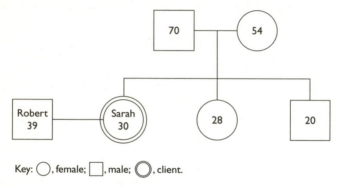

Key: ○, female; □, male; ◎, client.

Figure 5   Genogram of family members discussed by Sarah.

Referral and setting

Sarah was seen in the context of my placement in primary care in the Kentish Town Group Practice, London, UK. She was referred by her GP as describing 'symptoms of extreme anxiety'. She described feelings of helplessness that were causing her to wake up between three and four o'clock in the morning, thereafter she was unable to get back to sleep. She seemed preoccupied with feelings of an inability to perform well in her job.

Appearance and behaviour

The client arrived punctually for her appointment, and was dressed quite smartly. She was of medium build and appearance. Her manner was congruent with generalised anxiety, reflected in her rapid bursts of speech, the tension in her voice, as if fighting to control the tears from her stress and worries. Her body language and posture also reflected this. She seemed restless, occasionally fidgety, shifting between sitting upright and slightly forward with her elbows on her knees, suggesting she was tense, and too preoccupied with something to allow herself to sit more comfortably.

Contract

At the end of the first session it was proposed to Sarah that we could meet for a further five sessions and then review our progress accordingly. It was also pointed out to her that we may not always need to avail ourselves of the full number of sessions, but might decide that we had progressed sufficiently and satisfactorily enough to end therapy sooner. I also informed Sarah of issues of confidentiality and anonymity, and reminded her that she was free to withdraw from therapy at any time if she felt that her needs were not attended to satisfactorily.

Client's definition of the problem

Sarah mentioned that since returning from an idyllic honeymoon eight weeks previously, she had been very anxious about her job resulting in panic attacks, on average twice a week. At the time of counselling Sarah was taking two weeks off work on the pretext of a having caught flu. She worried that she 'was going mad and had lost the plot'. She was also very concerned about the stigma of not being able to 'hack it at work' and what her employers and husband might be making of all this if they really knew her reasons for the time off work. Sarah did not have a specific underlying fearful thought (such as 'I'm going to die') while she was panicking. There was no event at work to make her feel nervous (such as a performance review, upcoming extra responsibilities or a clash with her boss, etc.). The actual day-to-day nature of her work continued in its usual routine way, exactly as before she had left for her honeymoon. She reported that, prior to the holiday, she had experienced only the usual routine stress associated with a challenging job of her kind, but that she had also enjoyed the role because of its challenge, its prestige and its responsibility.

Counsellor's initial assessment

Given that sufficient questioning about Sarah's work environment didn't reveal any actual work-related incidents that might have precipitated the panic attacks, the focus of the initial hypotheses shifted to her recent honeymoon. This centred on Sarah experiencing some sort of shift in personal values, as a recently-married person taking a break from her usual environment, that caused this incongruence upon resuming her former life. Questioning along these lines proved fruitful, supporting the initial hypothesis that Sarah appeared to be experiencing a discrepancy between her previous highly-driven, career-woman identity and a newly-emerging role she felt she was inexorably gravitating towards. It seemed to support developmental stage theorists such as Erickson (1950), who suggested that the new demands, roles and decisions concerning the direction that will be taken in the future experienced by the individual during transition periods provoke an emotional crisis where one's identity may become confused (*diffuse*) and partly unglued. In this context, therefore, Sarah's insomnia and generalised anxiety were perceived as the physical manifestation of this 'psychic conflict' between her former and newly developing and emerging identity as a recently-married woman with all that that might imply for her. This psychic struggle was an immense drain on her nervous energy, and preoccupied her thoughts.

For the first time, Sarah was at a loss concerning what to do, and so panicked, telling herself that she was 'losing it'. Given her unbroken record in scaling all the heights that she had set herself, it was therefore an unprecedented episode in her history and so its impact provoked an exaggerated response. It caused her to doubt herself for the first time, and then, in turn, worry severely about what this must mean about her self-efficacy.

The therapeutic approach that was judged as best serving the interests of the client was one that favoured the use of questions that best elicited and reflected upon her new values and priorities in life, with the aim of reconciling the changing values and identities. As such the style and line of inquiry characteristic of a brief-therapeutic approach was favoured over a more orthodox cognitive-behavioural one. Applying standard CBT protocols for panic attacks was considered less relevant in Sarah's case. In my opinion, Sarah was just 'spooked' by this unprecedented experience precisely because she lacked previous experience of dealing with such uncertainty, resulting in confusion and angst over her next direction. Up to now her direction had been straightforward and nicely mapped out.

Thus CBT's emphasis on behavioural modifications for symptoms was considered of secondary importance to dwelling more exclusively on the use of questions to deconstruct this 'scary' experience for her. This would serve to separate her distress from her perception of not coping, while also reminding her of her previously demonstrated considerable coping resources and resilience.

It was likely that a consistent over-achiever like Sarah was probably used to having her mind focused in one clear direction (such as overcoming the various hurdles of qualification and promotion) when setting her sights at the top from an early age. If so, she would be less exposed and 'immunised' to the usual periodic bouts of doubt and indecision experienced by people whose career choice was never as clear cut from the start. In a sense, she needed to give herself permission to feel distressed and confused. A reflective approach is a good way for normalising this distress by the use of such questions as, 'In what way, specifically, is that a problem?'. This elegantly breaks the pattern of assumptions that, 'It must be bad to feel confused about one's next step in life'.

Theoretical framework

For the purpose of this study brief therapy refers to a therapeutic approach originating from the field of systemic therapy. Within this field, research at the Mental Research Institute and the Brief Family Therapy Centre gave rise to two more formal models commonly referred to as 'brief therapy': *brief strategic therapy* and *solution-focused therapy* respectively. A 'strategic-solution focused' approach (Quick 1996) was the model followed in the present case study. This combines elements of systemic circular questioning, brief strategic therapy's emphasis on precise clarification of *problems*, and solution-focused therapy's emphasis on detailed exploration and amplification of *solutions*. Precise clarification of the problem and detailed amplification of the solution lead to increased specificity and to deconstruction of global problems. Which component of the model is emphasised will shift, depending on the needs of the case and the position of the client.

Content of sessions and interventions

Session 1

After the introductory formalities, the client was asked to define her concerns in her own words. This is in line with deconstructing the presenting issues, allowing clarification and prioritisation of problems thus reducing them to small manageable chunks. Sarah offered just one presiding complaint, her anxiety about work, which affected her beliefs of self-coping and expressed itself physically as insomnia and panic-attacks.

Questions were then asked to determine whose reaction about her concerns she feared most. This revealed a hierarchy of fear, in order of priority – husband, family, colleagues.

It was decided that the anticipated fears would be examined in relation to each of these subjects in turn, but first it was necessary to gather more detailed background information on the client to elicit formative beliefs and experiences, and to gain an idea of Sarah's 'idealised' self. A genogram was constructed with the client, all the while asking the client further questions such as, 'What was that like?' (referring to school, etc.). Sarah was also asked, 'And what are you like, how would your family describe you to me?' The intention was to establish the measure by which Sarah valued or judged herself, with the future aim of examining it to see how realistic it was, or to determine in what ways she may have perceived herself as failing to live up to it.

Sarah's response to the latter question was enlightening: 'Go-getting, energetic, buzzing, driven, happy-go-lucky and ambitious'. In order to determine how Sarah judged a person (such as her current self) who lacked these qualities, she was then asked what the opposite of these qualities was. Again the rationale was to determine how the client views themself when they fail to meet the standards they have set for themself. Instead of a negative stream of adjectives, however, Sarah replied, 'Laid-back and relaxed'. She was then asked if this was 'necessarily such a bad state to be in?'. She replied that it wasn't but that was not who she was. This reply was puzzling. Was Sarah perceiving these opposites to her idealised behaviour as more attractive, possibly with a view to embracing them more in the future and hence making the change more acceptable and valid to herself?

The client was then asked the 'miracle question' (De Shazer, 1988). This is in line with a solution-focused approach and serves a number of functions. In this case, the aim was to explore what Sarah really wanted to be, or do, as opposed to how she felt she *should* be acting. Such responses would allow the basis for an exploration of the conflict that she may be experiencing. Sarah replied that she would actually like to leave her job as a director, but to 'save face' she would ideally have to be made redundant. This would neatly provide her with the excuse to take time out and consider her next option without implying to others that she wasn't up to the demands of the job, or had somehow failed to cope with it, or let it defeat her, in some way.

Further questioning along these lines revealed that Sarah was attributing negative conclusions to others around her and, therefore, was keenly worried about their judgements. It also revealed how her perceived sense of self-worth was bound up with her sense of continued high performance and achievement. She still saw herself as essentially being unable to live up to her former standards. Being 'less' of her former self implied that people must think less of her. Having now gained a measure of the core fears fuelling her anxiety, more information was gathered for later challenging her fears with the subjects that she had mentioned previously.

Her 'miracle scenario' was pursued with further questioning, urging her to consider whether she was already envisaging a time when she would leave the company, or planned to have a family, etc. This is also in line with solution-focused therapy's 'instances where exceptions are already happening' (De Shazer 1988). Sarah was encouraged to explore how she could move towards her goals. Choices and options were soon becoming more apparent to her, and she seemed visibly relieved. Exploring alternative scenarios such as part-time work, trying a different, less-demanding company with the justification that she was 'downsizing' in preparation for the eventual start of motherhood, etc. seemed productive.

At this point Sarah's considerable coping assets were brought into the conversation, reminding her that anyone who gets a first-class degree or undertakes an MBA undoubtedly possesses resourcefulness, is good at problem solving and working under pressure. She was asked to consider future scenarios that would be beyond her problem-solving skills once she put her mind to it. She sheepishly agreed that there were none.

The next phase, in line with brief therapy was to validate and normalise the client's concerns. Sarah was assured that she was not going mad, and that, in the course of normal development, ordinary life brings 'difficulties' to everyone when shifts in roles are necessary. The problems arise when ordinary difficulty was considered 'problematic' or when the existence of normal stage-appropriate difficulty is denied. It was suggested to Sarah that it was natural for people to outgrow their old values and priorities. It was a natural reaction, therefore, on her part to begin delving into new roles and values, having recently reached that symbolic age of thirty and also got married. Sarah was then complimented for her impressive achievements and for managing to 'keep it together' despite her dilemma. It was also put to her that she had already proved her worth in nine years of successful business, plus one year of doing an MBA. These were accomplishments that no one could overlook or take away from her, so she could hardly be construed as a failure by any reasonable standards.

The next phase was to challenge those previously-mentioned domains where she feared the worst reactions. It was decided to start in reverse order with the easiest first, in the hope of building upon this success and demonstrating a useful pattern for deconstruction of her other problems. Starting with the feared judgements of her co-workers and boss, Sarah was asked to imagine the opinions of her colleagues upon learning of her leaving the company. Her exaggerated negative replies were then put in context by eliciting her more favourable personal opinion of other staff who had left the company, then comparing the difference between these two judgements and finding out why they were different. Sarah was asked if she still recalled any emotion retained for a worker who had left a year ago. She could not. The point I aimed to put across was that, even in the worst case scenario where staff formed an unfavourable opinion of her for leaving the company, it was hardly likely that anyone would care in a short space of time anyway, because people have other things to occupy their thoughts and emotions. Besides, why was it so important what other people, whom she barely knew and was unlikely to ever see again, thought about her anyway? Could they possibly know enough about her to make an informed definitive statement of her worth, and then retain this emotion indefinitely? This appeared to sink in.

Next Sarah was asked to imagine the worst reactions of her family. She was asked if she truly believed that her family would stop loving her if she changed job, or opted out altogether to have a baby. She replied that they would always love her, but they had grown accustomed to seeing her as her old buzzing, go-getting self. Thus, the concern revolved around the habits of seeing people in different roles. She was then asked what was her experience of her family's reactions to daughters who gave birth to a first child? Would they still love her even though they would have to adjust their habit of relating to her in the accustomed way, and did she think the same would apply in her case? She smiled as she agreed that they would be happy for her. She realised that with these two domains she had exaggerated her fears, but she was genuinely worried about her husband's reaction as this was 'different'.

First, the issue of money was explored, to establish whether there was any practical obligation to continue employment regardless of circumstance. There was not, Robert's salary was substantial and could cover both of them when the time came for Sarah to have a baby. Sarah confessed her fears regarding disappointing her husband's high expectations if she left her job, Robert might think, 'that's not the girl I married'. He had met and married a girl who was ambitious, independent and exciting. Now she would only appear ordinary and boring in comparison, and her 'unused' brain 'would turn to mush'. Again, the theme of approval being linked to performance/achievement was evident. A similar reality-checking approach (asking her if this was necessarily the case) was pursued as before. Would she truly be unable to offer intelligent opinions on the world, or to comment on her husband's anecdotes from work? Moreover, presumably he had married her with some expectation of having children at some stage anyway. There may be some negotiation over timing but the tacit agreement that she would have to take time out or downsize her demanding work schedule at some stage of advanced pregnancy was always there regardless. Therefore, was it not better to elicit Robert's opinion herself rather than jump to conclusions about his worst reaction, and then worry about something that she did not know as a fact? To assist in this line of inquiry an empty-chair role-play was introduced. Sarah was asked to imagine that Robert was present and to fully say what was on her mind to him openly and honestly, while he listened intently. Quite tearfully, she explained to 'Robert' that she was unhappy at work but that she was too scared to move forward into the unknown, particularly because she was very afraid of his opinion of her leaving her job. In fact, her feelings and fears were so eloquently put that it was suggested to her that she repeat this conversation to Robert herself vebatim, allowing them to explore each other's feelings instead of imagining them.

In terms of treatment direction I envisaged being at a junction. One fork led to dwelling on the emotional impact in detail. The second fork led to putting the emotional consequences on hold for the time being, and exploring the premises behind the fears instead. If, at the end of this exploration, Sarah's fears and emotions were still unaffected, then they would be addressed in their own right. The approach that I was suggesting to the client was 'I'm willing to address the problems that are distressing you, but I'm not quite sure that these are necessarily problems in the first place, as opposed to normal reactions to where you are in life right now'. In reassessing this conceptual shift, Sarah's attitude towards her 'problem' changed, as then did the resulting emotions.

The session ended with a reminder of her considerable assets and coping resources, and that on the basis of past evidence, she would doubtless find a way of directing these resources to find the best solution to deal with whatever options she decided to pursue. For homework I gave her a handout from the *Mental Health Book* explaining the CBT rationale for panic attacks and anxiety symptoms. This covered the behavioural side of understanding her body's responses. We had not been able to cover this in detail during the session, other than to mention that her anxiety attacks were her body misinterpreting internal body cues. Being a highly-educated person, I knew that she would be able to educate herself on this physiological aspect without further assistance.

Session 2 (1 week later)

Sarah seemed visibly different. There was a marked difference in her demeanour, posture and tone, and she was smiling. She stated that a lot of our discussion had sunk in and she had not had any further anxiety attacks. She felt sufficiently confident with her abilities to cope with her changing priorities in the workplace. She wanted to see how things went before seeing if she needed counselling. Sarah had decided to stick with her job for another six months, then she could either move elsewhere or see how things went about starting a family with Robert. She mentioned the reminder of her options and flexibility in decision making as being particularly useful, and a huge relief for her, during counselling. Thus, she reframed her current job merely as a stepping-stone rather than a definitive measure of her worth. She felt able to handle things again. After only twenty minutes, we agreed to finish our sessions together, and she was reminded that the door remained open in the future in the unlikely event of her experiencing any reoccurrence of the anxiety attacks.

Summary and self-evaluation

The apparent success of this case was assisted, in large part, by the relatively straightforward presenting problem and a client who possessed very good problem-solving skills and a high degree of intelligence. She was able to accommodate and adjust to alternative perspectives relatively easily through reasoning. In other words, Sarah was an ideal client and would have made good progress with any brief therapy counsellor. This enabled the counselling process to proceed smoothly along the brief-therapy model. As such, this case was chosen not so much for its relative success but because it was the purest demonstration of brief therapy available in my recent practice. In most other instances brief therapy has been 'contaminated' by digressions into cognitive-behavioural techniques.

As a recent practitioner of this model, it was impressive to see the deconstruction of the client's problems with such forceful brevity by the employment of a style of questioning designed to elicit thought-provoking reflections. It was also encouraging to see how 'change is possible now' (Hoyt 1995) rather than from later; well into the allotted number of sessions. It impressed upon me the efficiency and parsimony possible with this approach. The theoretical simplicity of the model also allowed me to remember the steps of the model, as outlined in Quick (1996, Ch. 1, p. 12), with relative ease.

With hindsight, many other useful questions were omitted (such as, 'between now and time of referral what have you been doing?') in my haste to follow my own leads. More could also have been made of Sarah's linking her perceived sense of approval with an unrelenting state of driven achievement.

Use of supervision

Owing to the brevity of the case, by the time that I had my fortnightly meeting with my supervisor I had already seen Sarah for the second and final time.

References

De Shazer, S. (1988). *Clues, Investigating Solutions in Brief Therapy*. New York: W.W. Norton.

Erickson, E.H. (1950). *Childhood and Society*. New York: Lyle Stuart.

Hoyt, M. (1995). *Brief Therapy and Managed Care*, Ch. 7, On time in brief therapy. San Fransisco: Jossey-Bass.

Quick, E.K. (1996). *Doing what Works in Brief Therapy*. London: Academic Press.

Chapter 18

Client case study: a first attempt at psychodynamic individual therapy

with a case study by Antonia Reay

PRELUDE

We have chosen to present this case as it illustrates how confusion and uncertainty on the part of the therapist may be amplified in the wake of tensions between the 'push' of professional training and the 'pull' of supervision. Here, the author struggles with the anxiety of not knowing and the inherent tendency of many trainees to resolve their uncertainty in terms of a sense of some personal lack. People are complex, and working with people who are working towards change is even more so.

What is particularly unusual about this case is the ease with which the author reveals herself to the reader. She is honest and forthright and seemingly unaware of the immediacy that she creates between herself and her audience. Trainees often make the mistake of assuming that the reader, or assessor, of a report is only interested in the client or the subject of a case study or process report. This is far from the case. Indeed it is the unique interaction between the therapist and the client that makes for excellent reading. Great case studies and process reports account for what is happening both within and between the therapist and the client. Accounts of this nature require a comprehension of, and fluency with, the language of self and other – the simultaneous observation of the facts without and the ruminations and machinations within.

This case study raises interesting issues regarding the role of training in equipping the novice therapist with sufficient competencies to practise. It is clearly unethical to practise beyond one's own competencies. However, the evaluation of these competencies often becomes skewed by the feelings of self-doubt or anxiety that naturally arise when the stakes are high. Knowing when one has reached a level where it is safe to practise is a judgement that is not made on one fateful and momentous day; rather it is a recurring and iterative task that stays with us. This question may rise to the surface within sessions, later as we reflect alone or in consultation with colleagues. We often fail to present the whole picture of our work. Instead we choose instances and freeze them, as if they were available to us to sculpt and rewrite and ultimately ensure the idealised outcome. Such certainty is simply not possible in the bespoke and fluid craft of psychotherapy. It is indeed fundamental to development that we reflect upon our practice in the light of new learning, however rumination and perseveration are more often associated with self-punishment and self-deprecation than growth and development. We should not be fooled into thinking that it is either necessary or desirable to possess the capacity to 'see around corners'. Regardless of our stage of training or expertise we will always have to carry with us the humility of not knowing. Aspirations of one day 'knowing it all' imply that the answer is out there – that one size fits all. Thankfully, but sometimes painfully, it is never that simple.

> *Antonia Reay wrote this case study during the last year of her post-MSc in the Practice of Counselling Psychology, the final stage in the process of chartership. Antonia's reflective comments were added to her work some ten months after the original case study was conceived.*

Preamble

Why I chose this particular case

I chose to write about the first client that I saw for individual counselling. My choice was partly pragmatic for, at the time of writing, I was looking for a post and did not have any clients. However, I also chose this particular case because I found it challenging and complex for reasons that I think may be relevant to other trainee therapists.

There were three main factors that contributed to my difficulty. First, I think that there was a dissonance between the theoretical orientation of my placement and what I was being taught at the time. Second, my supervision group consisted of supervisees of far greater experience than me, which inhibited me from finding the group as useful and supportive as supervision undoubtedly can be. Third, and finally, I experienced the anxiety and self-doubt natural to a first-year trainee, which I think left me open to powerful countertransferential resonance with my client's low self-esteem and her apprehension and doubt about the process of therapy. At the time, I lacked the skill to be able to regularly take a step back from the content of the session and ask myself, 'What's going on here?' rather than being over-whelmed by a confusing mixture of my own and my client's emotions. The way in which these and other factors affected my work will be discussed fully in the later sections of this case study.

What I think and feel retrospectively about what I have produced

It has been interesting to review this case study again, now that I have recently finished my training. I am struck by my honesty about my own self-doubt and by the sense of what an enormous responsibility being an individual therapist seemed at the time. Experience has given me more faith in the process of therapy and in the client's own resources. Now that I am less weighed down by the pressure of being a 'good-enough' therapist, there is more room to think creatively.

It has also been useful for me to put my reaction to this first placement in the wider context of my experience of starting new posts or placements. I have chosen very different contexts for each of my posts and I now know from my personal therapy and from supervision that when faced with a new situation or when working with a client that I find very challenging, I am particularly vulnerable to feeling overwhelmed and inadequate or deskilled as a therapist. I am better able to tolerate these feelings because experience tells me that I can reframe them as a kind of professional 'growing-pain' and that they are a sure sign that I am learning a great deal and will feel competent and confident again in time.

What I learnt about the practice and theory of therapy

I learnt that it is acceptable not to be able to come up with spectacular interpretations, and that the harder one tries, the less likely it is to happen. Bion (1967) recommends that therapists 'abandon memory and desire in relation to your client', suggesting that in striving to remember what your client said and trying to get your counselling techniques 'right', one is distracted from the process of staying with the client.

I began to make a conscious effort to stop tracking the content of Maria's discourse every now and then in order to check how I was feeling (that is, scan my own reactions) or look for what I felt might be the metacommunication in the content. Rather than feeling that I had to keep all three levels in mind at once.

I learnt that I really wanted to try out a more structured, briefer cognitive approach and see how I found it, primarily because I wanted to put into practice the ideas that I was learning on my course. My understanding of the practice and theory of psychodynamic counselling has increased since seeing Maria, and I have used some of these insights to discuss the case. I think I needed time to digest the case, but also I became more used to juggling course reading requirements and assignments, with doing the reading necessary for particular clients.

CASE STUDY

Introduction

I saw Maria at the psychotherapy department of my local hospital, where I was beginning a placement as an 'honorary psychotherapist'. The honoraries were a mixture of trainee psychoanalysts, counsellors and psychiatric registrars, all of whom received once-weekly group supervision lasting ninety minutes, from one of two consultant psychotherapists. Referrals came from Community Mental Health Teams and were assessed by one of the consultants prior to being allocated to an honorary psychotherapists. The department's orientation was psychodynamic and clients were offered psychotherapy for a year on average.

I arranged my placement prior to starting the MSc course in Counselling Psychology at City University. I chose to work somewhere psychodynamic because I was familiar with psychodynamic concepts from having worked in a group setting for several years, so I felt that I had a foundation to work from. In retrospect, some of my anxieties may have been minimised had there been a better fit between what I was being taught in my training course and the theoretical orientation of my practice placement.

Summary of theoretical orientation

The objectives of psychodynamic therapy, as I then understood them, were to increase the client's insight into his/her desires and conflicts and how these link to past and current relationships (Jacobs 1999). The theoretical background to the case is post-Freudian, in particular drawing upon object-relations theory and, to a lesser extent, some concepts associated with ego-psychology as ideated by Erickson (1965) and Kohut (1971).

Although these two branches of post-Freudian thought do differ in theoretical emphasis, I feel that they are sufficiently compatible for my purposes, through sharing the same foundations and many of the same assumptions. The existence of an 'unconscious' is assumed, for example. The unconscious is a Freudian metaphor for the mental processes that we do not know about or do not understand, and which are not usually accessible to conscious thought, but whose presence 'must be inferred, discovered and translated' (Freud 1915), usually by the therapist in conjunction with the client.

Object-relations theory, unlike earlier psychoanalytic thought, sees humans as chiefly motivated by the wish to form relationships (Fairburn 1952). 'Object-relations' are the interpersonal relationships as they are depicted intrapsychically (internally). Other people, especially care-givers, are seen by the infant as potentially able to gratify his/her needs (physical and emotional), therefore the baby becomes attached to them. These early object-relations are the relationships that largely shape the infant's future interactions with people, including those as an adult. This occurs because the infant is said to internalise his/her perceptions of these key early relationships and they form the 'intrapsychic templates' (Mahler et al. 1975) of their experiences and expectations of others.

Object-relations theorists argue that a baby begins life in a state of psychological fusion or 'symbiosis' with its mother and gradually progresses towards separation. Mahler, an influential theorist of this school, argued that the negotiation and experience of this state of fusion and of the process of 'separation–individuation' is extremely influential to the pattern of the child's later relationships.

In my work with Maria the dynamic notions of transference, counter-transference and defence mechanisms had particular prominence. Psychodynamic theorists suggest that during the course of therapy a transference relationship (Freud 1915) develops, in which the client distorts the therapist–client relationship according to the templates formed by earlier relationships. That is, the emotions, experience and expectations of earlier relationships are played out in the counselling relationship and potentially provide the therapist with useful information on the organisation of the client's internal life.

Transference is seen as a central tool of psychodynamic counselling and, according to object relations theory, the therapist must work with the transference relationship, but essentially retain a positive, reality-based stance towards a therapeutic alliance. So the therapist can move between the two, reflecting back to the client discrepancies between the 'distorted' and 'realistic' experiences of the relationship.

Countertransference is thought of from a 'totalistic' viewpoint by most psychodynamic theorists (Kernberg 1965). This view sees countertransference as encompassing 'the total emotional reaction of the psychoanalyst to the patient in the treatment situation'. This includes the counsellor's own areas of emotional conflict, which through personal therapy, supervision and experience the counsellor learns to identify. It also involves countertransference proper, which involves the unconscious communication to the counsellor from the client's internal world through the transference relationship.

The counsellor has to monitor both his/her reactions to the client and the impact the client's discourse has on him/her and, if this is consistently felt, to use this as valuable information about the client's internal world. I take a totalistic view of countertransference as expressed by Sullivan (1953), who sees it as part of a continuous give-and-take between client and therapist in an interpersonal space.

Defences are a key psychodynamic concept. Perry (1993) defines them as 'an individual's automatic psychological response to internal or external stressors or emotional conflict'. Freud argued that defences were triggered by the anxiety caused by a conflict between one's wishes and what one's internal rules or external reality allows. Perry argues that character traits are partly made up of specific defences which individuals use repetitively across diverse situations. These become problematic when they are inflexible, block out conflicts from conscious awareness, are maladaptive (apart from, presumably, in the early situation in which they were learned) and interfere with positive outcomes.

The referral and convening the first session

Maria was referred by her GP, whom she had visited complaining of depression and anxiety. She was assessed by one of the two consultants, who was not my supervisor. I began the first session by introducing myself and emphasising the confidentiality of the session and what the limits of that confidentiality were. I acknowledged that Maria had already been assessed, so I had some idea of what brought her to counselling, but I asked her to tell me in her own words what she hoped that we could work on together.

Maria was a very attractive 26-year-old woman from South America. She was smartly dressed, confident in manner – having good eye contact, a clear voice and smiling often. However, I wondered if she was quite anxious underneath, as she sat forward on her chair, clutching her handbag in front of her. She described her main problem as one of depression and that sometimes she wanted to die, but felt that she would never try to kill herself because she had a 5-year-old son to look after. She was expansive about what was wrong with her marriage and her husband John. It seemed harder for her to talk about what she was like in the marriage and when I questioned her about it, she quickly reverted to talking about John.

Maria described how the relationship began with her husband by saying, 'we were like two butterflies', but that John had two faces and that now she felt they were so near and yet so far apart. She also described herself as having two faces – one looking fine from the outside, but a very different face on the inside. She described how initially her GP had not believed that she was depressed. She said she had coped with feeling down when she was in South America by going out dancing with a friend, but that she knew no young people here, as her husband was older and boring and she did not like his friends. She had spoken to the other mothers at her son's school initially, but had decided they were not her 'sort' and also wondered what they thought of her.

Maria said she had sometimes felt unhappy while growing up, as her mother and father had divorced when she was five and, thereafter, her mother had worked very long hours and would return in the evenings, tired and irritable. Maria had one elder sister, with whom she got on, but described her as 'reserved'. Nonetheless, she wished they were near her now, as she felt isolated and trapped at home with her small son. (See Figure 6, Appendix A.)

The session ended with Maria asking, 'if [I thought] she had problems, was there something wrong with her?' I asked about her expectations of therapy and she said she had none, but wanted advice on whether to leave her husband or not. I explained that psychotherapy did not involve giving advice, but aimed to increase self-knowledge and the confidence to find one's own answers. Maria said that it would be good, at least, to have someone to talk to every week.

Initial formulation of the problem

Maria's presenting problem was her feelings of depression, which she described as springing from feeling trapped and isolated. She also described feeling very anxious and panicky when left alone in the house. Her anxiety and depression seemed linked to my impression of her as someone who found relationships with others difficult, her metaphor of 'two faces' suggested a possible lack of trust in people being what they seemed. It sounded as if it was hard for her to take the risk of getting to know the mums at school – easier to decide they 'weren't her sort', rather than face possible disappointment or rejection. I did not know what possible cultural differences might be making social contact more difficult to negotiate, even after six years in Britain, but made a mental note to explore this further when it came up again.

I wondered about Maria's levels of self-esteem. She described herself as 'weak' and her concern about the sort of impression that she made on others could be a symptom of low self-esteem, but also of a lack of self-knowledge, or a fear that what was inside her was unacceptable in some way. She had said heatedly that she could not stand people who did not say what they thought, I had asked if she felt that I was not doing so and she had replied 'maybe, yes'. I wondered if low self-esteem or poor self-image played an important part in her depression.

I also wondered to what extent Maria was able to take responsibility for her problems and decisions, for example, it seemed more comfortable to focus on John's shortcomings as the cause of her unhappiness, rather than to reflect on herself. Moreover, her isolation seemed to be the fault of the boringness or unsuitability of others, rather than any difficulty on her part. This might fit in with her wanting me, whom she had just met (albeit that I was the professional), to advise her on whether to leave her husband.

Negotiating a contract and therapeutic aims

I explained the boundaries of the counselling session, in terms of time and frequency of sessions – once a week for fifty minutes. I also said that this time was available to Maria for up to a year. In the second session, I felt we needed to spend time negotiating therapeutic aims, as Maria's expectations were of advice and diagnosis. Maria had named curing her depression as one aim. I suggested that this was not something that could happen overnight, but that gradually we could explore her depression and understand it more. Maria also said that she wanted to increase her confidence. I replied that through Maria talking with me, and obtaining my feedback, her self-knowledge and self-acceptance should increase and so, hopefully, would her confidence.

Biographical details of the client

Maria was 26 years old, one of two daughters of a divorced couple. She was born in South America and her mother and sister still lived in her city of origin. She was in contact with them by phone and letter and visited them once a year with her son. Her husband went there too, for the first time while she was in therapy. Her mother has had therapy and Maria says she gets on better with her as a result, as her mother now accepts that she was a difficult mother, and wants to make amends. Her sister was currently seeing a psychiatrist following a 'breakdown'. She has only met her father on rare occasions throughout her life. He had been married three times and had three sets of children. He reportedly had a bad temper and was sometimes violent to her mother while they were still married. Maria came to England six years ago to study English. She had a brief romance with John and found that she was pregnant. Maria says that John refused to pay for an abortion, so she returned to her country of origin while pregnant. John phoned her there and eventually persuaded her to come back to Britain and they got married. She feels that his friends think that she trapped John into marriage. John is about 10 years older than Maria and has a well-respected job, to which he is very committed. This sometimes involves him in working unsocial hours, which Maria resents. Her son, Alex is five and has now started school. Maria works for a photographic development shop part-time.

The therapeutic plan and main techniques used

The initial therapeutic plan was to establish a 'therapeutic alliance', that is sufficient levels of collaboration to enable Maria to open up to me and let me try to understand the nature of her distress (Horvath et al. 1993), even though this might be a painful process at times. My aim was to do this by listening attentively, reflecting back what I heard and keeping the boundaries of the session, thus fostering Winnicott's (1958) 'safe, holding environment'.

An important theme for Maria, as already discussed, seemed to be her view of herself as 'weak', disempowered and needing to look outside herself for the power over her situation – to her husband for the state of her marriage, to me for the answers to her problems. I felt that her focus on John in our sessions was a symptom of her feeling that she was insubstantial, and did not have an internal view of herself. I hoped that by feeding back what I heard and interpreting it (once the alliance was established) she might begin to be more sure of herself. I aimed to model acceptance of what Maria brought to the session, in the hope that she might begin to accept herself more.

The use of interpretation in my work with Maria was at times laboured. It is the process of linking themes, defences, what is left unsaid and what the counsellor feels is happening between him/her and the client in the session, in order to suggest to the client the possibility of 'unconscious feelings and ideas, of which the client may not be fully aware' (Jacobs, 1999). My interpretations were largely dismissed by Maria, which may have been the result of poor timing, inaccuracy and/or defensive activity on Maria's part, which I was failing to address (McLoughlin 1995). Possibly this defensive activity could have been due to the very act of my listening and trying to understand Maria, as that might have been eroding her defence of keeping people at arms length, and thus causing her anxiety.

I made few interpretations of the transference relationship between Maria and myself, even though I often felt, as did my supervision group, that there was material in her discourse which seemed highly relevant to our counselling relationship, at the same time as being about external relationships and situations. Some of this caution was due to my perception that it was part of my job to hold on to my inferences about a client until such time as they brought an implied awareness of them, or at least relevant material about which I could proffer my suggestion. Bion (1959) concieves of the therapist's role as partly that of a container, which holds the client's disturbing feelings until a time when he/she can accept those feelings as his/her own. I was also aware of the 'temptations of power and certainty' (Amundson et al. 1993), about having too much faith in one's hypotheses as a therapist. Moreover, on a much more practical note, as a trainee counsellor, it was very hard to formulate the parallel process that I felt was happening in the session into some sort of useful and digestible form, while continuing to attend to the client's discourse. On many occasions, by the time I had spotted a recurring theme or made a connection in the client's discourse and had formulated what I wanted to say into some coherent form, the client had moved on to talk about something else. Of course this was not necessarily a bad thing, albeit frustrating, for if something needs to be interpreted it should be about a theme that recurs in different forms from time to time, so there should be other opportunities for the counsellor to say what he/she feels needs saying.

My main reluctance to make transference interpretations centred around, what I now know to be a misunderstanding of, how one should try to feed back transference hypotheses to the client. Theoretically, I knew that transference is not about the counsellor, but about the way the counsellor is experienced in terms of the client's inner world, or as a reflection of his/her discourse. However, in the intensity of the session, it felt hard to frame my insight into words other than, 'I wonder if this is also how you feel about me?' or, 'is that also what happens here, between us?' This also seemed to be the manner in which my supervision group spoke of feeding back transference interpretations to the client, or it may have been my inexperience which misinterpreted them. Essentially, what I and Maria missed was the 'as if' quality (McLoughlin 1995) of what happens in therapy, which might have made such interpretations easier for me to say and for her to hear.

Instead such interpretations often felt too bald (Meltzer 1967) and presumptuous to say. This was partly due to the fact that Maria almost always refused to acknowledge that anything I said or did (including breaks) affected her in any way, or that any of her discourse had any relevance to the therapeutic relationship. I could also have been feeling countertransferentially, the feelings of disorientation and anxiety that Maria felt whenever she had to depend on anyone, which may have resonated with my own fears about my performance as a counsellor.

With hindsight, apart from not trying so hard, I should probably have done more to address and explore Maria's anxiety about letting people near her. Also, according to Malan (1979), for an interpretation to be taken on board it needs to have three elements: (1) the here and now of the counselling relationship, (2) factors current in the client's life situation, and (3) issues relating of the client's past. Although, worrying that I managed to include all three parts in my interpretation every time would have increased my anxiety.

An example of an occasion when I felt that there was material in the session probably relevant to the therapeutic relationship occurred when I missed a session. Maria had told me the week before that she could not make the session due to the demands of work. I had, therefore, used the time to do other things and had not gone to my placement. However, Maria had turned up after all and had, according to the secretary, been furious, demanding, 'Well, should I come next week or not?' I had felt awful about not being there, even though Maria had her part in it, as my supervision group pointed out. At the following session, I tried to facilitate Maria saying how she felt about me not being there. She insisted, with a smile, that it had not mattered at all and that she had much more important things on her mind. However, I felt that there were angry feelings underneath and she stared hard at me over her smile. I now understand that Maria's reluctance to say that she was angry may have sprung from her anxiety that expressing negative feelings towards me would result in rejection. In our later sessions in therapy she acknowledged harbouring fears about an older, needed but annoying, friend and conceded that there might have been a parallel in our relationship. I also wondered if there might have been cultural factors that made it hard to be anything but polite to a professional.

The rest of the session was spent with her describing how angry she felt when John ignored her and she went into detail for the first time about one of their more dramatic fights. She said her anger was like a 'fire' and that she had stopped hitting her husband during fights because the strength of her feelings scared her and she did not know where it came from. I felt she was letting me know that she was angry with me too, and that she was a force to be reckoned with. I drew a parallel between her anger at being ignored by John and her possibly feeling overlooked last week and that she had talked of feeling dismissed by her mum as a child. She acknowledged that she had felt overlooked last week, but said it was not at all the same as with family and that she felt more angry with John than with anyone. I also wondered whether being ignored resonated with her own feelings of insubstantiality and emptiness. It also seemed to be an example of how it was difficult for her to let people get it right for her, but I felt that she had partially acknowledged what I had said and I left anything else for another session.

Difficulties in the work and the use of supervision

A major difficulty in the work with Maria was that she missed roughly one in three of our sessions, sometimes giving me notice, sometimes not. She was also often late. Usually Maria's reasons for her lateness or absence were to do with child-care problems, work demands or transport problems. Clearly there were practical difficulties which interfered with Maria's regular attendance, but I felt that there must have been a psychological aspect as well, for there to be such consistent difficulties to attend at a time that we had agreed together. My supervision group felt that Maria was expressing her resistance to allowing a fruitful discourse between us, which would involve her feeling and expressing vulnerabilities. They suggested that I review my progress with Maria and ask her if deciding on a date to end would feel containing and help her to use her time more fully. I put this to Maria, who shrugged and said she did not mind, but then asked was this because I was angry that she could not always come. I did feel annoyed and disappointed when she did not attend. However, I found it difficult to know how to discuss this further, although I did try, as I partly interpreted her absence in terms of myself – as a comment on my inadequacies and as confirmation of my concern that this type of therapy was not helping Maria. I did bring my fears that I was not a 'good-enough' counsellor to supervision, but did not let them know the extent of my anxiety. I think, at least initially, I was concerned that the group might confirm my fears. In supervision, it was suggested that when in doubt I stick to Rogers' (1975) qualities of being empathic, congruent and accepting, qualities which have relevance across therapeutic models (Horvath and Luborsky 1993). These authors also pointed out that a significant part of what I was feeling was very probably the result of countertransferential processes – that my self-doubt as a trainee therapist was resonating with Maria's powerful feelings of anxiety and her low self-esteem. I felt supported by their comments, but still felt like a rabbit caught in the headlights of a car at times. I also took my concerns to personal therapy, where we discussed them in terms of countertransference and my self-esteem and established that I knew I was a safe counsellor really, if not a very proficient one yet.

The comments of Bion and McLoughlin suggest that my anxieties were not uncommon among those beginning psychodynamic work. However, I also think that the degree of anxiety and doubt that I felt about the model and my work, were exacerbated by three other factors: (1) the complexity of the model and its emphasis on the self as the major tool in therapy, (2) the lack of fit between me and my supervision group, and (3) the difference in emphasis between work in placement and the taught component of my MSc training.

The complexity of the model

Psychodynamic counselling is a highly complex and rich process. It requires the therapist to attend to the client's discourse at several different levels – to track the content, to attend to deeper communication or themes, which may be contained in that content, about the client's internal world and how this relates to what is occurring in the session between counsellor and client.

Such reliance on the self of the counsellor is a tall order for a trainee therapist. McLoughlin (1995) argues that the counsellor needs to split him/herself into a participating part and an observing part – warning that he/she needs to maintain the detachment of the therapeutic stance and not burden it with too much feeling. Moreover, I think that the lack of concrete tasks and developmental markers within the psychodynamic model make it feel a rather nebulous process at times, as it is hard to judge if progress is occurring. The process of psychodynamic counselling requires a great deal of faith.

The lack of fit between me and my supervision group

My supervision group was supportive, but consisted of two other super-visees who were far more experienced than I was and who had been members of the supervision group for at least a year. One member was a trainee psychoanalyst, whom I had worked with in a group setting, and who was near completion of his training after six years, and the other was a counsellor on a post-qualification course. My supervisor was a consultant psychotherapist of great humour and energy who, although supportive, was genuinely puzzled by my anxiety and lack of confidence given my group psychotherapy experience. I think my course tutor may well have been accurate when he commented, after marking this case study, that perhaps the supervision group failed to spot the degree of my anxiety, because I was worried about showing it, in a process parallel to that occurring in therapy, where Maria rarely showed me the degree of the anger and sadness she described, probably for fear of rejection.

The theoretical dissonance between my training course and my placement

I found it hard to have the necessary faith in psychodynamic counselling while I was studying other theoretical orientations during my training. Particularly as cognitive behavioural therapy (CBT) and systemic models (which I was learning about at the time) emphasise a more collaborative, active and transparent approach, addressing symptoms more directly, which was attractive to me. Although I also feel that these other approaches benefit greatly when they acknowledge the dynamic nature of the thera-peutic relationship in the way that psychodynamic counselling does. Also, I did not do enough reading around the case, partly due to the academic demands of my course.

I think my lack of confidence in the work Maria and I were doing was partly due to my sympathy with her discontent that we were not directly addressing either her depression or her anxiety. I felt her interpersonal difficulties would also have come up if we had worked collaboratively on concrete tasks (Ryle 1975).

The therapeutic ending

About six months into the therapy my confidence in the work Maria and I were doing increased somewhat and I felt that the relationship became warmer. Maria's self-confidence had increased and she described feeling more at home in Britain. She had begun to socialise with her work colleagues for the first time and had developed a flirtation with one of them – a 19-year-old man. She felt that he had helped her to discover her 'real self' – outgoing, fun-loving and young. She saw this side of herself as having been oppressed by her husband John, with whom her relationship had deteriorated. I thought that she was increasingly projecting the depressed, isolated, responsible, cold and violent side of herself on to him. I tried to challenge this split by suggesting she had both sides to herself, which she fleetingly acknowledged.

Around this time Maria began to struggle with questions about whether she was lovable, what did love constitute, could it be non-physical, and when was it OK to hug someone? This was catalysed by her deciding to break off her relationship with her young colleague, because she was frightened by the strength of her feelings and felt that it was not going to work because of his youth. These difficulties and important questions that Maria brought to the sessions were counterpoised by a new tendency for her to cut off a topic after a while, with phrases like, 'well it doesn't matter, I just live day by day at the moment' or, 'anyway, I met a new man this weekend'. My supervision group felt that she was at a crossroad between taking more responsibility for her difficulties, such as her marriage, which she saw as increasingly doomed, and really looking at herself, or taking refuge in going out more and more, seeing less of her son and husband and not thinking about her life.

Three weeks before we were due to break for the summer holidays, Maria told me at the end of a session that she wanted to end her therapy. I asked her to come back for the next two sessions or so, so that we could talk about her decision. Maria came back for the final session before the break. She explained that she did not want to talk about her problems any more, even though they would probably 'catch up with her'. She went on to say that she did not feel that she was getting any further with the question of whether she should leave John or not, although, when I challenged her about this, she admitted that she did not actually want to make that decision, for fear of the consequences either way.

I said that I felt there was more that we could work on together, but that it was her decision whether to continue or not. I raised, not for the first time, that an approaching break was often a difficult time in therapy and clients were sometimes surprised by how much it affected them. Maria said it was nothing like that, but it seemed a good time to end. I then suggested that we review what we had done together. Maria agreed and said that she had valued having somewhere to come and talk. She added that although she knew nothing about me and I knew everything about her, she still trusted me. I suggested that it sounded like she had made important progress, as she had spoken to me at the beginning of not trusting anyone. When asked what she had not found helpful, she said, 'Do you really want to know? You not saying much.' I fed back that I felt that her self-knowledge and confidence had increased during the six months, but that I would have liked to have seen more of the depressed and angry sides of her that she had spoken about. We talked about her hopes and fears for the future and she asked about further psychotherapy in the future, should she need it.

Evaluation of the work

It has been hard to condense six months' work into this brief case study, I have just sketched an impression by giving a few examples of typical interchanges. I still feel that a more structured, problem-focused approach to Maria's difficulties would have suited her more and would have given her concrete skills for the future, moreover, that was what she said she wanted. I think it was important that she managed to stick to counselling for six months and to open up to me, far more than she had done to anyone previously, and to have an experience of being taken seriously and accepted. I think her insight into herself did increase and, hopefully, should she seek psychological treatment in the future, she will find it easier to take part.

I think that I managed to be a safe practitioner, although had I been more secure in my model and supervision, I might have been better able to look at the countertransferential issues and thus have been a more effective therapist. I remember feeling that I was not feeding back enough of what I thought, through lack of confidence. I would now add to that that I did not challenge or explore Maria's pushing of the time boundaries nearly enough, nor did I spend enough time talking with her about her culture and what cultural differences might be affecting both the work that we were trying to do and her external life.

I decided to leave the placement after Maria had finished. I found one that suited me better and paid for individual supervision. I found this far more containing. My supervisor was very matter-of-fact about my anxieties and I was far more open about my process. I taped some of my sessions and found that knowing that he had listened to them and thought that I was doing OK was immensely reassuring. It also lead to detailed and specific feedback.

Liaison with other professionals

I wrote to the GP who had initially referred Maria, to tell him of her decision to terminate therapy. I said that I agreed with Maria's opinion that her depression might well 'catch up with her' and that at such a time, further psychological intervention should be considered, but that it was my opinion that a more focused approach, such as CBT or cognitive analytic therapy would suit Maria better, as she had found it hard to engage in psychodynamic therapy initially, and had wanted more concrete solutions.

References

Amundson, J., Stewart, K. and Valentine, L. (1993). Temptations of power and certainty. *Journal of Marital and Family Therapy*, 19(2), 111–123.

Bion, W.R. (1959). Attacks on Linking. In (1967) *Second Thoughts*. London: Heinemann.

Bion, W.R. (1967). *Second Thoughts: Selected Papers on Psychoanalysis*. London: Maresfield Reprints.

Erickson, E. (1965). *Childhood and Society*. Harmonsworth: Penguin.

Fairburn, W.R.D. (1952). *An Object-relations Theory of Personality*. New York: Basic Books.

Freud, S. (1915). The Unconscious, 14, 159–215. In *The Standard Edition of the Complete Works of Sigmund Freud*, Vols 1–24. London: Hogarth Press.

Horvath, A., Gaston, L. and Luborsky, L. (1993). Chapter 14, The Therapeutic Alliance. In Miller et al. (eds) *Psychodynamic Treatment Research*. New York: Basic Books.

Horvath, P. and Luborsky, S. (1993). The Therapeutic Alliance. *Journal of Consulting and Clinical Psychology*, 61(4), 561–573.

Jacobs, M. (1999). *Psychodynamic Counselling in Action*, 2nd edn. London: Sage Publications.

Kernberg, O. (1965). Notes on Countertransference. *Journal of the American Psychoanalytic Association*, 13, 38–56.

Kohut, H. (1971). *The Analysis of the Self*. New York: International Universities Press.

Mahler, M.S., Pine, F. and Bergman, A. (1975). *The Psychological Birth of the Human Infant: Symbiosis and Individuation*. New York: Basic Books.

Malan, D.H. (1979). *Individual Psychotherapy and the Science of Psychodynamics*. London: Butterworth Heinemann.

McLoughlin, B. (1995). *Developing Psychodynamic Counselling*. London: Sage Developing Counselling Series.

Meltzer, D. (1967). *The Psychoanalytic Press*. Perthshire: Clunie Press.

Perry, J.C. (1993). Chapter 15, Defenses and their Effects. In Miller et al. (eds) *Psychodynamic Treatment Research*. New York: Basic Books.

Rogers, C. (1975). Empathic: an unappreciated way of being. *The Counselling Psychologist*, 5(2), 2–10.

Ryle, A. (1975). *Frames and Cages*. New York: International Universities Press.

Sullivan, H.S. (1953). *The Interpersonal Theory of Psychiatry*. New York: Norton.

Winnicott, D.W. (1958). *Through Paediatrics to Psychoanalysis*. London: Hogarth Press.

Appendix A

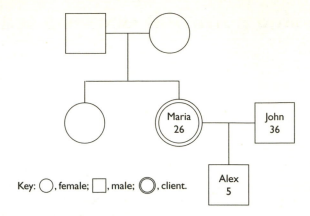

Key: ◯, female; ▢, male; ◎, client.

Figure 6 Genogram of family members discussed by Maria.

Chapter 19

How not to write a client report: discussing common errors a trainee makes

The previous chapters described the requirements for presenting case studies and process reports. Numerous examples of actual work were included to give the reader a clearer idea of the level and breadth required of this work in postgraduate academic settings. Once having grasped what is required of you in a case study or process report, there may still be some uncertainty about how best to describe your clinical experience. Indeed, many students perform well in the counselling context with clients and are able to give a balanced account of their clinical practice in supervision sessions, but are let down by the poor quality of their written work. Most often this is due to one or more of the following faults:

1   Failure to fully justify one's actions or interpretation of psychological process.
2   Making claims that are not borne out in the transcript or case study.
3   'Forcing' one theoretical model on to case material that is quite clearly presented from another theoretical perspective.
4   Making extravagant (and usually unbalanced) claims that do not accurately reflect the complexity of the situation.
5   Resorting to generalisations and gross assertions in order to simplify process and, presumably, impress the reader.
6   Using technical terms (including diagnostic categories) inappropriately, or resorting to psychobabble.
7   Being overly descriptive of psychological process without adequate critical reflection on what is happening in the session.
8   Having no clear rationale or objective for the session, and consequently providing no focus for the person assessing the work.
9   Poor grammar, typographic errors and untidy presentation of written material or inaudible audio tapes for process reports.

The remainder of this chapter illustrates, through excerpts from case studies and process reports, some of these and other errors. The excerpts are accompanied by tutor's comments in order to improve your understanding of what tutors are looking for in coursework. In our experience, we have found that it is unusual to come across a student who produces outstanding case studies and process report at the start of their training. Because most tutors have the ability to identify key problems and deficiencies quickly in coursework pertaining to clinical material, you stand a good chance of significantly improving the quality of your work, and enhancing your assessment grade if you learn to remedy these before submitting work for assessment. Much like learning any new and unfamiliar task, it takes prac-tice and a willingness to respond positively to the feedback given by tutors.

We apologise to readers for not providing a complete background to, and case history of, the clinical excerpts below. This would take up too much space and also potentially compromise the anonymity of the work we have included. We have intentionally left in spelling and stylistic errors. These give as bad an impression as conceptual problems, but are easier to prevent by careful proofreading of work before it is submitted.

1   Client background:

Stephen is a 9 year-old male. He is a student in ***** school. He is average build and height and he has blond hair and blue eyes. He wears the school uniform with the school logo.

Not only is this not written in correct English, but the material presented does not directly connect with the subheading of 'client background'. Also, what is the relevance of his hair and eye colour, and the school logo, other than to say that you were observant? Why choose these items or features and not others?

2   Physical appearance and personality:

Marie is a 40 year old married woman with shoulder length blonde hair and blue eyes. She is 5 ft 5 inches tall with a medium build. She has been separated from her husband for the last four years who lives in Canada. Marie has two boys one is 19 and the other is 15 years old. The eldest son is in U.K. living with his friend's family and the youngest son is in Canada with his father. Marie came across as a warm and friendly person with a posh outlook. She seemed relaxed and had a calm look on her face. She was wearing light blue jeans, black and white stripped top and sat on the chair a bit slouched. As the session progressed she became quite emotional however, towards the end seemed to have calmed down and appeared happy.

Much of the material presented has nothing to do with personality. Also, physical appearance and characteristics are only partially relevant to the problem. A list of the client's physical characteristics is neither here nor there. While you describe how she was at the beginning of the session and again later on, you have not included anything on the interaction and sequences between yourself and the client. Some of the terms you use are colloquial and imply judgement, e.g. 'posh'.

3   COUNSELLOR: What was his reaction?

This question was asked as a follow-up from the previous question to explore how the husband reacted when the client told him how she felt about what he was doing. This was done on my part to gain some idea about how important or interested was the husband to save his marriage and his relationship with client and whether he made any effort whatsoever to do so.

Yes, but you must remember that you can only glean the client's perception of her husband's view of the relationship, rather than a 'true' and effective sense of their relationship.

4   Another example of the ABC model can be given where the client expressed her remorse, as she feels she was not a good mother to her children when she was drinking. The activating event A was she was drinking and taking drugs, the consequence C was she missed her children's childhood and feels guilty and the beliefs B are 'I missed my children's childhood,' 'I'm a bad mother,' 'my children don't think I'm a good mother' and 'it's awful to be a bad mother.' These feelings of guilt and remorse makes the client seek refuge in drinking and drugs which makes her unable to carry on living a normal healthy life and she feels like a failure. This leads her to feel depressed and the whole cycle is repeated. The client also seems to suffer from insecurity and lack of control. These feelings along with a fear of relapse prevent the client to look positively to the future.

The way that you have delineated this in an A B C scheme does not make sense. You have tried to make a complex series of interactions seem quite linear. You are also trying to find a 'cause' for her taking drugs and drinking, whereas another way to look at it could be that these are symptoms within an ecology of dysfunctional relationships. Your use of conditional language is appropriate, but take care not to try to simplify complex material with unsubstantiated ideas about causation.

5   **Cognitive behavioural profile:**

Cognitive factors: e.g. 'my stomach is full so my whole body must have swelled up' and 'I only have to look at a chocolate bar and my arse grows', jumping to conclusions and mind reading e.g. 'everyone will think I'm disgusting if I am fat' and 'if my friends see me eating to much they will think that I'm a fat pig', should statements e.g. 'I should loose another half a stone' and 'I have to eat two burgers every time I go in to MacDonald's'.

Your noting specific utterances by the client and categorising them is good, however you need to include the specific terms used in CBT for these cognitive factors that you are trying to illustrate.

6   Kate's early life history indicated characteristics of a dependent personality which had led her to seek care and protection from others and by so doing prevented her from self learning by confronting difficulty situations (Young 1990). Now, it seemed that she was displaying similar behaviours in order not to confront difficulties faced at her place of employment. This led me to question Kate's motivation for therapy and her perception of her symptoms. I questioned the validity of the presenting difficulties and what part 'secondary gains' namely seeking early retirement played. This concept of 'secondary gains' favours certain behaviours in order to fulfil a desired function although these same behaviours may themselves become problematic in themselves and become the source of difficulties experienced, (Hawton et. al. 1996 pp.34).

Despite the typographical errors, this is well written and shows that you have sought to interpret the psychological process and substantiated this from recent literature. However, if you use clinical concepts such as 'dependent personality' you should probably justify this in terms of DSM criteria and also demonstrate your awareness of the politics of clinical diagnosis and labels.

7   Client is 18. female and family history. Natural mother left family home when stepdaughter was 2. Father has enmesheed relationship with stepdaughter until second wife on the scene. Father takes a back seat and allows step-mother to dominate relationship over step-daughter. Step-daughter feels over controlled by step-mother and under supported by her family.

These are incomplete sentences. There are typographical errors and colloquialisms. It is inappropriate to submit work in telegraphic style.

8   When Lisa was feeling confident she would talk rapidly and often interrupt interventions. I would try to hold on to themes in her conversation with which to make connections and would quite often feel a bit overwhelmed. I would find myself waiting for the chance to make many comments on her material. At some point in the session Lisa would abruptly stop and give me a look which seemed to indicate that I was supposed to supply something now.

You make some interesting observations. Many of them describe the client's behaviour. There is no clear sense, however, of your reactions and the client's subsequent response to your reactions. In other words, you could say more about the patterns of interaction, or process.

9   Presenting problem:

Since it was not his idea to start counselling therapy the client at the first meeting he informed me that he did not know anything about the agency and what was his role in this room. Although when he began to talk about himself and his family he expressed his distress with his parents. The problem was that his younger sister receives all the attention and not himself.

You have not proofread this (e.g. you use counselling and therapy in the same sentence). More importantly, none of the material presented relates to the client's presenting problem. Furthermore, you do not indicate how you handled the interaction with the client.

10   THERAPIST: 'That must be very hard for you.'

By saying that I am trying to show empathy to the client by accepting the fact that it was difficult for him not meeting for 4 weeks

CLIENT: 'I went to my father for Easter, did you remember I told you I was going to go?'

The client probably does not want to have further insight of his worry that I forget him of the fact that the break was too long as he admitted. And he continues the conversation by commenting with whom he spent his Easter. Saying that his facial expression changed and he looked happier.

It is not clear how this is in any way empathic. You might have quite easily picked up on his anger or disappointment that he did not see you for four weeks. The client then returns to this issue reminding you that he told you he was going to his father. The tape conveys his irritation with you, but you do not pick this up. There are some typos and your final interpretation does not make sense.

11   Session 3: Aims

The aim was to:
1   Evaluate to client's insight into the cause of his problems.
2   Explore the strength of his ego defence mechanism.
3   Try to be empathic.
4   Discuss other issues.

These all seem to be worthy aims but you have failed to provide a rationale for any of them.

12 Lead into session (summarise what has happened prior to the point at which the transcript begins).

The transcription has been written on the 3rd session, towards the end of the session. Before this point the client said that he had enough of been ill (stomach problem, back pain). He feels worried because his landlord wants him out. The stomach problems began in August and I am truing to find out whether the emotional pain experienced subsequent to the break up of his relationship is being denied and has been expressed in term of physical pain (although the pain seems reel, I don't think that he is hypochondriac). Simon has been told that the lower back pain isn't due to a slipped disk or a muscle pulled, there is no real explanation for it. he has been given a machine with contain batteries and provides vibration which the client wears against the affected area and which provides relief from the pain. We speculated that it might have be the cold or sleeping in a bad position.

You are now contradicting yourself. In a previous section you suggested that the problem might have been a psychosomatic one. This section suggests that you are taking his somatic problems at face value. Also, proofread your work!

13 Presenting problem:

The client is depressed, he was going out with this girl (C), whom he grew very fond of. They stay together for two years. He describes her as embodying both the family and friends that he left behind when he came to England. He once caught her kissing someone else. Shocked and horrified he decided to end the relationship and never to see her again. Mike has few friends, does not socialise and doesn't want to get involved in another relationship for fear of being hurt again. He gave me the metaphor of a chair saying that if he gets attached to the chair (it's safe) it won't hurt him. Lately his landlord has been trying to evict him. The client goes out but does not socialise, he describes liking his own company. He doesn't drink for religious reasons and does not like noise and being around smokers.

There are several points covered in a single sentence. Present your material more simply. Stick to one tense, preferably the past tense. Do not use any abbreviations. Rather than saying 'the client is depressed,' perhaps you can state that he 'appeared' depressed (and then justify how you made this assessment) or he was referred because he presented as being depressed. Some of the material has nothing to do with the presenting problem. Confine the scope of the material to the relevant heading.

14 Initial assessment

George was the only child for almost eight years, and he get used to have all the attention of his parents and his stepfather. Although when his mother got pregnant, he stopped to be the only child and attract all the attention. Obviously it was a hard for him to adjust to a new situation providing that he had already faced his parents divorced. Moreover his biological father who has a good relationship with him leaves in Newcastle. Therefore the only way to attract the attention is by being naughty.

This is not written in plain English and shows that you have not proofread this material. You have made an assumption about his difficulty in adapting to the new situation, and have given no supporting evidence to justify this.

15 The content of the three sessions included an understanding of her family tree which included other step mums, the disengagement and enmeshment in acquiring and having personal possessions removed and the ramifications of how such relationships with her stepmother are affecting her social life and how she chooses friends and boyfriends.

These statements are unfounded. You have not established enmeshed or disengaged family relationships. These are psychological terms but you use them as action terms in concrete events. You cannot meaningfully link them in this way. The use of the term 'step mums' is inappropriate in a piece of clinically-oriented work.

16 This would have provided the space to address interpersonal issues (Safran & Segal, 1990) and facilitate her understanding that evidence of all kinds, negative as well as positive, is relevant to therapy without her loosing my respect. Secondly, sensitive and empathic exploration of the early experiences, which had given rise to the development of negative core beliefs, would have guarded against her feeling blamed in any way. This would also have facilitated a strengthening of the working alliance, which Beck et al., (1990) state is crucial when working with deeper personality issues.

You demonstrate good reflection, however there is a danger in sticking too strongly to the technique described in textbooks. The tape conveys a confident and sympathetic relationship with the client and you can easily afford to be more relaxed and less driven by technique.

17 The process seemed to change quite markedly after the fourth session when I was silent for much of the session and began to make interpretations. Following these interpretations Bill began to talk more freely than at any time before. His play began to be more constructive

and creative. It also stopped being hostile and instead he seemed to display positive feelings towards me. For example, he began to invite me to play more games with him, and during our fifth session he spent much of the time pretending to prepare food for us to eat together.

During my supervision session, my supervisor and I concluded that Bill appeared to be more securely attached to me by this point. He was making lots more eye contact and smiling at me quite frequently. I also noticed changes in my own countertransference feelings. As Bill became more playful I began to enjoy our sessions together and found his narratives to be rich in material. I no longer felt as much anxiety over my role and what I should be doing, and instead let myself be led by Bill's unconscious communications.

This is a very well written section. Your reflections on the psychological process are balanced and take into account metacommunications, i.e. the reciprocal influence of process of client and therapist.

18 Client's profile

L, is of medium build with brown hair and brown eyes and usually wears tracksuits. On first impression L's manner was polite, but quite. He never talks out of the therapeutic room and he often looks serious and sceptical.

What is a 'client profile'?! You have not included anything that gives the reader an impression of the person you are working with. How old is he? Is he employed? Was he easy to engage? How did he describe his problem? A few random remarks about the client hardly constitutes a well-formulated assessment based on your observations.

19 Lines 120, 122 and 124 (commenting on process)

Here I am introducing the idea of talking to this friend about her sexual abuse. I feel that it would be liberating for Annie to be able to tell her close friends the secret that she has had since childhood. I am taking a bit of a risk as I am not sure how her friend will respond but I think that she has feared people's responses all her life because she was ashamed. I hope that a friend's positive response will help her to feel that she did nothing wrong.

This certainly is a risk. If you feel that this could be pushing the client too fast and in a direction she may not want to go, you should openly discuss your dilemma with her. You need to be more transparent about your impressions. In this way, the client need not feel coerced by you.

20 Summary

This is not a very good session technically. It does not demonstrate any advanced counselling techniques. However it does demonstrate how I have tried to encourage Annie to make changes in her life. Most of the session is quite behavioural in orientation but this client needed to make changes, as her life had become one of caring for others and working all the time. This was not helping her depression. In other previous sessions we had explored the abuse and the effects that this had on the way she felt about herself. Annie had understood this well and she had shown some relief when she was able to understand why she felt as she did. However the final stage of therapy needed to look at making changes in her life in order that she could move on in a positive way, enjoying life for the first time.

This seems honest! However, your description that the session was quite behavioural is not entirely consistent with your audio tape. I wonder whether you are confusing the use of some behavioural techniques with a behavioural approach. It is appropriate at this stage of your training to develop a more integrative approach to your work.

21 Culture/Ethnicity

The family was subject to contradictory cultural influences. The Spanish element reflected a defiantly free-living attitude to marriage and children. Bianca's grandmother had three children from three different fathers, and Stephanie, Gina's mother, was illegitimate at a time when such matters were a source of shame in Spanish culture. Stephanie herself had been pregnant with Gina when she married Pepe (*father*).

If you are going to make such sweeping generalisations you will need to provide some evidence.

22   Therapy (a process of change facilitation) becomes a co-operative undertaking in which new meaning, understanding and expectations is co-constructed by the therapist/client-observer system, rather than imposed by the therapist Tomm (1984) feels that continual change and evolve-ment is natural. The therapist is co-influencing the direction of change in an existing pattern of change. The therapist's function is to support clients to become agents of their own choices (change).

In this process of be-ing and be-coming the client system has some choice in the direction of the change but not in whether to change or not. From this perspective the existence of a constant, stable self or social-system becomes an illusion. Because people are brought up and educated to have a predominantly Newtonian mechanistic worldview they expect stability, predictability and control in all forms at most levels of life. This is the cause of much pain and disillusionment to many people, on a personal level but also in their experience of social life. This illusion of stability is created by the smooth nature of first-order change in an ever-changing, self-organising system within a complex, dynamic larger eco-system.

It is better to put complex ideas in to plain English. Also, you have not demonstrated any link between these ideas and the case you have presented. This material would be better off in an essay.

23 COUNSELLOR: 'Sorry, who is "she"?'

(My attention apparently wandered here. There is no ambiguity in what JB has actually said. The confusion is entirely mine. Or am I picking up some non-verbal communication?)

Good point. Why do you think your attention may have wandered?

CLIENT: 'Lisa.' (*wife*)

COUNSELLOR: 'Can we just try something? Let's just separate for a moment, since you made the separation in the context of your own up-bringing, between having some financial advantages but emotional deprivation. You tell me that the emotional deprivation is by far the more significant of those, and I'm hardly likely to disagree with you am I? If there was emotional deprivation then and there is now extra love now isn't it like someone's making up the deficit, to express it in financial terms? Isn't it like you were born with an emotional overdraft and now someone's giving you some credit, so why shouldn't you just accept that there was a time when there was less than you deserved and now maybe there's a time when there's more than you deserve and at the moment the balance is looking kind of OK?'

(I in turn ignore him and return doggedly to my own agenda)

Again, you make an observation about your own behaviour, but do not offer an explanation as to why you return to your own agenda.

24 CLIENT: 'A lot of people would say "Oh, you're a spoilt brat, you should be a better person"; Yeah, I probably am in a lot of ways.'

COUNSELLOR: 'Explain to me what you mean by that.'

(Attempt to draw him out)

CLIENT: 'A lot of people would say the kind of upbringing I've had put one hell of a silver spoon in my mouth, and therefore what I've had is a lot more than other people would get. But then I think that isn't everything because as far as my emotional development goes I was totally massively starved, and I think that's a hell of a lot more important than any financial upbringing you can possibly have. I think I'm a perfect example of that. I'm emotionally starved.'

There is no lead in to the tape. I have no idea about the context of your sessions, the background to this particular session, or the client's problem. You need to contextualise your work for the reader.

25 After some discussion of the limitations of brief therapy (me) and the improbability of some Freudian interpretations (him), we agreed that the prime objective our remaining session would be to reduce his feelings of anger and that our criterion for success would be that his wife ceased to be frightened of him.

I then asked him to talk about his two recent attempts to kill himself. Both attempts had been at home, spontaneous events involving modest quantities of alcohol and painkillers while sleeping separately from his wife after a row. On both occasions he had woken up unharmed and feeling rather silly. No one else, no even his wife, knew of these attempts and on neither occasion had he been hospitalised. I disclosed to him that I had, for several years, worked as a Samaritan. We made a verbal contract that he would make no attempt to kill himself. If he found himself inclining that way he would call me on my mobile. In the event of not being able to contact me he would leave a message and call the Samaritans. I considered the suicide risk to be low and my supervisor concurred.

There are some important and highly-sensitive issues here, but you seem to be glossing over them. For example, what limitations of brief therapy were discussed? How did he respond? How did you come to agree on the objective for the session? Is it within his control for his wife to stop being frightened of him? Why did you feel that your work as a Samaritan was helpful? Is it policy within your agency to give clients your mobile phone number?

26 Contract and therapy plan:

Sean has been engaged in therapy for the past ten weeks. Therapy was aimed at anger management. I selected a CBT plan for working with Sean since studies have demonstrated that cognitive behavioural therapy is particular effective for depression and anxiety disorders (Corey 1996).

How have you arrived at CBT for depression and anxiety when the presenting problem was anger management? There seems to be a leap without cueing the reader into your assessment of the client and his problem.

27 CLIENT: 'Anger. My flat mate was also out so I could deal with it in private.'

I had tried to address this recurring problem in the past. Since depressed individual's assume a state of learned helplessness (Dobson, 1996), I have often asked Sean whether allowing himself to suffer in silence is going to help matters.

Be careful not to generalise and become categorical about the direction of causality. Sometimes people become depressed because of learned helplessness.

28 This Process Report and the work done with the client so far is an amalgamation of the structure that Pallazzoli Selvini et al (1980) brings to Systemic Therapy (used here interchangeably with Family Therapy), the narrative metaphor (Hoffman 1993) and Watzlawick et al (1974) principles of the formulation of problems and there resolution.

This theoretical description seems rather ambitious to say the least. If you are going to refer to an author, the least you can do is to ensure that the reference is accurate. The reason for this is that the author's name is in fact Selvini Palazzoli.

29 Lisa explained that whenever she was in a crowded and noisy environment, such as a busy train station or crowded bar, she felt unwell. Specifically, she described feeling tightness in her chest causing her difficulty to breathe, as well as a feeling of nausea, combined with headaches and dizziness. Lisa went on to explain that when she began experiencing these symptoms she felt she was 'having a heart attack' and feared that she would draw attention to herself by fainting or collapsing, which would result in 'everyone staring at her'. The first time this had happened was approximately five months after the assault. It coincided with a dinner engagement organised with her colleagues arranged at a busy restaurant/bar. Lisa explained that she had been aware of this event for some time, but as the day drew closer, she became increasingly anxious about attending. She significantly recalls during the week leading up to the event, she began to experience strong headaches and nausea. Thoughts of attending the dinner began to consume her thoughts and effected her sleep, and by the day of the engagement, she knew she would not be able to attend. Her biggest fear was that she would relive these symptoms, which would cause her to collapse in front of her colleagues, thereby attracting attention to herself.

This is very well written. Wherever possible, use the client's own words to illustrate points made as this can be very powerful and shows the teacher that (a) you have attended to the client's story and (b) it serves as a justification for your interpretations.

30   The client did not accept this reasoning immediately, but did eventually understand the rational basis of the argument I was attempting to convey.

How did she display or convey rejection of these ideas? What explanation do you have for her initially rejecting the ideas?

31   I wondered whether a cognitive approach would be useful for her stress symptoms, but it proves difficult to keep her focused on tasks.

This reads like a personal diary entry.

32   Children will not tell their therapist what their real problems are, not only because they cannot speak with ease but also because the acute anxiety they suffer from only permits them to employ a less direct for of representation, i.e. toys (Klein, 1989).

Maybe children also do not have the vocabulary, but this is not really a psychological problem.

33 Appearance and behaviour

At the assessment session, H appeared nervous at first – her head bowed and glancing to the door when somebody walked past – but very quickly relaxed. Maintenance of eye-contact, speed of response and non-verbals all suggested a fairly high level of self-confidence although these were incongruent with her habit of prefixing much of what she said with 'I know it sounds ridiculous' and 'this is going to sound really stupid'. She will also occasionally play with her hair and this is notably before a disclosure that embarrasses her. She wore a long sleeved top, which covered her wrists and part of her hands. Verbally, H was coherent and articulate, responding and acting in an appropriate manner. Her mood appeared generally flat but did fluctuate, and at time over the course of therapy she was tearful and at other times would smile cheerfully.

This is very good. It could be enhanced by your including something on your reactions to her and how you felt in the session.

34 Biographical details

Mr. B is a 33-year-old male, single and lives with his girlfriend. Mr. B is presently starting up his own company after having worked for an IT firm where he was a consultant manager for a computer company. When the client was first referred he was still working but due to a lapse of depression was forced to stop working to receive sick leave. Since therapy started he has just started to work in the office but has left the company to start his own business based from his home. He has got a large supportive network of friends and family and has a great interest in cooking and enjoys sport activities such as squash and tennis.

You should only include relevant detail. Some of this sounds a bit like a CV for a dating service.

Conclusion

Some of the material presented here makes for uncomfortable reading. After all, few of us welcome criticism or negative commentary. You can expect your tutor to be more lenient at the start of your training and gradually to raise his or her expectations of your coursework as you progress through the course. It is an unfortunate fact that many students are almost exclusively interested in their grade and largely ignore comments and feedback. Sadly, such students are destined to repeat some of the errors described in this chapter. In an increasingly competitive job market, there is little room for borderline or mediocre practitioners. Always set your sights on submitting exemplary coursework.

Chapter 20

Conclusions

The case studies and process reports represented in this volume have both reflected diverse themes and crystallised a range of issues of relevance to trainees and accomplished practitioners alike. We are indebted to the honesty and bravery shown by our authors, as they shared their work, and their thinking behind it, with us. As with much that is personally engaging and provocative, we were able to put ourselves in the shoes of the therapist and client as they worked toward some kind of helpful and shared understanding of the difficulties central to each case. Our rationale for selecting these particular case studies and process reports for inclusion in this volume varied enormously. However, some recurring themes emerged. In particular, ruminations about therapist confidence and preparedness for practice surfaced regularly, so too did the importance of self-awareness and the capacity to be involved in, while simultaneously observing, the therapeutic process. The task of managing one's feelings throughout therapy appeared to be a concern shared by a number of our therapists. These feelings sometimes arose from the provocative content of the client's material. However, more common were the anxieties of being a 'good enough' therapist. Rumination and self-doubt crept in to several of the accounts provided by our author–practitioners. The creativity and risk-taking of many of our contributors is evident in their accounts of their practice. It was apparent that courage, sufficient to cope with moving from the familiar to the unfamiliar, was required of both the therapist and the client as they worked towards growth and change.

Confusion and uncertainty on the part of the therapist is amplified as a result of tensions between the push of professional training and the pull of supervision combined with the unique set of opportunities and limitations afforded by the client and therapist in the therapy setting. Therapists have to be strong emotionally to retain integrity when they are subject to so many spheres of influence. A professional identity that is not contingent on 'knowing it all' is critical if the therapist is to escape the trap of confusing the evolving nature of knowledge with evidence that they are failing and thus not sufficiently prepared for practice. Trainees, in particular, are vulnerable to the tendency to resolve their uncertainty in terms of some sense of a personal lack. As we have seen from the case examples offered by our colleagues, clients are complex and therapeutic understanding emerges and unfolds. The capacity to stay with uncertainty, and to engage in iterative formulation and reformulation, is fundamental to genuine engagement with the humanity of the 'problem'. However, this stance demands bravery, confidence and the good will of both client and therapist alike.

The honesty and openness of the therapist/authors is plainly apparent throughout the foregoing clinical accounts. Such transparency requires much more than excellent recall and the capacity to represent the 'facts' accurately. It requires the reflexive understanding of theoretical knowledge. Therapists have to know what to look for, which in turn is contingent upon knowledge of why it is important. To the absorbed reader, caught up in the story, the authors' articulation of their account disguises the mechanics of knowing what to attend to – like a theatre audience that enjoys the performance without any knowledge of how the cast were selected or the set constructed. Good therapeutic story telling often obscures the theory that chartered the territory and provided the map of markers and things to look out for. In order for our therapist/authors to describe their encounters they draw upon assumptions associated with what matters, what is of significance, and what factors are likely to have a bearing on process and outcome. This rendering of knowledge 'second nature' can, at times, appear to be the goal of therapist training and development. However, this is neither necessary, nor wholly desirable. If the rationale for practice is allowed to become wholly tacit the capacity of the therapist to teach is diminished. Regardless of our stage of training, we must strive to maintain the capacity to articulate why we engage in therapy the way we do.

As readers, we are privileged to gain an intimate insight into the person of the therapist. Our authors are honest and forthright, creating immediacy through the telling of their story. Trainees often make the mistake of assuming that the reader, or assessor, of a report is only interested in the client or the subject of a case study or process report. This is far from the case. Indeed, as we have seen, it is the unique interaction between the therapist and the client that makes for excellent reading. Great case studies and process reports account for what is happening both within and between the therapist and the client. Accounts of this nature require a comprehension of, and fluency with, the language of self and other – the simultaneous observation of the facts without and the ruminations and machinations within. This, we believe, is the essence of the dynamism that characterises therapy. Therapists must be knowledgeable about themselves. They must possess a preparedness to examine their place in the moment-to-moment practice of therapy. This knowledge is built, in part, upon an understanding of the biases, prejudices and preferences that shape who we are and, in turn, colour the interpretations and judgements reflected in our practice.

Several of the client studies, in particular Chapters 7 and 17, raise interesting issues regarding the role of training in equipping the novice therapist with sufficient competencies to practise. What is clear is that it is unethical to practise beyond one's own competencies. However, the evaluation of these competencies often becomes skewed by the feelings of self-doubt or anxiety that naturally arise when the stakes are high. Knowing when one has reached a level where it is safe to practise is a judgement that can not be made on one fateful and momentous day. Rather, it is a recurring and iterative task that stays with us throughout our career, as we work with the uniqueness and diversity that is an inescapable reality of interacting with people. Questions of competence may rise to the surface within sessions with our clients, or later as we reflect, either alone or in consultation with colleagues. We are never in a position to present the entirety of our work. Even though we may become highly skilful in recording detailed clinical notes, when we refer back to them we will struggle with the tendency to attend to particular instances selectively. The instances that catch our eye are often those which particularly concern us. Either they touch upon issues that overlap with our own concerns or they represent instances that validate or invalidate our own core values. As a consequence of the inevitability of the presence of the 'self' of the therapist in the therapeutic relationship, we must develop both self-knowledge and the capacity to self-censor. That is, we must possess the ability to sense what are often provocative feelings, while recognising that both the origins of these feelings and responsibility for managing them, reside with us, the therapist.

Striving for perfectionism is a thread common to a number of the chapters presented. You will recall that 5 in their work with 15 discussed their desire to do more and better with the benefit of hindsight. Trainees have a tendency to ruminate over the micro aspects of practice. They may isolate instances in the session where they said, or could have said, something that they have now come to think of as critical. Often these ruminations have as their origin the desire to get it absolutely perfect first-time round, as if there is only one possible way to do therapy. It is ironic that this desire to become more competent may actually undermine effective practice if it is allowed to go unmoderated. If, in the evaluation of practice, we adopt an exclusively micro (as apposed to macro) focus we run the risk of reducing therapy to its minutiae. The consequence of such short-sightedness is the objectification of events and the divorcing of instances, such as therapeutic strategies or utterances, from their context. When we extract events from their context we tend to validate the underlying assumption that the event could have only one meaning. For example, for the therapist whose first language is not English there is a complex and furious process of translation, taking place to and from English and their language of birth, as they seek to understand the experience of the client. The minor time lags arising from this process of translation may result in the therapist missing an opportunity to clarify, challenge or empathise. These experiences can be frustrating and deeply invalidating for the novice therapist. However, rather than indicating weakness on the part of the trainee therapist they may be more illustrative of underlying strivings for perfectionism and fears of inadequacy. Experienced therapists tend to accept that what is important will return. A missed opportunity to comment provides a further chance to test a hypothesis. A chance to increase confidence in one's construction of what is going on for the client. Isolating and freezing events in therapy implies that they are available to us to sculpt and rewrite to achieve an idealised outcome. Such certainty is simply not possible in the bespoke and fluid craft of psychotherapy. It is indeed fundamental to professional development that we reflect upon our work in the light of new learning, however, rumination and perseveration are more often associated with self-punishment and self-deprecation than growth and development. We should not be fooled into thinking that it is either necessary or desirable to possess the capacity to see around corners. Regardless of our stage of training or expertise we will always have to carry with us the humility of not knowing. Aspirations of one day 'knowing it all' imply that the answer is out there – that one size fits all. Thankfully, but sometimes painfully, it is never that simple.

When reporting work in a complex case, with multiple presenting issues and a therapeutic style that transcends more than one 'essentialist' approach, clarity of writing style is an enormous achievement. This achievement was attained by a number of our contributors, who demonstrated that it is possible to be coherent and measured in the face of seemingly insurmountable difficulties. We have described this style as one of 'poise rather than panic', suggesting that it constitutes one of the benchmarks of therapists' development. In practice, it may be observed either in the way that the therapist selects technique, or in the technical execution of their work. In particular, Nicola Gale, in Chapter 4, illustrated how it was possible to integrate directive, cognitive and behavioural (CBT) techniques into an exploratory approach grounded squarely in the therapeutic relationship. She, and other authors who can capture the essence of this style, is clearly conversant with the theoretical and empirical literature, and confident, calm and measured in her approach.

Many of the therapeutic stories comprising this series of case studies and process reports are illustrative of the spirit of joint enquiry that is indicative of broadly constructivist approaches to collaboratively developing understanding and facilitating change. We are reminded that relational ways of working are critical where clients are ambivalent about, or unconvinced of, the possibility of change. This collaborative approach places the power and impetus for change squarely between the therapists and the clients, rather than wholly within either parties. Both therapists and clients are dependant upon one another to elucidate, refine and mould understandings. The clients retain their status as 'experts' in *what* they see in their world, while the therapists add value in terms of their capacity to conceptualise and account for *how* the clients see their world. Thus, together clients and therapists are able to chart a unique and personally meaningful course for change that often demands flexibility on the part of the therapists as much as the clients.

In every therapy session, therapists are faced with a set of circumstances not encountered before and so must choose to make particular interventions on the basis of probability rather than certainty. It is arguable that in brief therapy the pressure to take therapeutic risks is high, given that clients often present with deep-rooted problems and the time available to help is short. Novice therapists probably err on the side of caution, frequently letting opportunities to work with core aspects of their clients' psyche go unexploited. A number of the cases presented in this volume capture something of the spirit of adventure that pushes therapists beyond their usual ways of working, thus illustrating the tensions that arise when taking responsibility for directing the course of therapy. Tension and anxiety in therapists may not necessarily portend danger, rather they are the natural consequence of moving out of the comfort of the known; the familiar or the routine.

Whatever your stage of training, or the extent of your experience, enormous opportunities to learn and develop are afforded through systematic reflection on practice. Case studies and process reports provide frameworks that require the structuring of experiences into coherent narratives. Although our authors' have provided us with insight into particular and unique examples of their practice, in doing so, they have raised a number of issues that are likely to resonate with all of us. These issues should not be seen as definitive. They only represent a few of the considerations and challenges facing those of us who seek to work with people psychotherapeutically. There is so much more that could be written. Psychotherapy is truly a fascinating and wholly engaging business that will continue to provoke much thought and debate. One thing is sure, however, each enterprise holds the potential to be unique in its course and, in turn, to provide an impetus for change and growth within both client and therapist.

Index